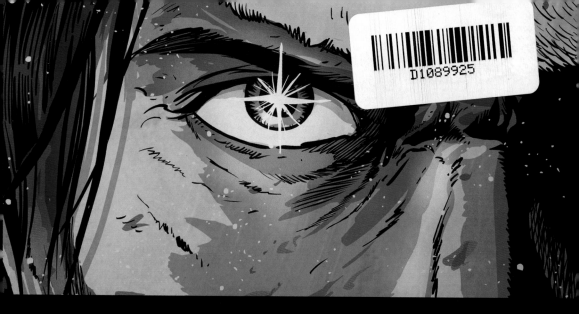

NAUGHTY LIST

NICK SANTORA

LEE FERGUSON

JUANCHO!

PIPPA BOWLAND

SIMON BOWLAND

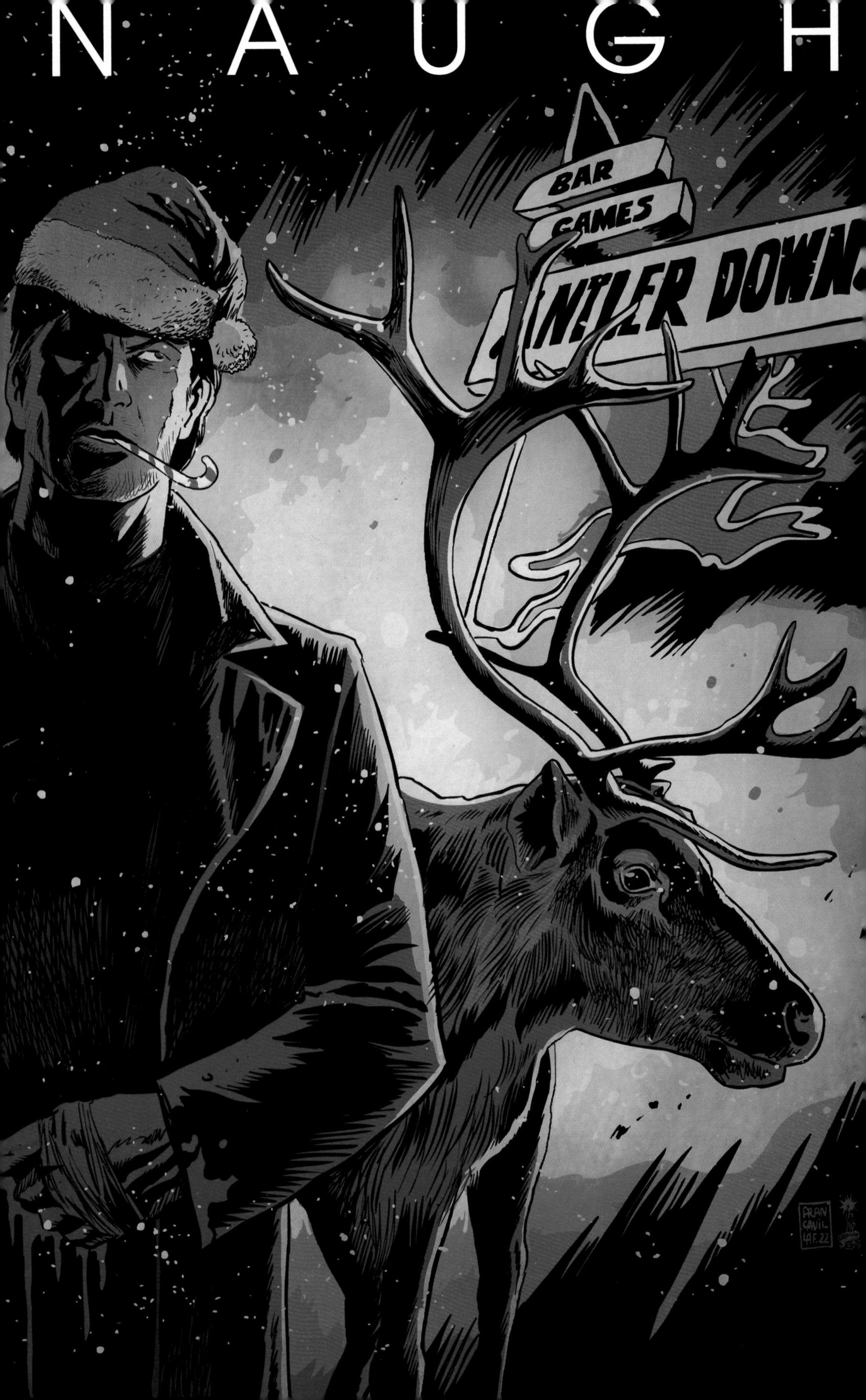
N A U G H
BAR
GAMES
NTLER DOWN

TY LIST™

NICK SANTORA writer
LEE FERGUSON artist
JUANCHO! & **PIPPA BOWLAND** colorists
SIMON BOWLAND & **DAVE SHARPE** letterers

FRANCESCO FRANCAVILLA front and original covers
LEE FERGUSON & **JOSE VILLARRUBIA** incentive cover

GARY BEDELL logo designer
CHARLES PRITCHETT issue #1 backmatter designer
COREY BREEN book designer
MIKE MARTS editor

created by **NICK SANTORA**

AFTERSHOCK™

MIKE MARTS - Editor-in-Chief • JOE PRUETT - Publisher/CCO • LEE KRAMER - President • JON KRAMER - Chief Executive Officer
STEVE ROTTERDAM - SVP, Sales & Marketing • DAN SHIRES - VP, Film & Television UK • CHRISTINA HARRINGTON - Managing Editor
MARC HAMMOND - Sr. Retail Sales Development Manager • RUTHANN THOMPSON - Communications Specialist
ANNE RANDULIC - Manager, Social Media & Engagement • KATHERINE JAMISON - Marketing Manager • KELLY DIODATI - Ambassador Outreach Manager
BLAKE STOCKER - VP, Finance • AARON MARION - Publicist • LISA MOODY - Finance • RYAN CARROLL - Director, Comics/Film/TV Liaison
JAWAD QURESHI - Technology Advisor/Strategist • CHARLES PRITCHETT - Design & Production Manager • COREY BREEN - Collections Production
TEODORO LEO - Associate Editor • SARAH PRUETT & GIGI WILLIAMS - Publishing Assistants

AfterShock Logo Design by COMICRAFT
Publicity: contact AARON MARION (aaron@publichausagency.com) & RYAN CROY (ryan@publichausagency.com) at PUBLICHAUS
Special thanks to: ATOM! FREEMAN, JAKE GERMANY, IRA KURGAN, MARINE KSADZHIKYAN, KEITH MANZELLA, ANTHONY MILITANO, ANTONIA LIANOS, STEPHAN NILSON & ED ZAREMBA

PRINTED IN CANADA. First Printing: September 2022. 10 9 8 7 6 5 4 3 2 1

AFTERSHOCKCOMICS.COM Follow us on social media

I N T R O D U C T I O N

Some of the most wonderful memories of my life are from Christmas time. Being inside a warm home when it's cold outside. Making tree-shaped cookies with mom. Giving and getting gifts. And just being thankful for family and friends. Christmas is special.

So, I never understood why people always got so negative every December...

"I hate shopping during the holidays!" "I don't want to visit Uncle Morty this year!" "I didn't get the one thing I really wanted!"...it just seems like Christmas was getting pooped on a lot, and it just boggled my mind. Why did so many people have a problem with such a wonderful day?!

NAUGHTY LIST is Christmas getting tough and pushing back against all the complaints! It also lets "The Good" (giving, kindness, goodwill) defeat "The Bad" (cruelty to animals, violence against women, murder). And when "The Good" wins, that's always a good thing! But at the end of the day, it's just supposed to be fun, silly and a little weird—and definitely not for kids!

NICK SANTORA
August 2022

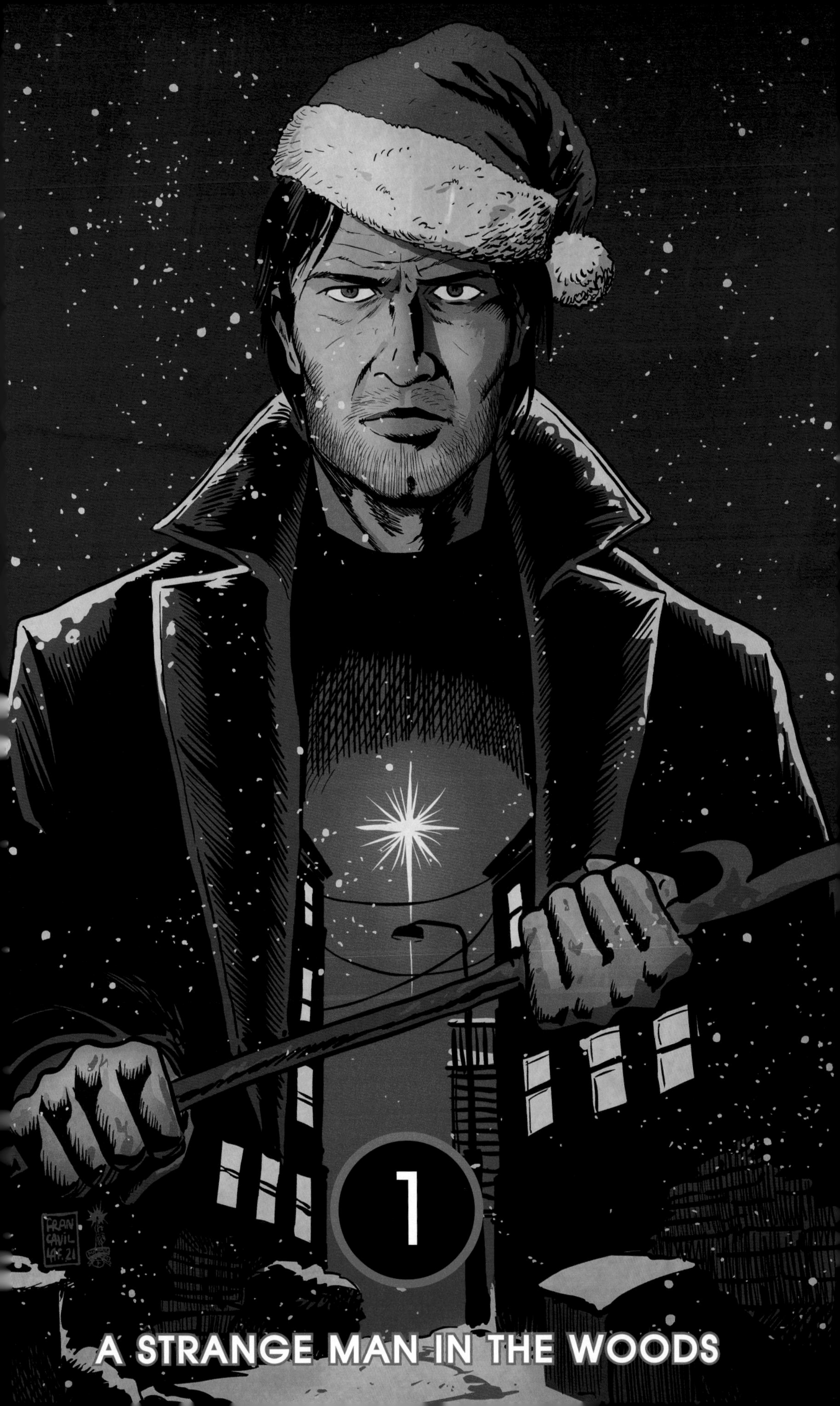

1

A STRANGE MAN IN THE WOODS

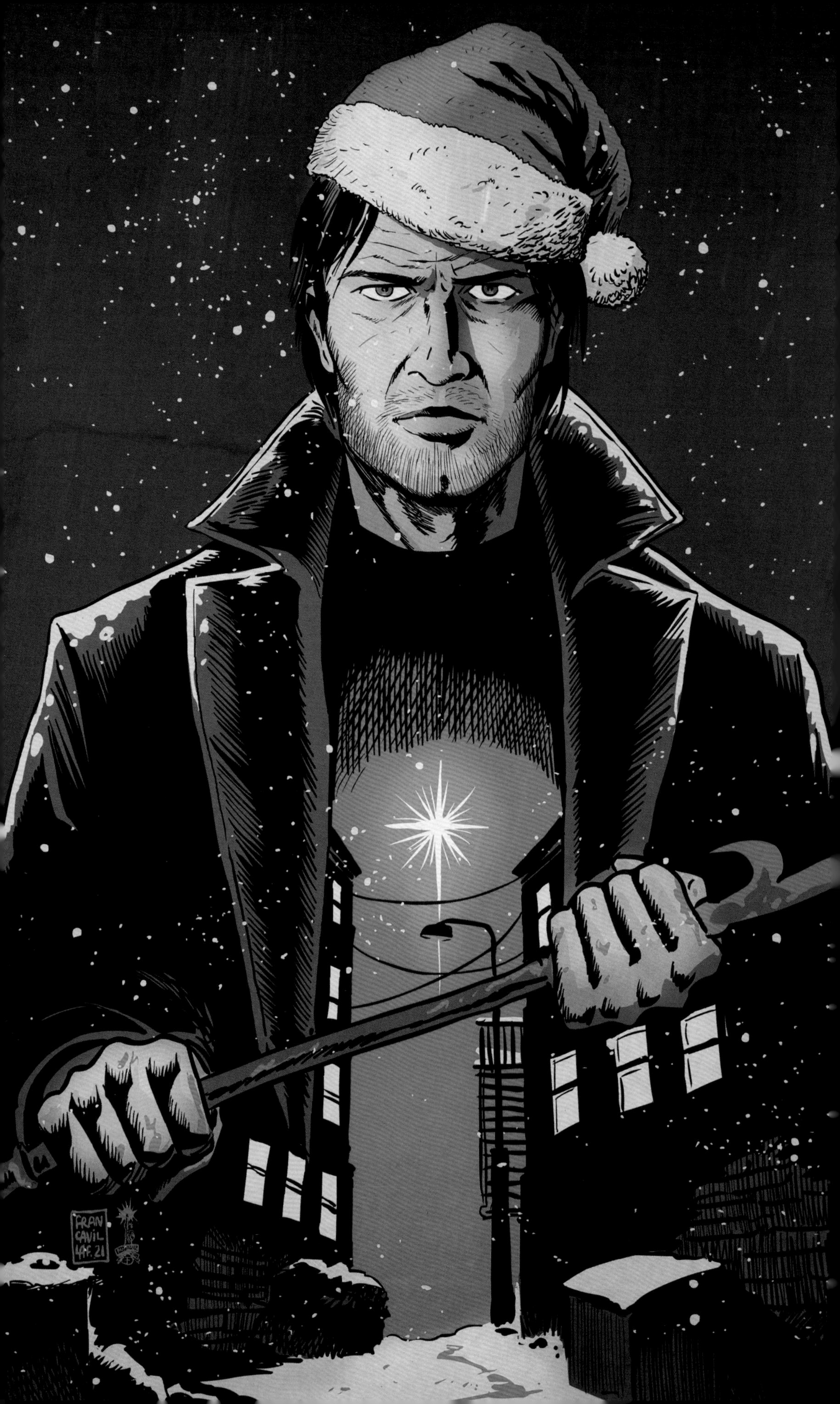
FRAN
CAVIL
4F. 21

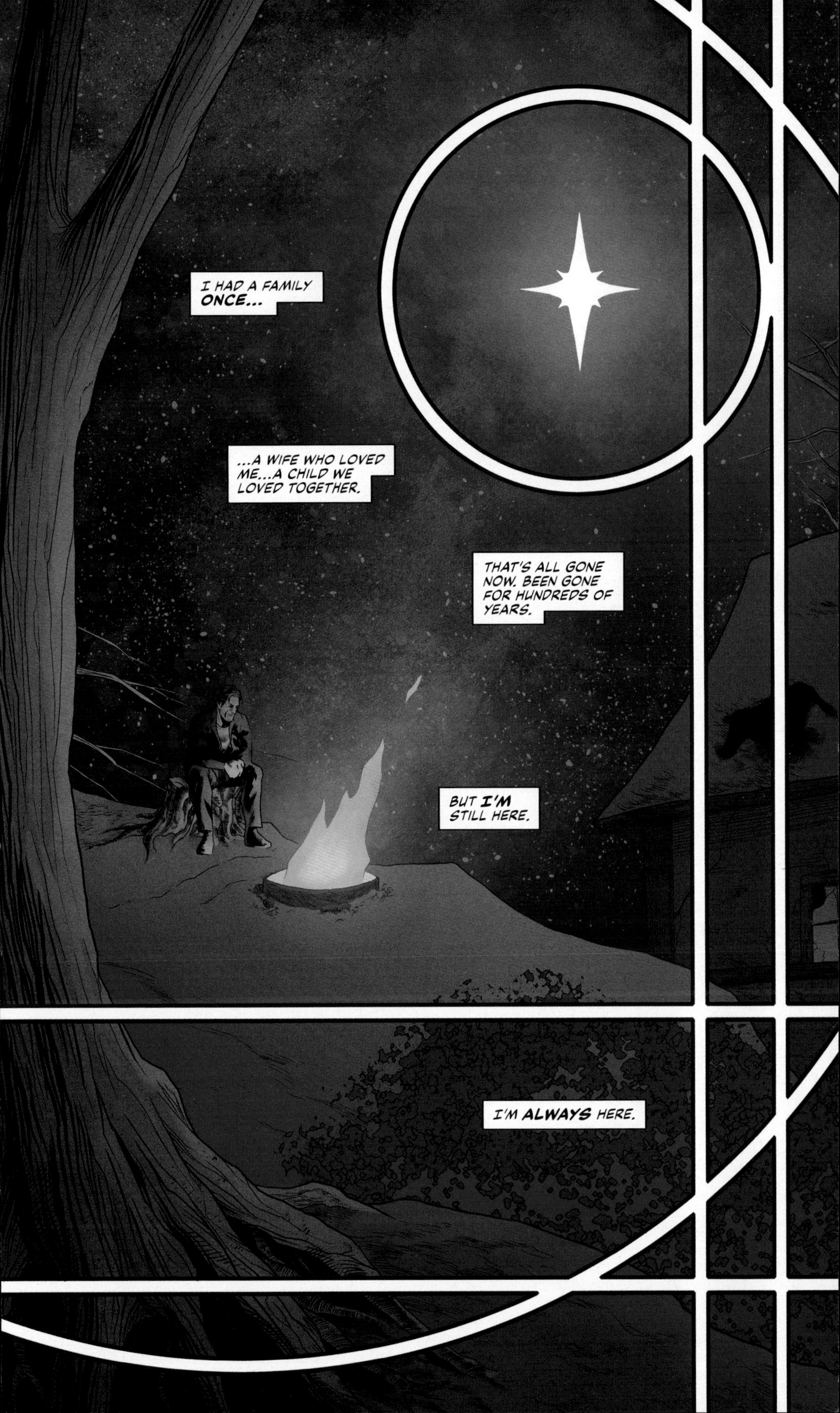
I HAD A FAMILY ONCE...
...A WIFE WHO LOVED ME...A CHILD WE LOVED TOGETHER.
THAT'S ALL GONE NOW. BEEN GONE FOR HUNDREDS OF YEARS.
BUT I'M STILL HERE.
I'M ALWAYS HERE.

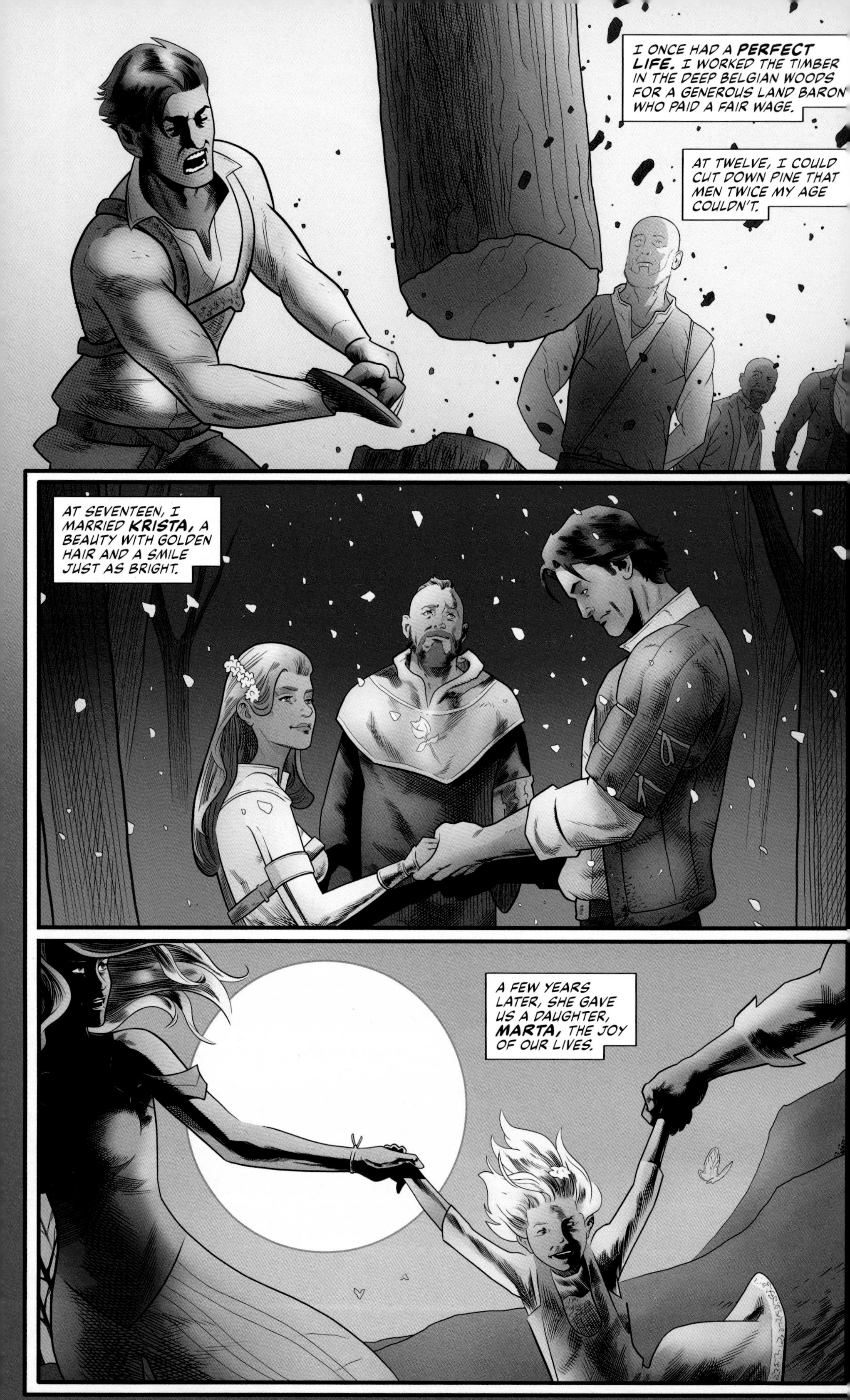
I ONCE HAD A PERFECT LIFE. I WORKED THE TIMBER IN THE DEEP BELGIAN WOODS FOR A GENEROUS LAND BARON WHO PAID A FAIR WAGE.
AT TWELVE, I COULD CUT DOWN PINE THAT MEN TWICE MY AGE COULDN'T.
AT SEVENTEEN, I MARRIED KRISTA, A BEAUTY WITH GOLDEN HAIR AND A SMILE JUST AS BRIGHT.
A FEW YEARS LATER, SHE GAVE US A DAUGHTER, MARTA, THE JOY OF OUR LIVES.

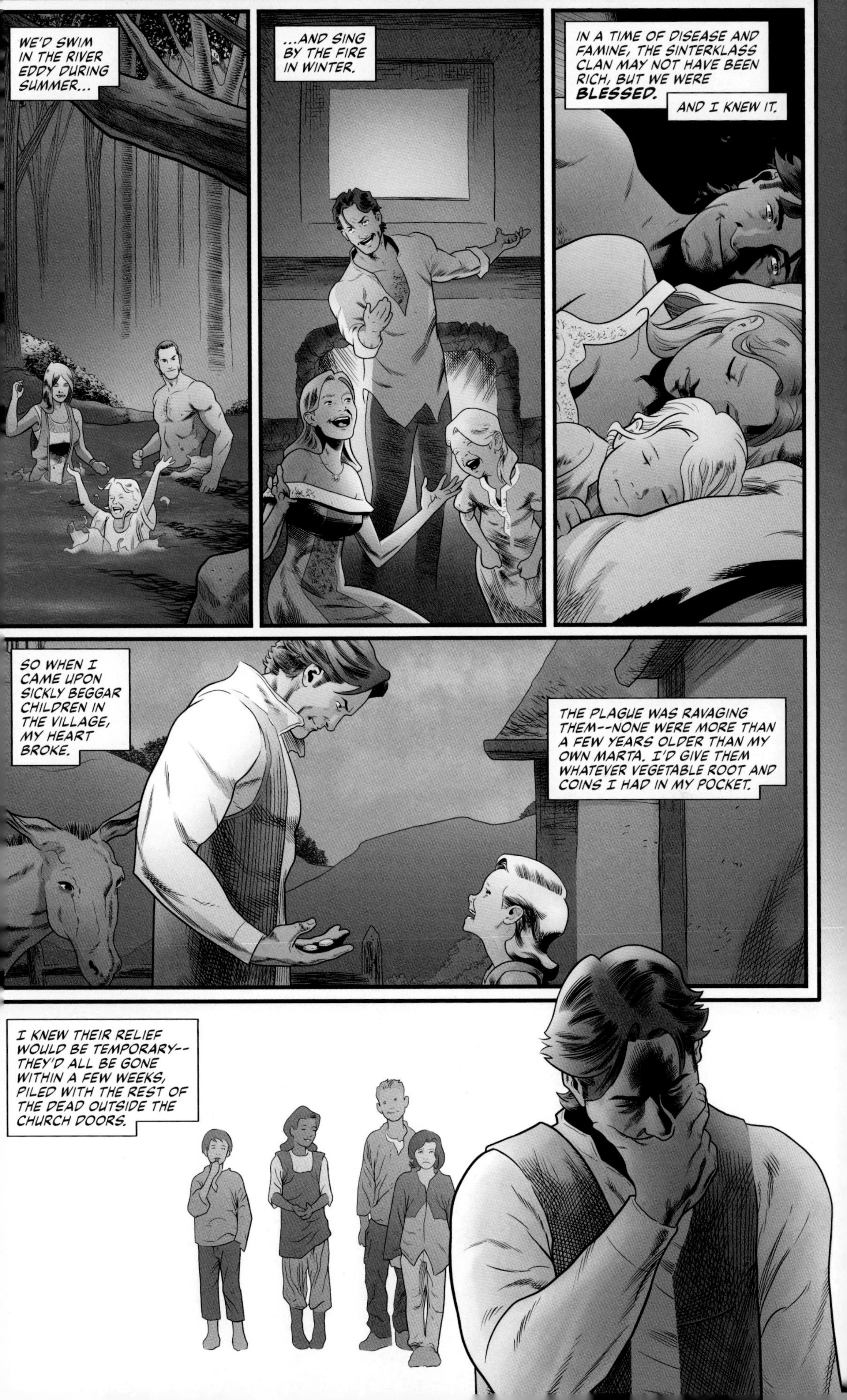
WE'D SWIM IN THE RIVER EDDY DURING SUMMER...
...AND SING BY THE FIRE IN WINTER.
IN A TIME OF DISEASE AND FAMINE, THE SINTERKLASS CLAN MAY NOT HAVE BEEN RICH, BUT WE WERE **BLESSED.**
AND I KNEW IT.
SO WHEN I CAME UPON SICKLY BEGGAR CHILDREN IN THE VILLAGE, MY HEART BROKE.
THE PLAGUE WAS RAVAGING THEM--NONE WERE MORE THAN A FEW YEARS OLDER THAN MY OWN MARTA. I'D GIVE THEM WHATEVER VEGETABLE ROOT AND COINS I HAD IN MY POCKET.
I KNEW THEIR RELIEF WOULD BE TEMPORARY--THEY'D ALL BE GONE WITHIN A FEW WEEKS, PILED WITH THE REST OF THE DEAD OUTSIDE THE CHURCH DOORS.

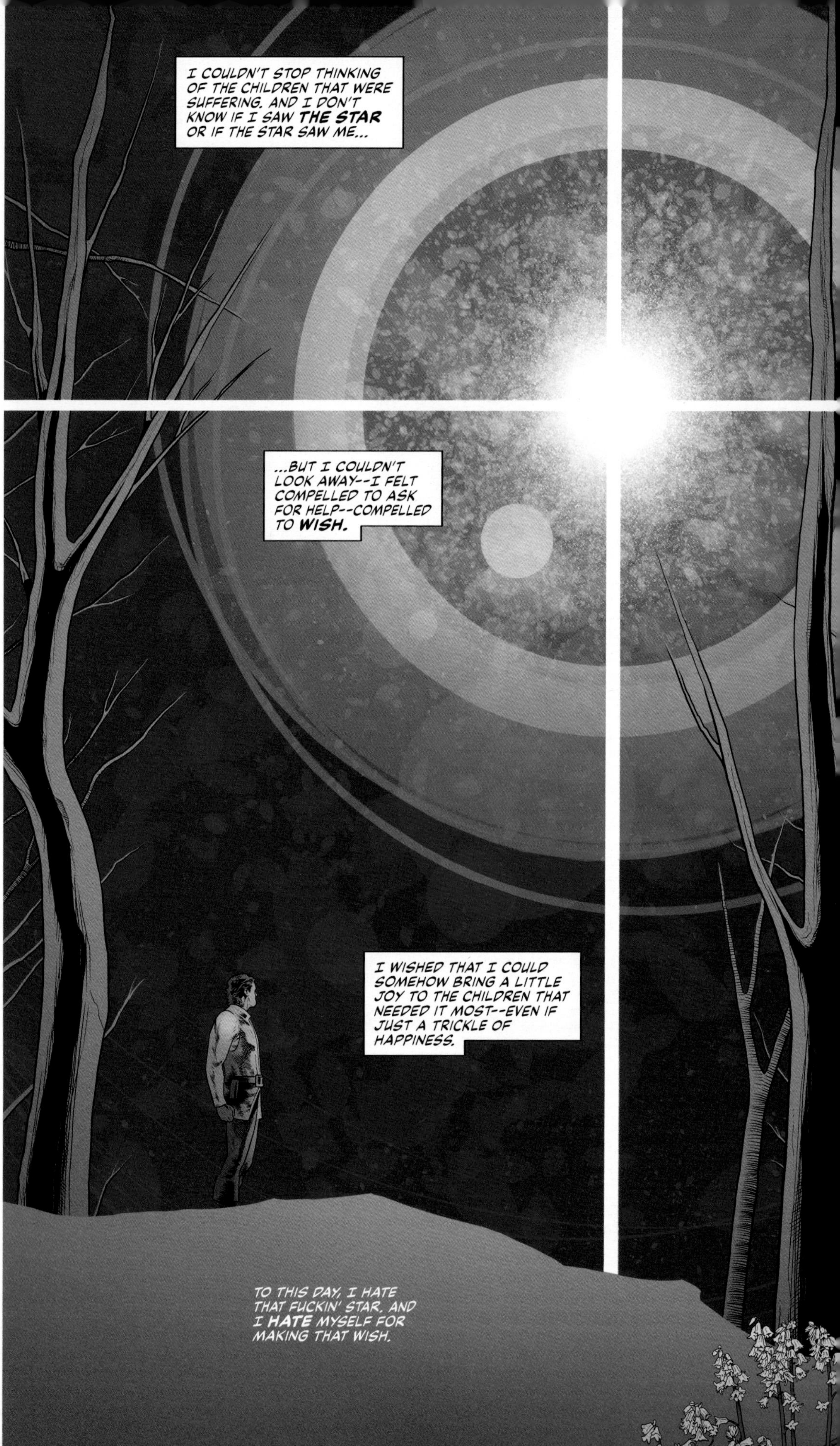
I COULDN'T STOP THINKING OF THE CHILDREN THAT WERE SUFFERING. AND I DON'T KNOW IF I SAW **THE STAR** OR IF THE STAR SAW ME...
...BUT I COULDN'T LOOK AWAY--I FELT COMPELLED TO ASK FOR HELP--COMPELLED TO **WISH.**
I WISHED THAT I COULD SOMEHOW BRING A LITTLE JOY TO THE CHILDREN THAT NEEDED IT MOST--EVEN IF JUST A TRICKLE OF HAPPINESS.
TO THIS DAY, I HATE THAT FUCKIN' STAR. AND I **HATE** MYSELF FOR MAKING THAT WISH.

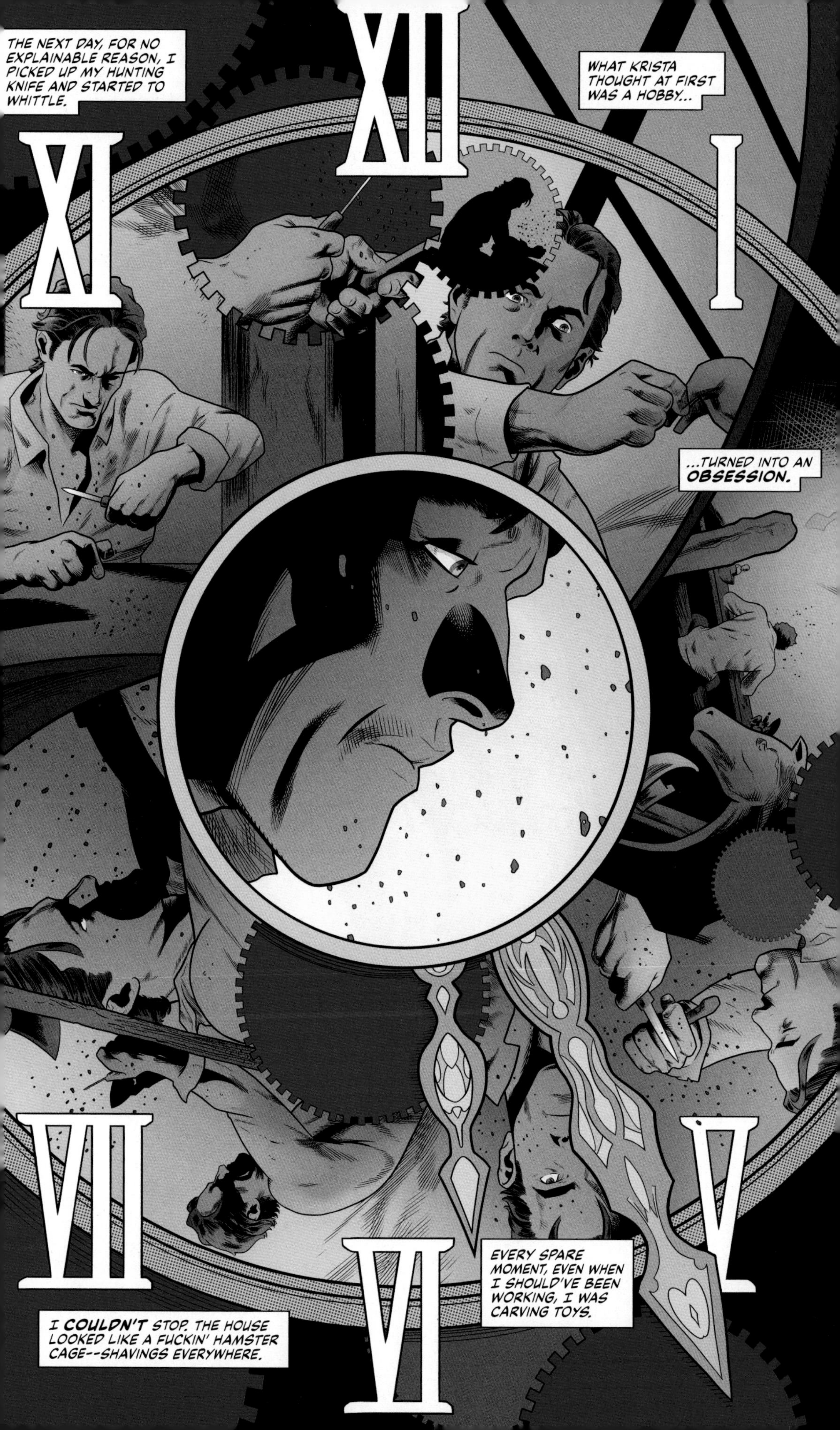
THE NEXT DAY, FOR NO EXPLAINABLE REASON, I PICKED UP MY HUNTING KNIFE AND STARTED TO WHITTLE.
WHAT KRISTA THOUGHT AT FIRST WAS A HOBBY...
...TURNED INTO AN **OBSESSION.**
EVERY SPARE MOMENT, EVEN WHEN I SHOULD'VE BEEN WORKING, I WAS CARVING TOYS.
I **COULDN'T** STOP. THE HOUSE LOOKED LIKE A FUCKIN' HAMSTER CAGE--SHAVINGS EVERYWHERE.

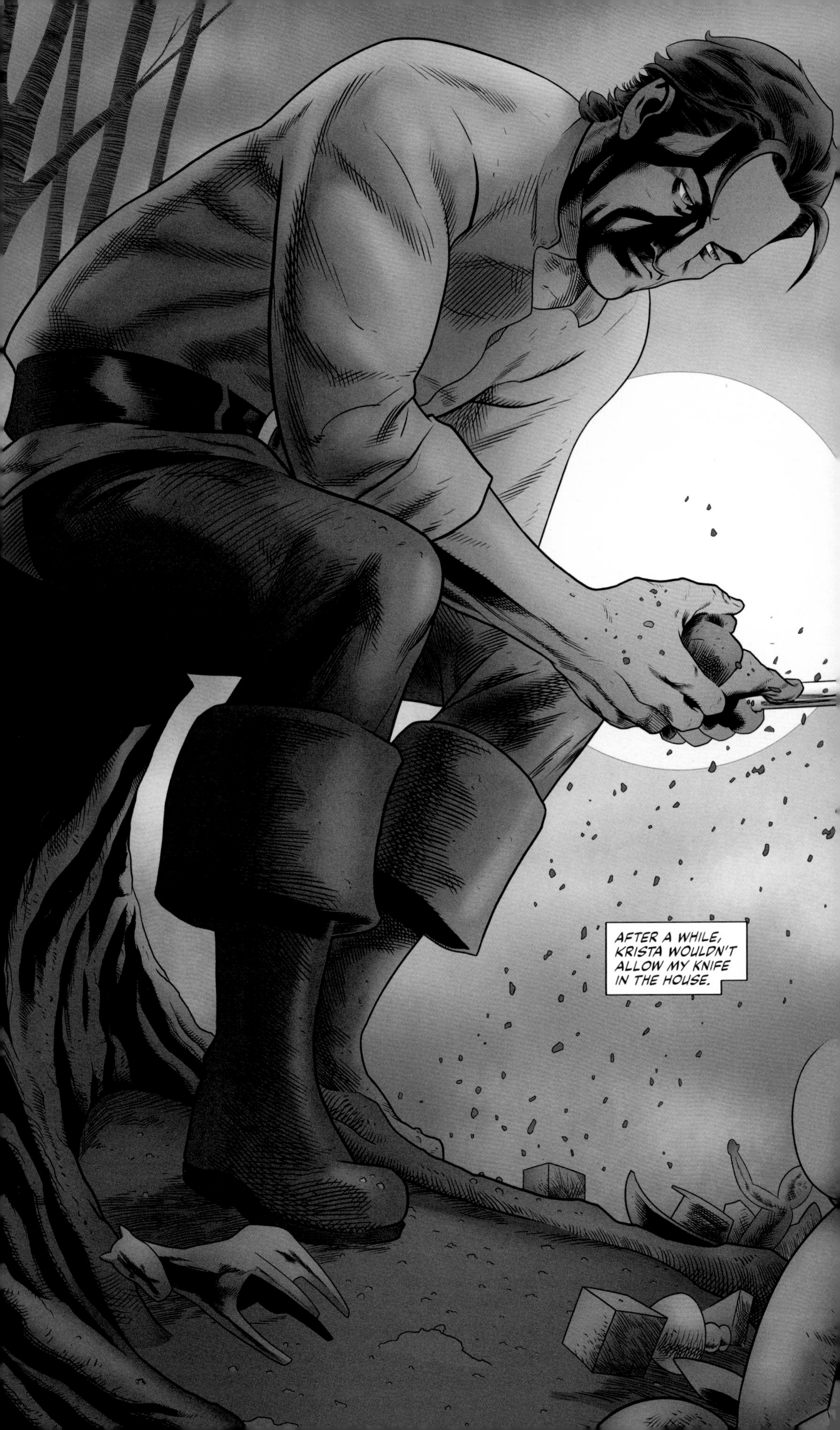
AFTER A WHILE, KRISTA WOULDN'T ALLOW MY KNIFE IN THE HOUSE.

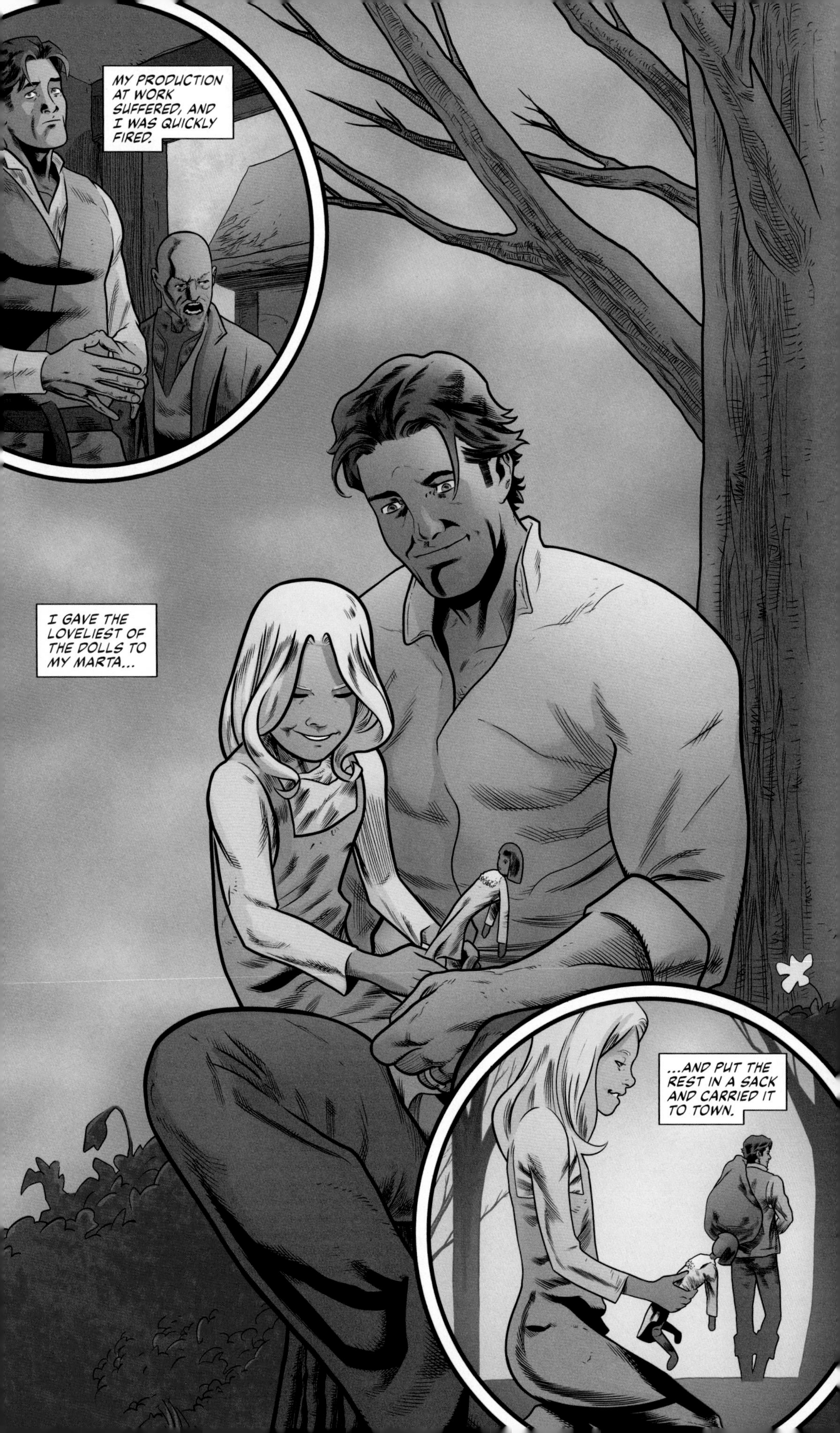
MY PRODUCTION AT WORK SUFFERED, AND I WAS QUICKLY FIRED.
I GAVE THE LOVELIEST OF THE DOLLS TO MY MARTA...
...AND PUT THE REST IN A SACK AND CARRIED IT TO TOWN.

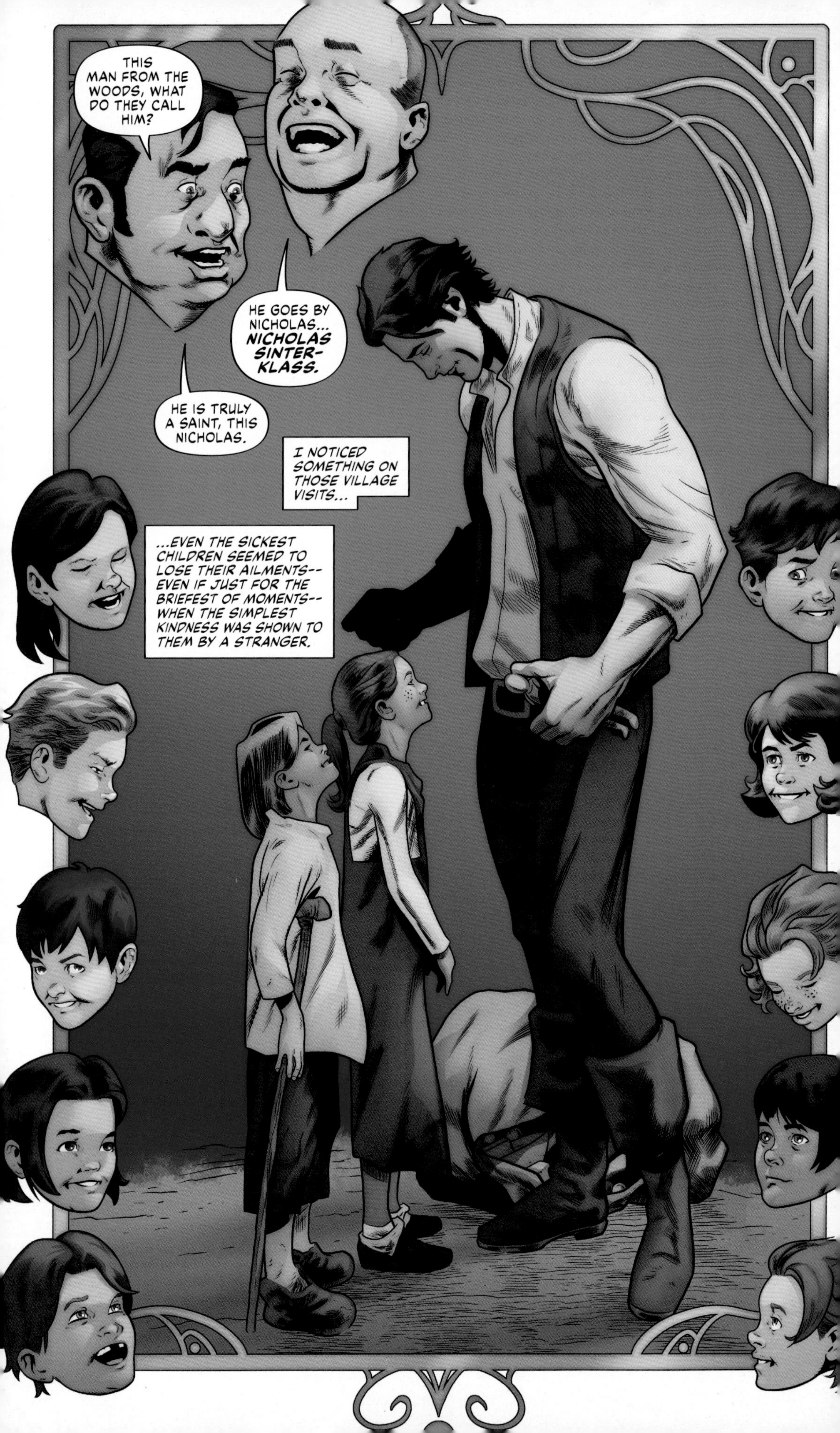
THIS MAN FROM THE WOODS, WHAT DO THEY CALL HIM?
HE GOES BY NICHOLAS... NICHOLAS SINTER-KLASS.
HE IS TRULY A SAINT, THIS NICHOLAS.
I NOTICED SOMETHING ON THOSE VILLAGE VISITS...
...EVEN THE SICKEST CHILDREN SEEMED TO LOSE THEIR AILMENTS--EVEN IF JUST FOR THE BRIEFEST OF MOMENTS--WHEN THE SIMPLEST KINDNESS WAS SHOWN TO THEM BY A STRANGER.

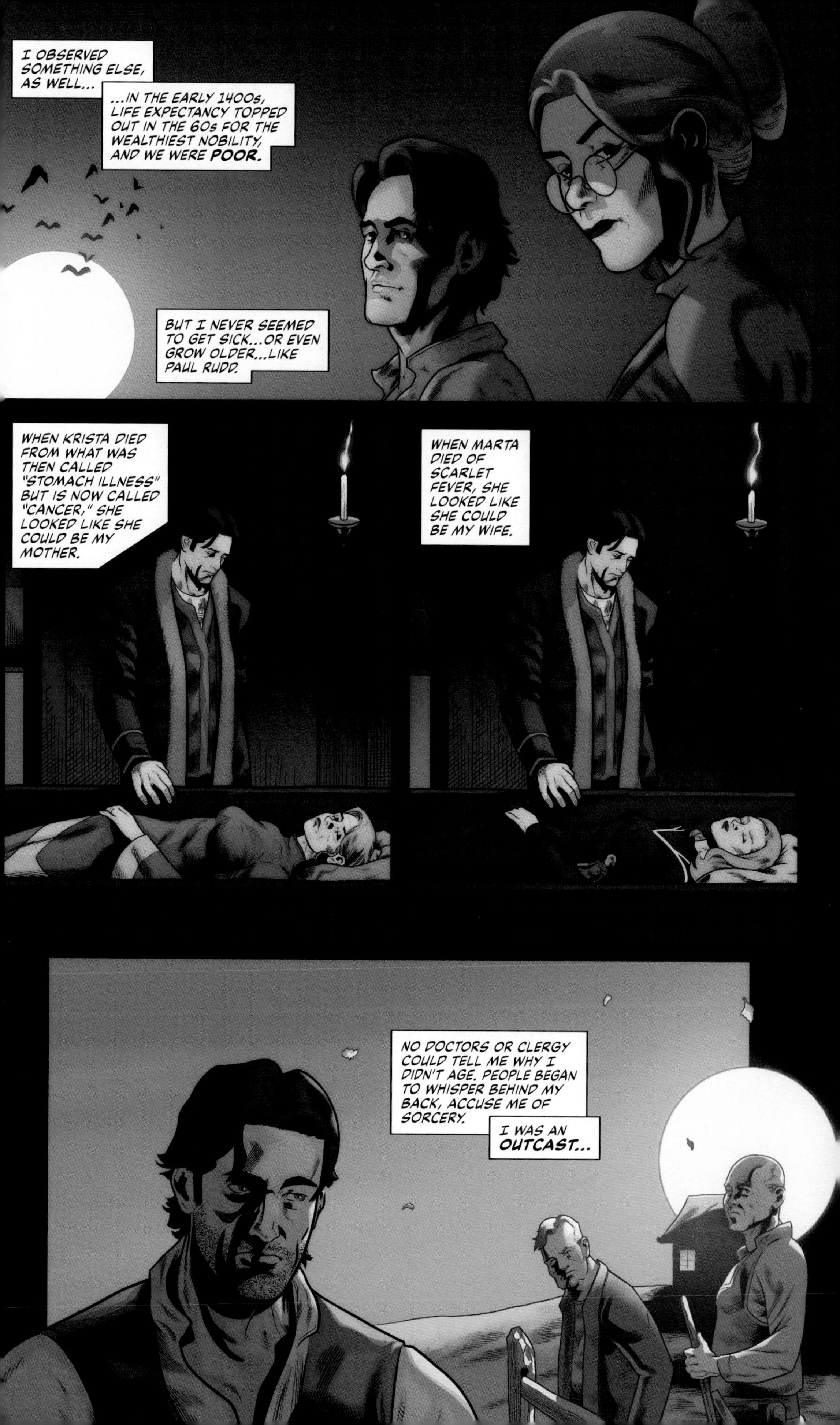
I OBSERVED SOMETHING ELSE, AS WELL...
...IN THE EARLY 1400s, LIFE EXPECTANCY TOPPED OUT IN THE 60s FOR THE WEALTHIEST NOBILITY, AND WE WERE POOR.
BUT I NEVER SEEMED TO GET SICK...OR EVEN GROW OLDER...LIKE PAUL RUDD.
WHEN KRISTA DIED FROM WHAT WAS THEN CALLED "STOMACH ILLNESS" BUT IS NOW CALLED "CANCER," SHE LOOKED LIKE SHE COULD BE MY MOTHER.
WHEN MARTA DIED OF SCARLET FEVER, SHE LOOKED LIKE SHE COULD BE MY WIFE.
NO DOCTORS OR CLERGY COULD TELL ME WHY I DIDN'T AGE. PEOPLE BEGAN TO WHISPER BEHIND MY BACK, ACCUSE ME OF SORCERY.
I WAS AN OUTCAST...

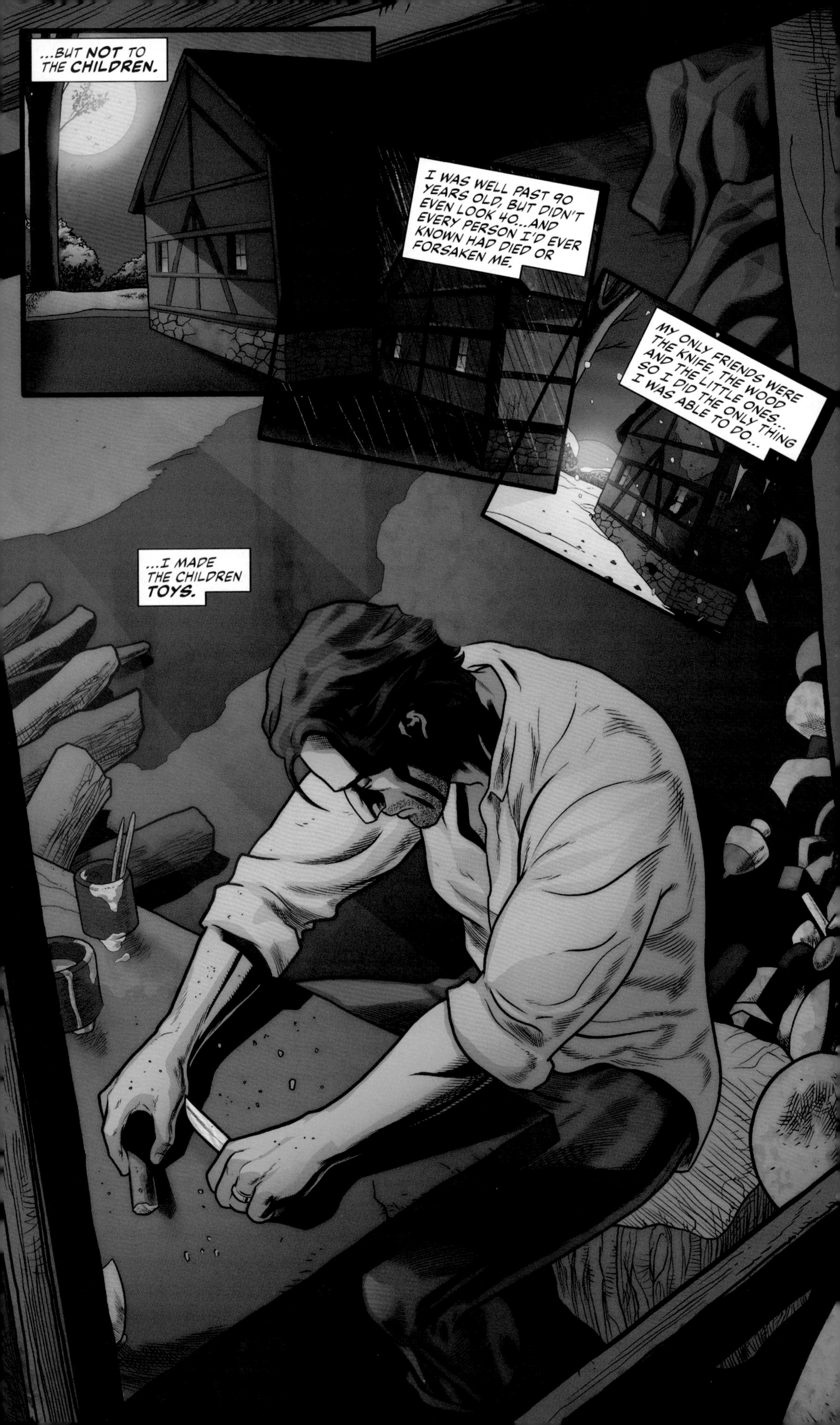
...BUT NOT TO THE CHILDREN.
I WAS WELL PAST 90 YEARS OLD, BUT DIDN'T EVEN LOOK 40...AND EVERY PERSON I'D EVER KNOWN HAD DIED OR FORSAKEN ME.
MY ONLY FRIENDS WERE THE KNIFE, THE WOOD AND THE LITTLE ONES... SO I DID THE ONLY THING I WAS ABLE TO DO...
...I MADE THE CHILDREN TOYS.

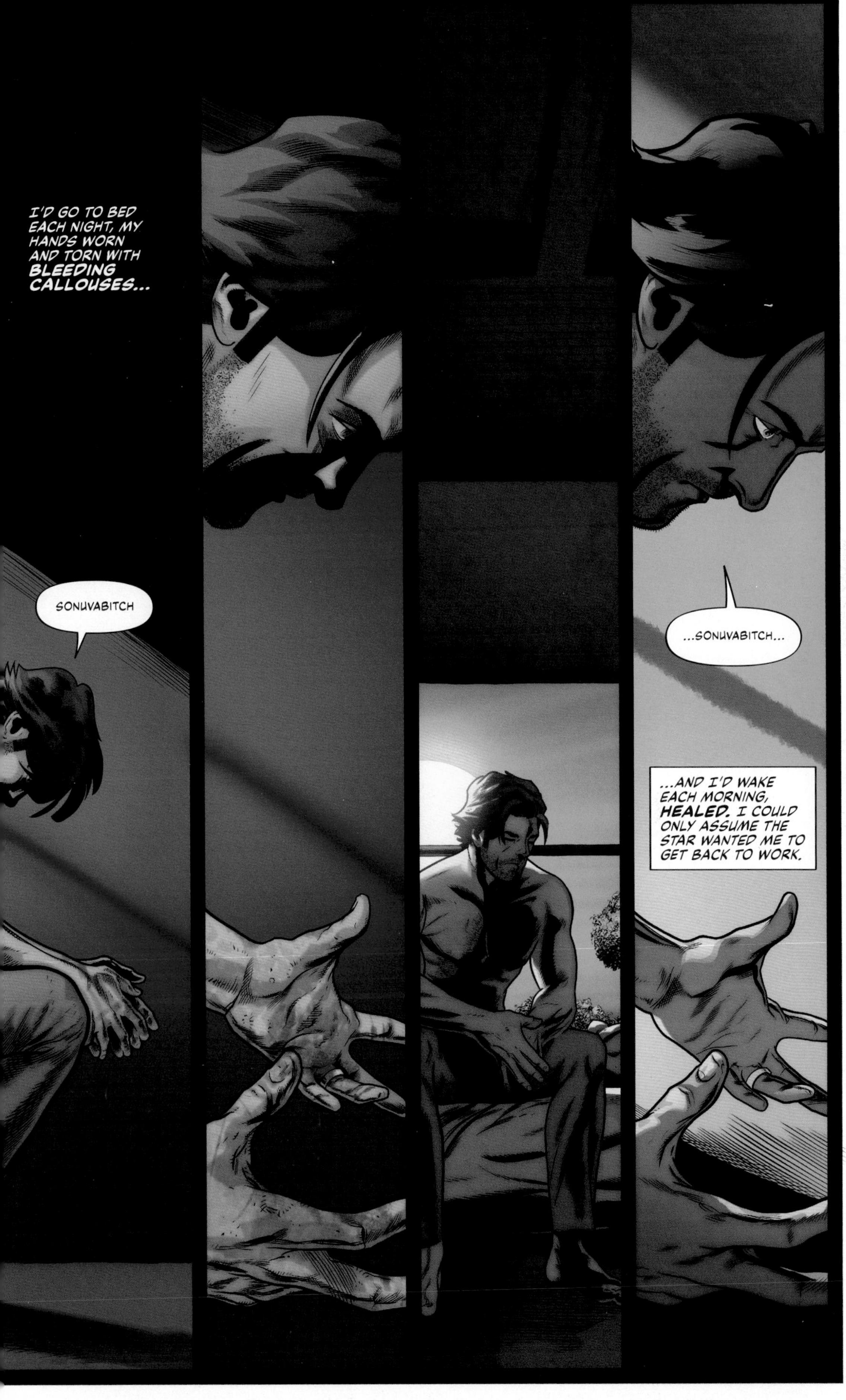
I'D GO TO BED EACH NIGHT, MY HANDS WORN AND TORN WITH BLEEDING CALLOUSES...
SONUVABITCH
...SONUVABITCH...
...AND I'D WAKE EACH MORNING, HEALED. I COULD ONLY ASSUME THE STAR WANTED ME TO GET BACK TO WORK.

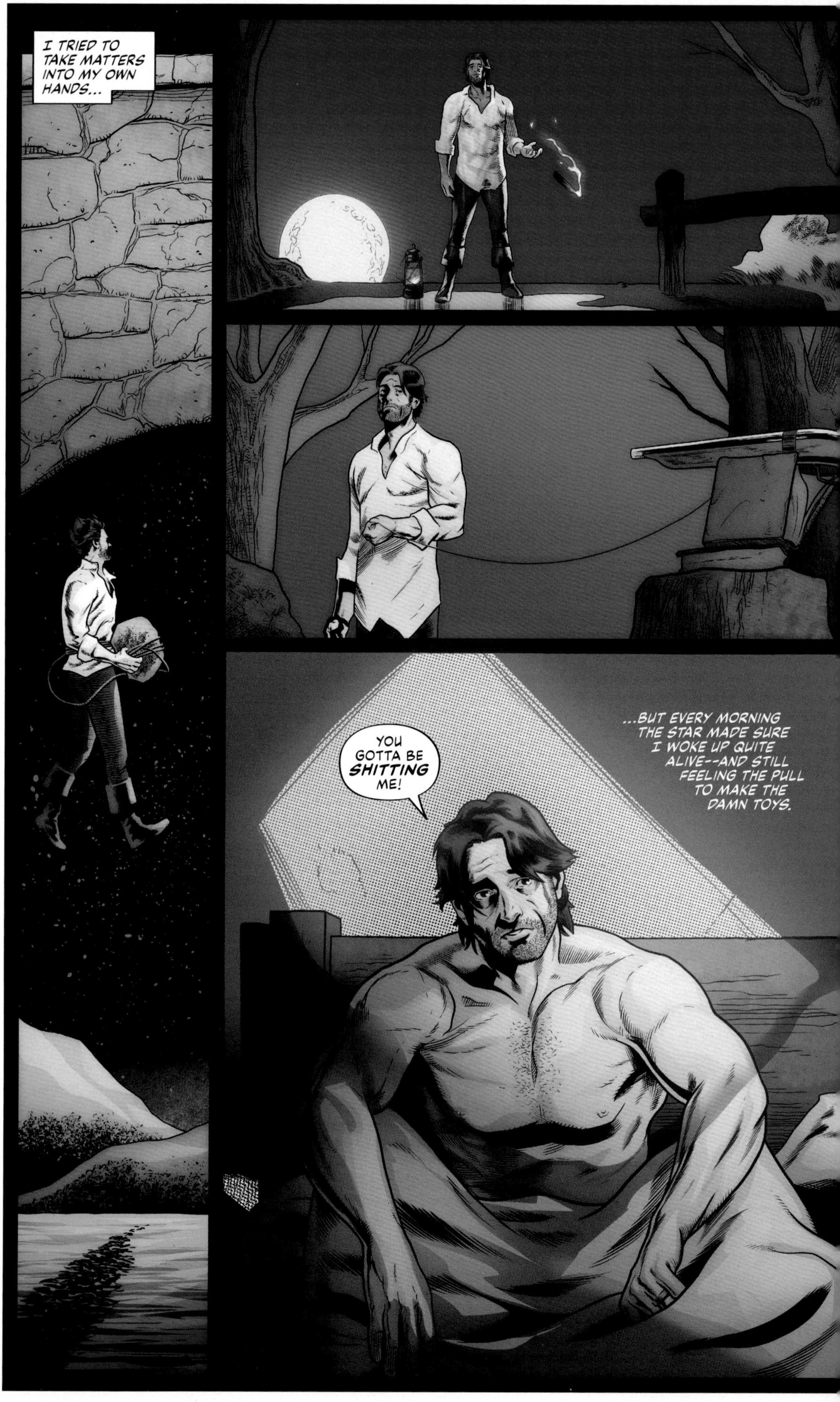

I TRIED TO TAKE MATTERS INTO MY OWN HANDS...
YOU GOTTA BE SHITTING ME!
...BUT EVERY MORNING THE STAR MADE SURE I WOKE UP QUITE ALIVE--AND STILL FEELING THE PULL TO MAKE THE DAMN TOYS.

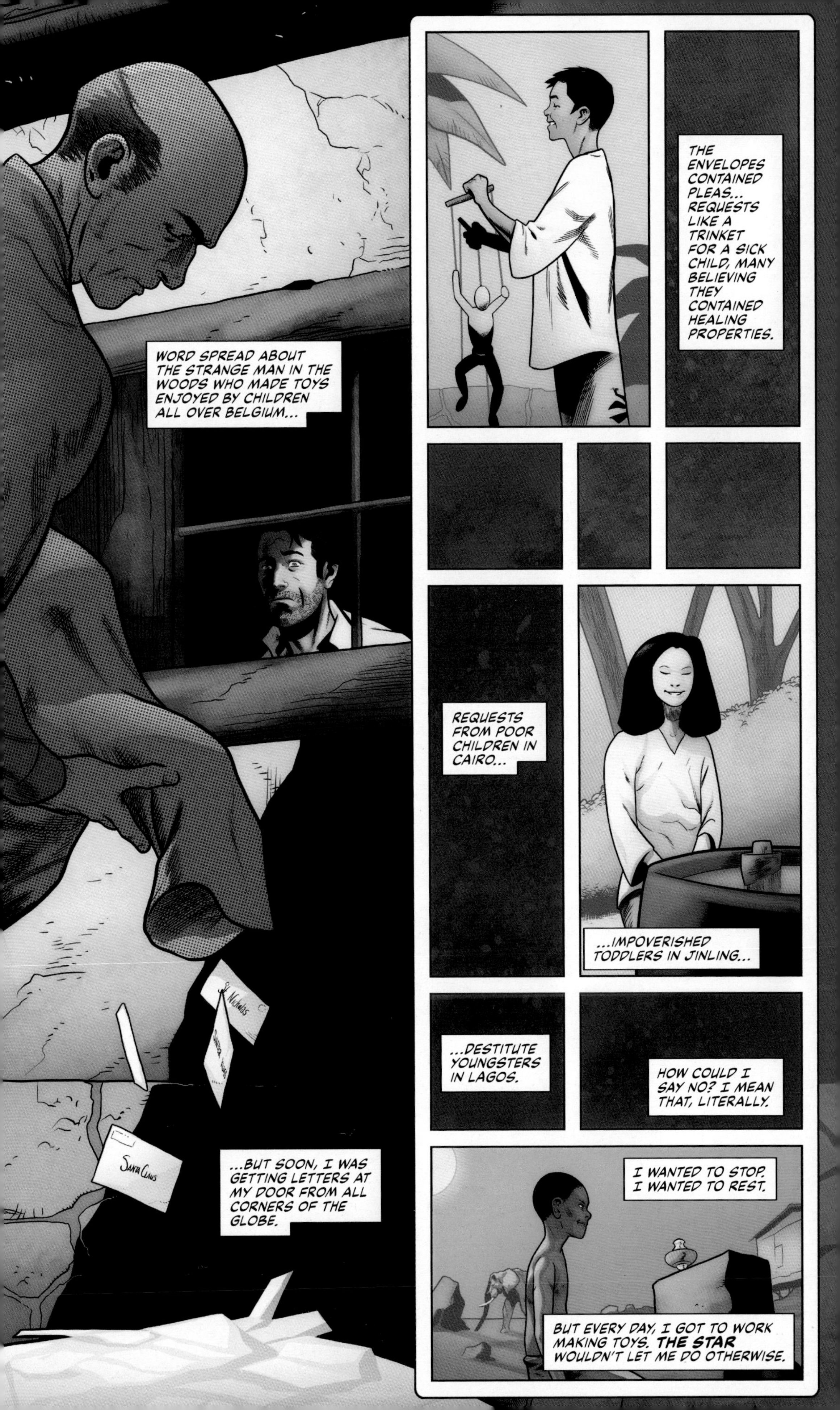
WORD SPREAD ABOUT THE STRANGE MAN IN THE WOODS WHO MADE TOYS ENJOYED BY CHILDREN ALL OVER BELGIUM...
St. Nicholas
Santa Claus
...BUT SOON, I WAS GETTING LETTERS AT MY DOOR FROM ALL CORNERS OF THE GLOBE.
THE ENVELOPES CONTAINED PLEAS... REQUESTS LIKE A TRINKET FOR A SICK CHILD, MANY BELIEVING THEY CONTAINED HEALING PROPERTIES.
REQUESTS FROM POOR CHILDREN IN CAIRO...
...IMPOVERISHED TODDLERS IN JINLING...
...DESTITUTE YOUNGSTERS IN LAGOS.
HOW COULD I SAY NO? I MEAN THAT, LITERALLY.
I WANTED TO STOP. I WANTED TO REST.
BUT EVERY DAY, I GOT TO WORK MAKING TOYS. THE STAR WOULDN'T LET ME DO OTHERWISE.

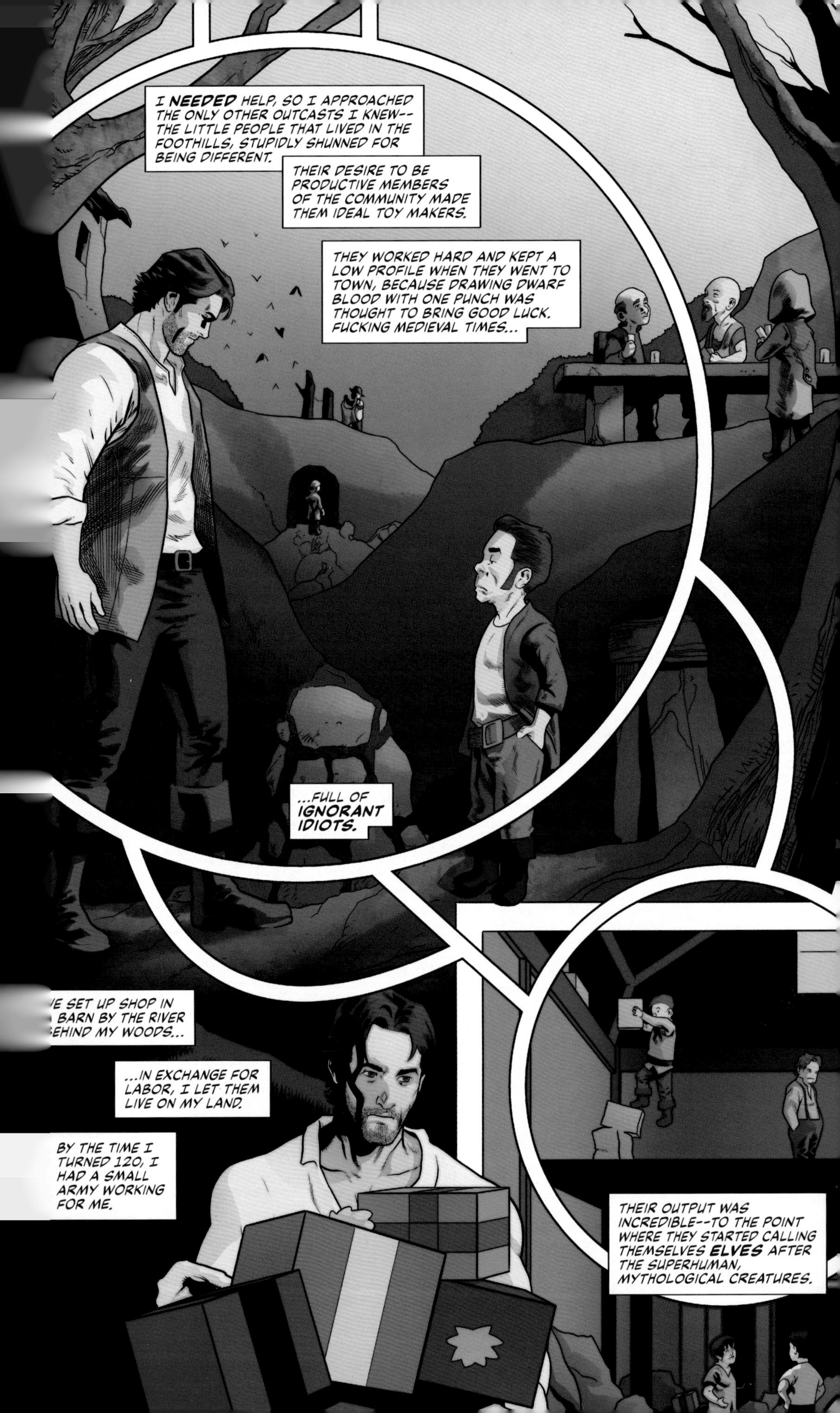

I NEEDED HELP, SO I APPROACHED THE ONLY OTHER OUTCASTS I KNEW-- THE LITTLE PEOPLE THAT LIVED IN THE FOOTHILLS, STUPIDLY SHUNNED FOR BEING DIFFERENT.
THEIR DESIRE TO BE PRODUCTIVE MEMBERS OF THE COMMUNITY MADE THEM IDEAL TOY MAKERS.
THEY WORKED HARD AND KEPT A LOW PROFILE WHEN THEY WENT TO TOWN, BECAUSE DRAWING DWARF BLOOD WITH ONE PUNCH WAS THOUGHT TO BRING GOOD LUCK. FUCKING MEDIEVAL TIMES...
...FULL OF IGNORANT IDIOTS.
E SET UP SHOP IN BARN BY THE RIVER EHIND MY WOODS...
...IN EXCHANGE FOR LABOR, I LET THEM LIVE ON MY LAND.
BY THE TIME I TURNED 120, I HAD A SMALL ARMY WORKING FOR ME.
THEIR OUTPUT WAS INCREDIBLE--TO THE POINT WHERE THEY STARTED CALLING THEMSELVES ELVES AFTER THE SUPERHUMAN, MYTHOLOGICAL CREATURES.

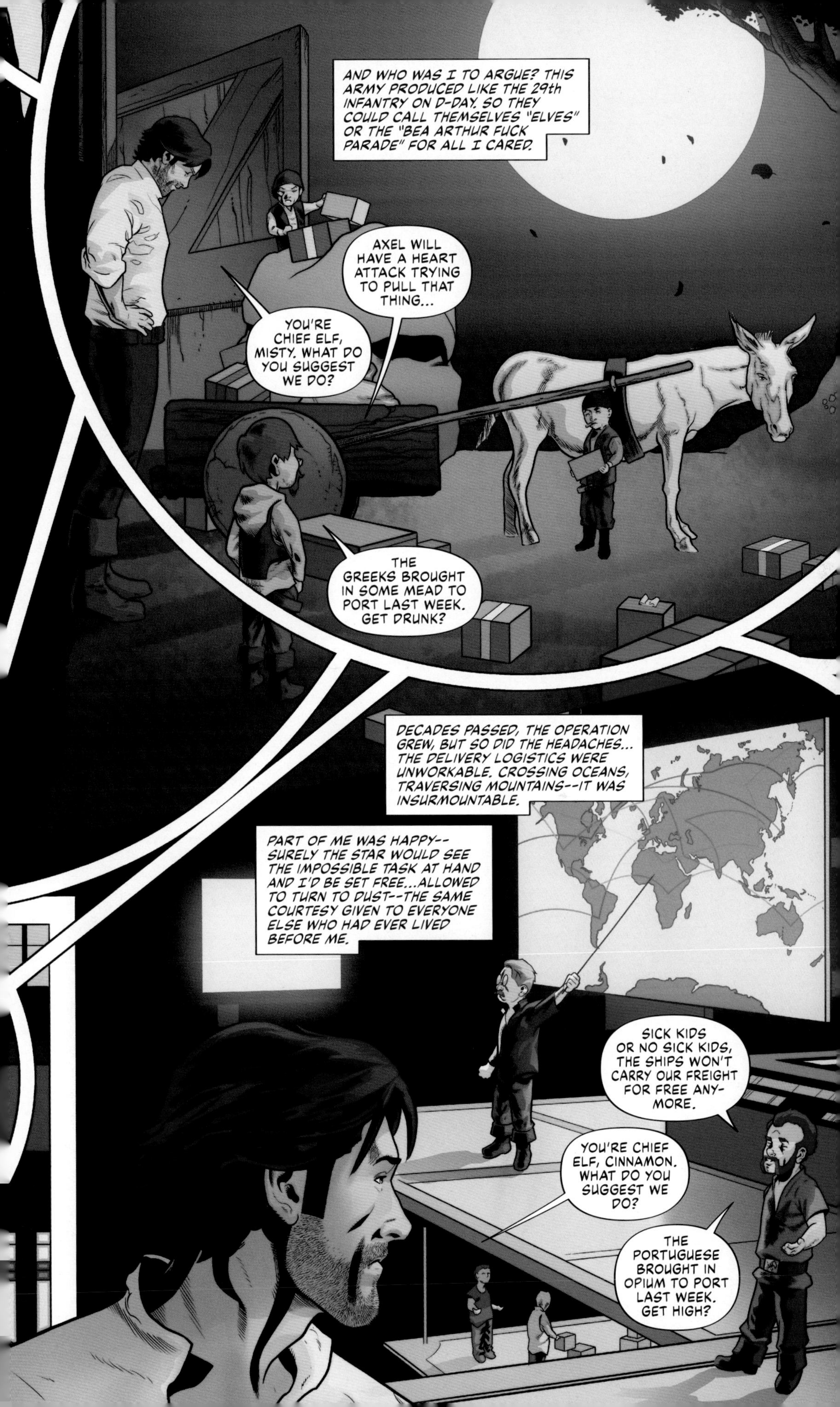
AND WHO WAS I TO ARGUE? THIS ARMY PRODUCED LIKE THE 29th INFANTRY ON D-DAY. SO THEY COULD CALL THEMSELVES "ELVES" OR THE "BEA ARTHUR FUCK PARADE" FOR ALL I CARED.
AXEL WILL HAVE A HEART ATTACK TRYING TO PULL THAT THING...
YOU'RE CHIEF ELF, MISTY. WHAT DO YOU SUGGEST WE DO?
THE GREEKS BROUGHT IN SOME MEAD TO PORT LAST WEEK. GET DRUNK?
DECADES PASSED, THE OPERATION GREW, BUT SO DID THE HEADACHES... THE DELIVERY LOGISTICS WERE UNWORKABLE. CROSSING OCEANS, TRAVERSING MOUNTAINS--IT WAS INSURMOUNTABLE.
PART OF ME WAS HAPPY--SURELY THE STAR WOULD SEE THE IMPOSSIBLE TASK AT HAND AND I'D BE SET FREE...ALLOWED TO TURN TO DUST--THE SAME COURTESY GIVEN TO EVERYONE ELSE WHO HAD EVER LIVED BEFORE ME.
SICK KIDS OR NO SICK KIDS, THE SHIPS WON'T CARRY OUR FREIGHT FOR FREE ANY-MORE.
YOU'RE CHIEF ELF, CINNAMON. WHAT DO YOU SUGGEST WE DO?
THE PORTUGUESE BROUGHT IN OPIUM TO PORT LAST WEEK. GET HIGH?

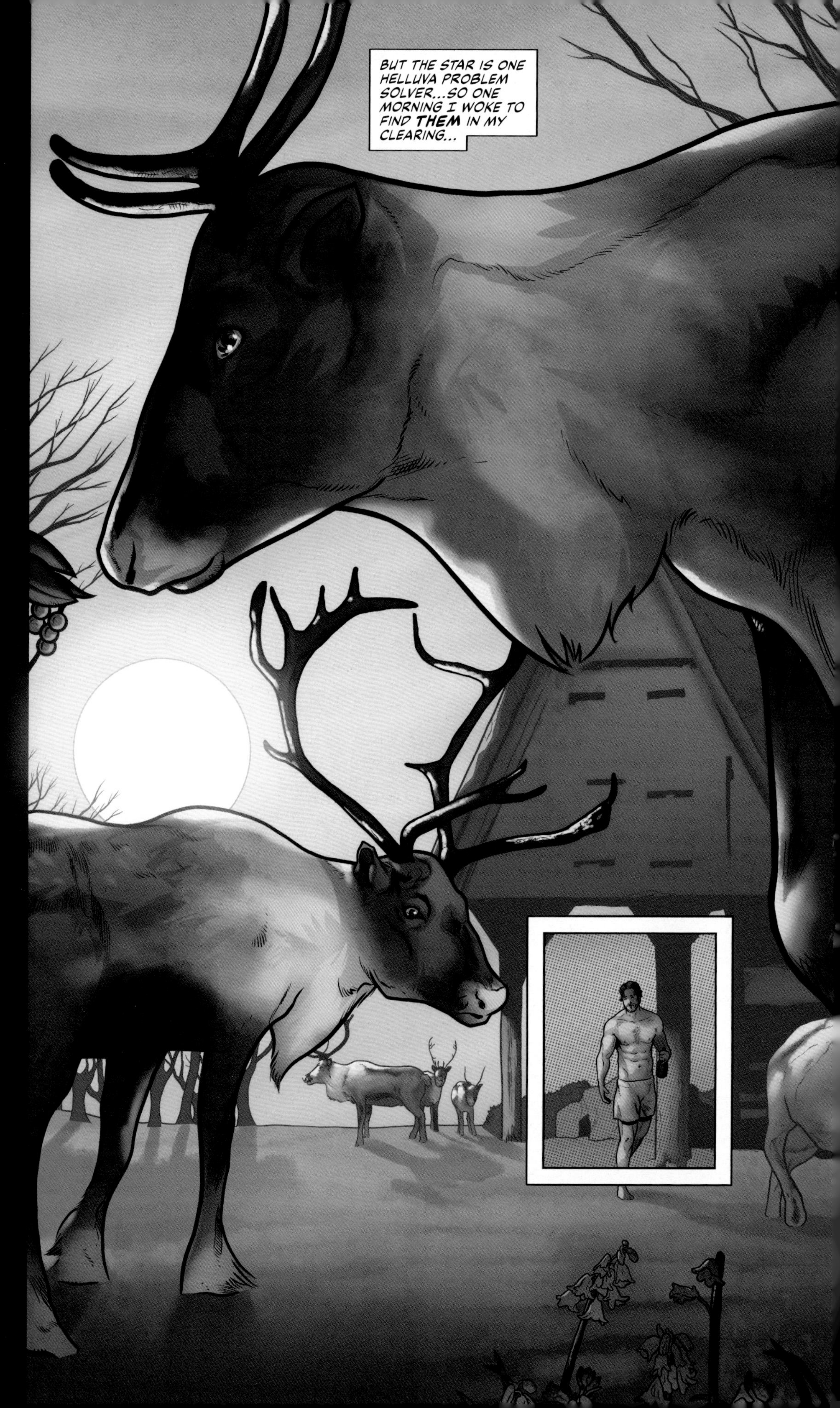
BUT THE STAR IS ONE HELLUVA PROBLEM SOLVER...SO ONE MORNING I WOKE TO FIND **THEM** IN MY CLEARING...

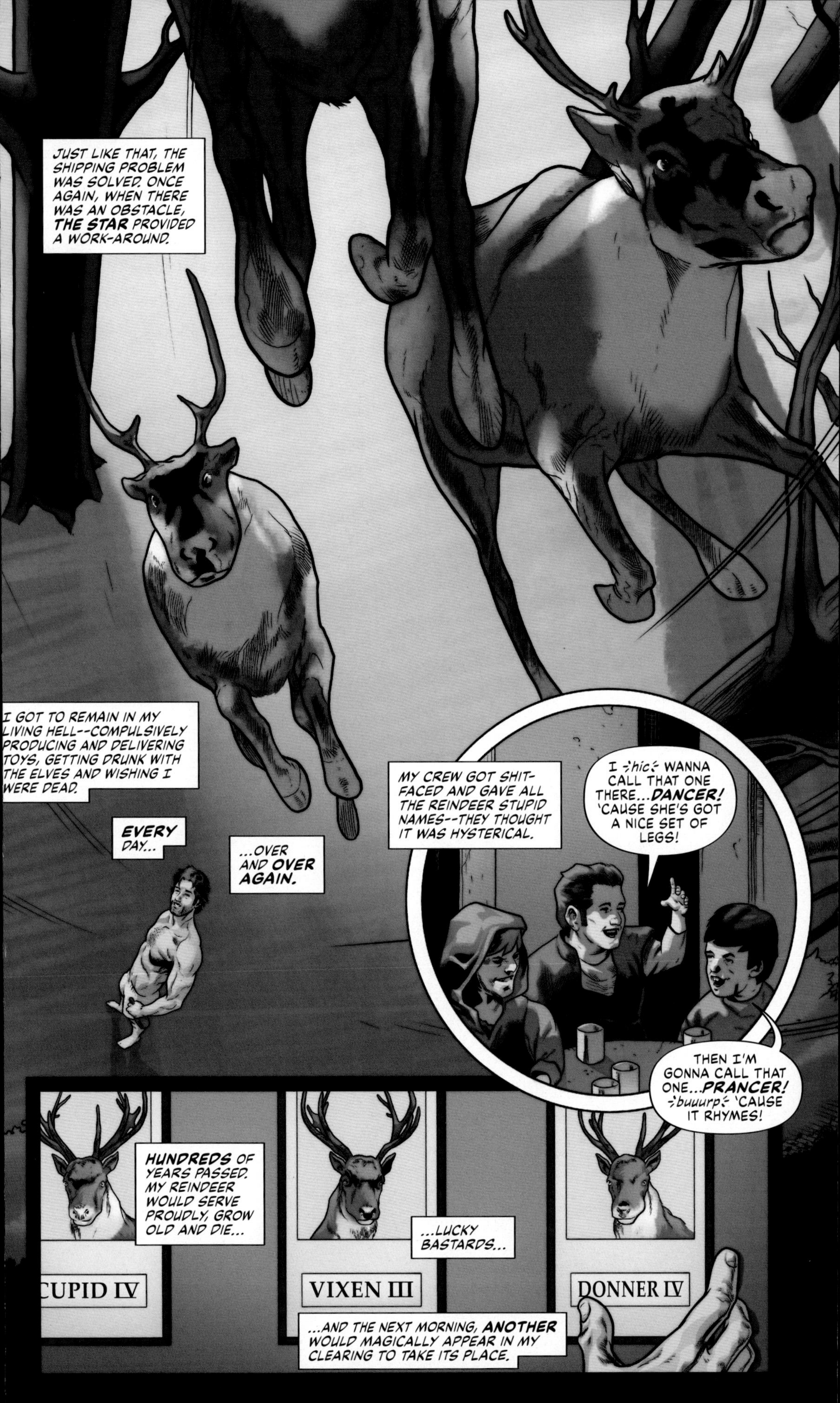

JUST LIKE THAT, THE SHIPPING PROBLEM WAS SOLVED. ONCE AGAIN, WHEN THERE WAS AN OBSTACLE, THE STAR PROVIDED A WORK-AROUND.
I GOT TO REMAIN IN MY LIVING HELL--COMPULSIVELY PRODUCING AND DELIVERING TOYS, GETTING DRUNK WITH THE ELVES AND WISHING I WERE DEAD.
EVERY DAY...
...OVER AND OVER AGAIN.
MY CREW GOT SHIT-FACED AND GAVE ALL THE REINDEER STUPID NAMES--THEY THOUGHT IT WAS HYSTERICAL.
I -hic- WANNA CALL THAT ONE THERE...DANCER! 'CAUSE SHE'S GOT A NICE SET OF LEGS!
THEN I'M GONNA CALL THAT ONE...PRANCER! -buuurp- 'CAUSE IT RHYMES!
HUNDREDS OF YEARS PASSED. MY REINDEER WOULD SERVE PROUDLY, GROW OLD AND DIE...
CUPID IV
...LUCKY BASTARDS...
VIXEN III
DONNER IV
...AND THE NEXT MORNING, ANOTHER WOULD MAGICALLY APPEAR IN MY CLEARING TO TAKE ITS PLACE.

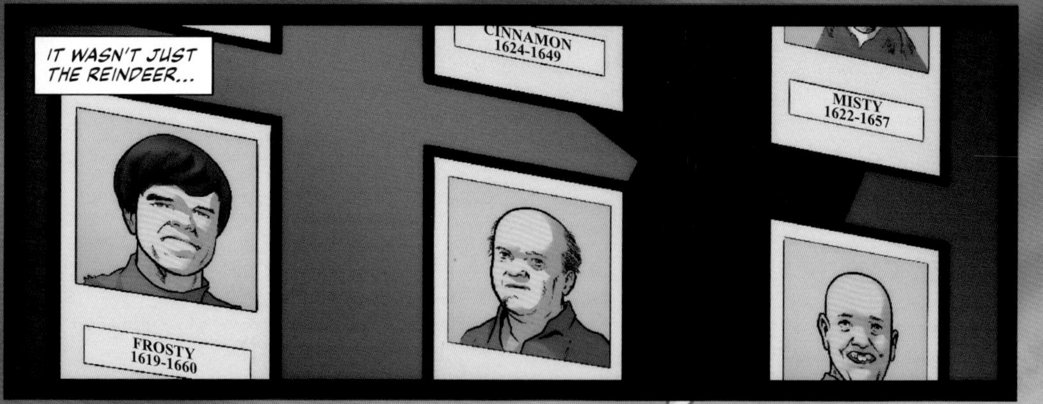
IT WASN'T JUST THE REINDEER...
CINNAMON 1624-1649
MISTY 1622-1657
FROSTY 1619-1660

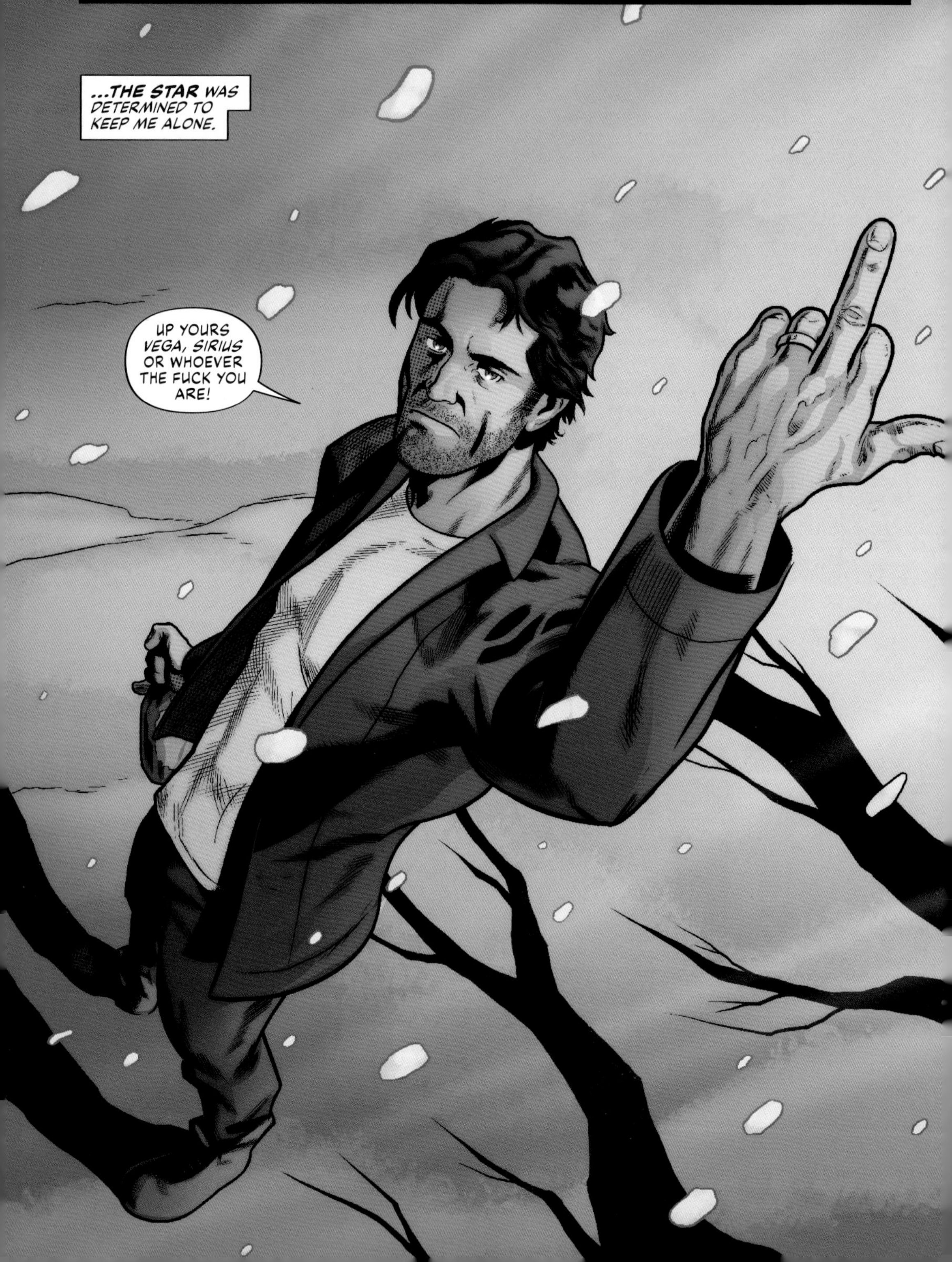
...THE STAR WAS DETERMINED TO KEEP ME ALONE.
UP YOURS VEGA, SIRIUS OR WHOEVER THE FUCK YOU ARE!

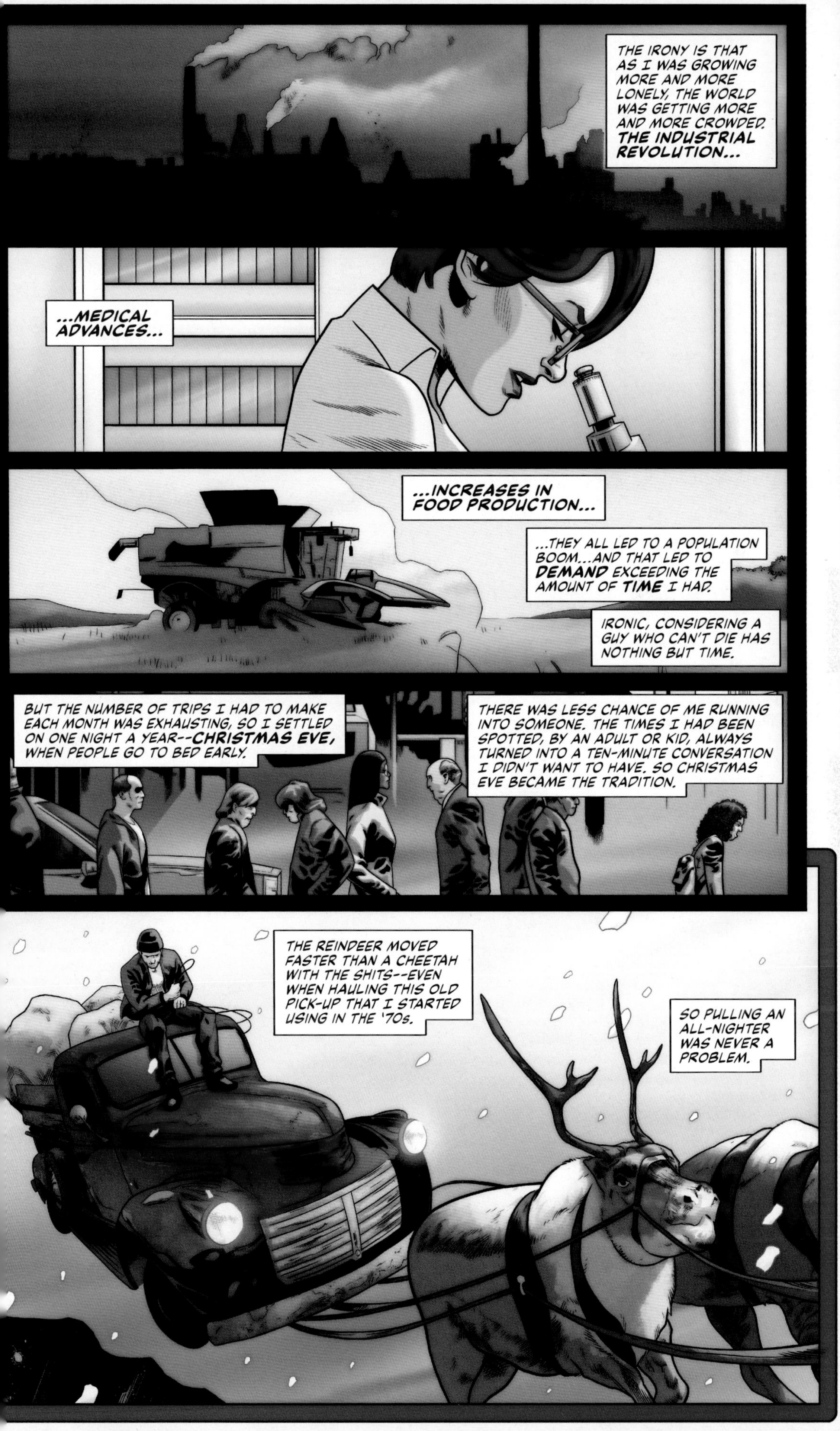
THE IRONY IS THAT AS I WAS GROWING MORE AND MORE LONELY, THE WORLD WAS GETTING MORE AND MORE CROWDED. THE INDUSTRIAL REVOLUTION...
...MEDICAL ADVANCES...
...INCREASES IN FOOD PRODUCTION...
...THEY ALL LED TO A POPULATION BOOM...AND THAT LED TO DEMAND EXCEEDING THE AMOUNT OF TIME I HAD.
IRONIC, CONSIDERING A GUY WHO CAN'T DIE HAS NOTHING BUT TIME.
BUT THE NUMBER OF TRIPS I HAD TO MAKE EACH MONTH WAS EXHAUSTING, SO I SETTLED ON ONE NIGHT A YEAR--CHRISTMAS EVE, WHEN PEOPLE GO TO BED EARLY.
THERE WAS LESS CHANCE OF ME RUNNING INTO SOMEONE. THE TIMES I HAD BEEN SPOTTED, BY AN ADULT OR KID, ALWAYS TURNED INTO A TEN-MINUTE CONVERSATION I DIDN'T WANT TO HAVE. SO CHRISTMAS EVE BECAME THE TRADITION.
THE REINDEER MOVED FASTER THAN A CHEETAH WITH THE SHITS--EVEN WHEN HAULING THIS OLD PICK-UP THAT I STARTED USING IN THE '70s.
SO PULLING AN ALL-NIGHTER WAS NEVER A PROBLEM.

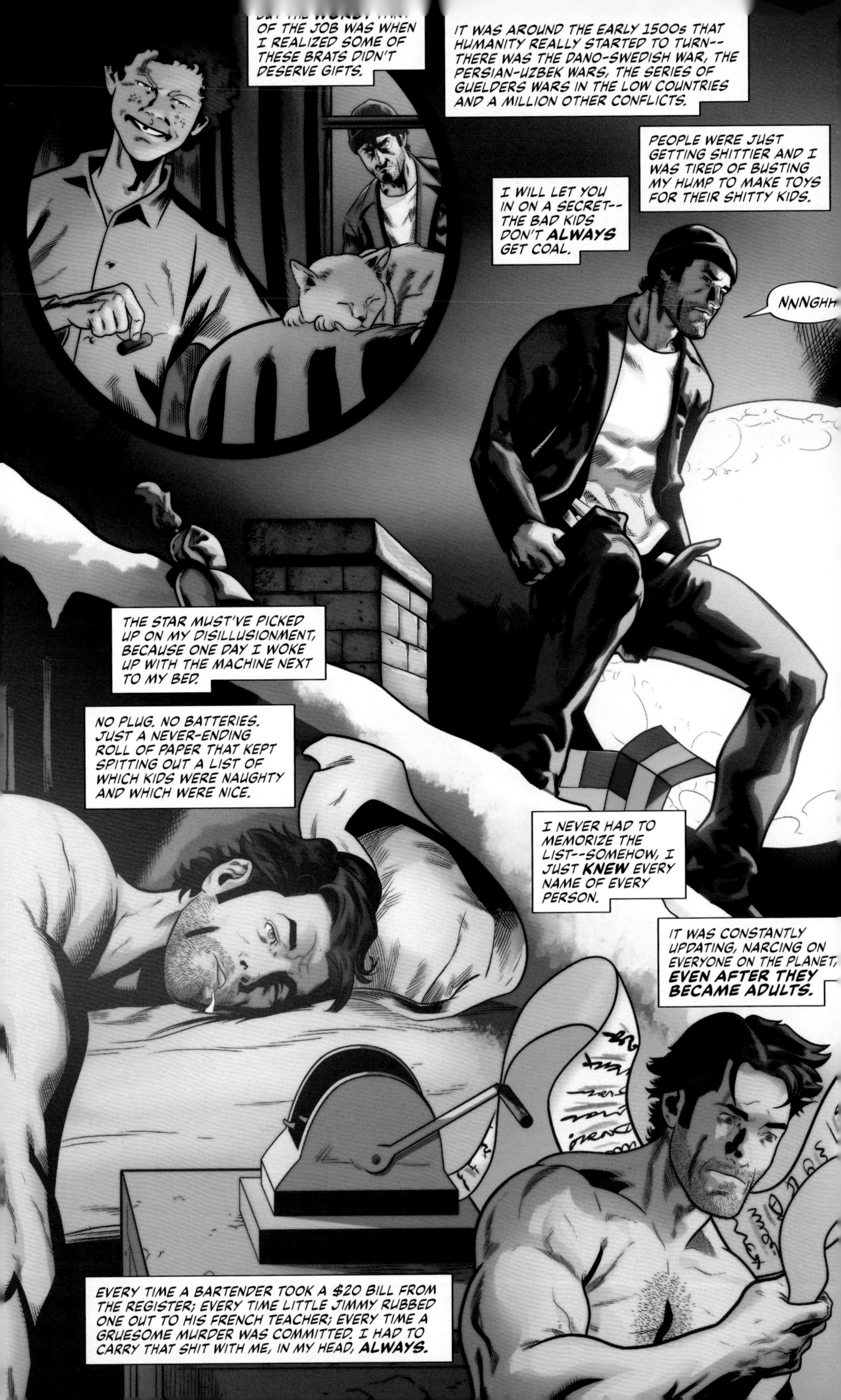
OF THE JOB WAS WHEN I REALIZED SOME OF THESE BRATS DIDN'T DESERVE GIFTS.
IT WAS AROUND THE EARLY 1500s THAT HUMANITY REALLY STARTED TO TURN-- THERE WAS THE DANO-SWEDISH WAR, THE PERSIAN-UZBEK WARS, THE SERIES OF GUELDERS WARS IN THE LOW COUNTRIES AND A MILLION OTHER CONFLICTS.
PEOPLE WERE JUST GETTING SHITTIER AND I WAS TIRED OF BUSTING MY HUMP TO MAKE TOYS FOR THEIR SHITTY KIDS.
I WILL LET YOU IN ON A SECRET-- THE BAD KIDS DON'T **ALWAYS** GET COAL.
NNNGHH
THE STAR MUST'VE PICKED UP ON MY DISILLUSIONMENT, BECAUSE ONE DAY I WOKE UP WITH THE MACHINE NEXT TO MY BED.
NO PLUG. NO BATTERIES. JUST A NEVER-ENDING ROLL OF PAPER THAT KEPT SPITTING OUT A LIST OF WHICH KIDS WERE NAUGHTY AND WHICH WERE NICE.
I NEVER HAD TO MEMORIZE THE LIST--SOMEHOW, I JUST **KNEW** EVERY NAME OF EVERY PERSON.
IT WAS CONSTANTLY UPDATING, NARCING ON EVERYONE ON THE PLANET, **EVEN AFTER THEY BECAME ADULTS.**
EVERY TIME A BARTENDER TOOK A $20 BILL FROM THE REGISTER; EVERY TIME LITTLE JIMMY RUBBED ONE OUT TO HIS FRENCH TEACHER; EVERY TIME A GRUESOME MURDER WAS COMMITTED. I HAD TO CARRY THAT SHIT WITH ME, IN MY HEAD, **ALWAYS.**

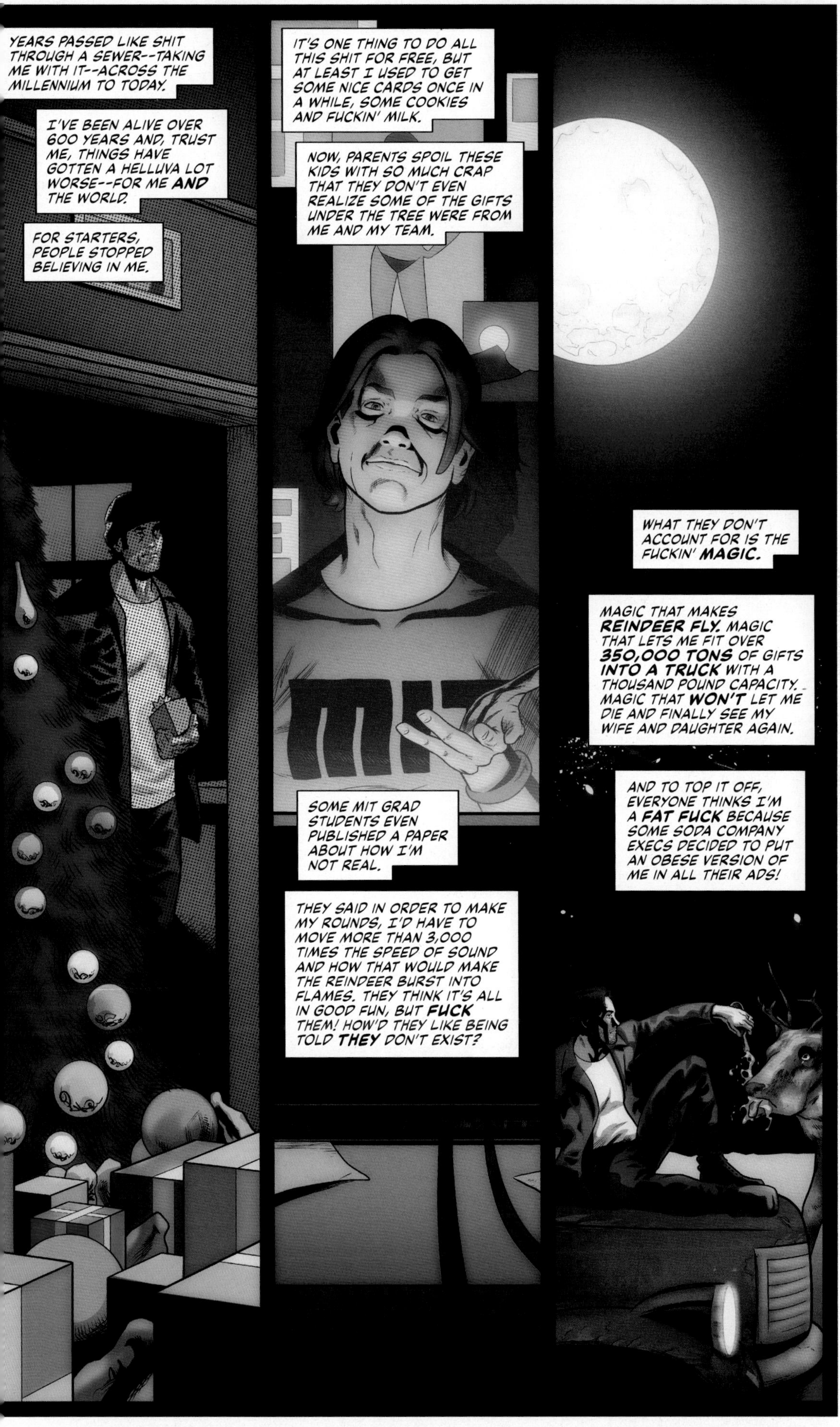
YEARS PASSED LIKE SHIT THROUGH A SEWER--TAKING ME WITH IT--ACROSS THE MILLENNIUM TO TODAY.
I'VE BEEN ALIVE OVER 600 YEARS AND, TRUST ME, THINGS HAVE GOTTEN A HELLUVA LOT WORSE--FOR ME **AND** THE WORLD.
FOR STARTERS, PEOPLE STOPPED BELIEVING IN ME.
IT'S ONE THING TO DO ALL THIS SHIT FOR FREE, BUT AT LEAST I USED TO GET SOME NICE CARDS ONCE IN A WHILE, SOME COOKIES AND FUCKIN' MILK.
NOW, PARENTS SPOIL THESE KIDS WITH SO MUCH CRAP THAT THEY DON'T EVEN REALIZE SOME OF THE GIFTS UNDER THE TREE WERE FROM ME AND MY TEAM.
MIT
SOME MIT GRAD STUDENTS EVEN PUBLISHED A PAPER ABOUT HOW I'M NOT REAL.
THEY SAID IN ORDER TO MAKE MY ROUNDS, I'D HAVE TO MOVE MORE THAN 3,000 TIMES THE SPEED OF SOUND AND HOW THAT WOULD MAKE THE REINDEER BURST INTO FLAMES. THEY THINK IT'S ALL IN GOOD FUN, BUT **FUCK** THEM! HOW'D THEY LIKE BEING TOLD **THEY** DON'T EXIST?
WHAT THEY DON'T ACCOUNT FOR IS THE FUCKIN' **MAGIC.**
MAGIC THAT MAKES **REINDEER FLY.** MAGIC THAT LETS ME FIT OVER **350,000 TONS** OF GIFTS **INTO A TRUCK** WITH A THOUSAND POUND CAPACITY. MAGIC THAT **WON'T** LET ME DIE AND FINALLY SEE MY WIFE AND DAUGHTER AGAIN.
AND TO TOP IT OFF, EVERYONE THINKS I'M A **FAT FUCK** BECAUSE SOME SODA COMPANY EXECS DECIDED TO PUT AN OBESE VERSION OF ME IN ALL THEIR ADS!

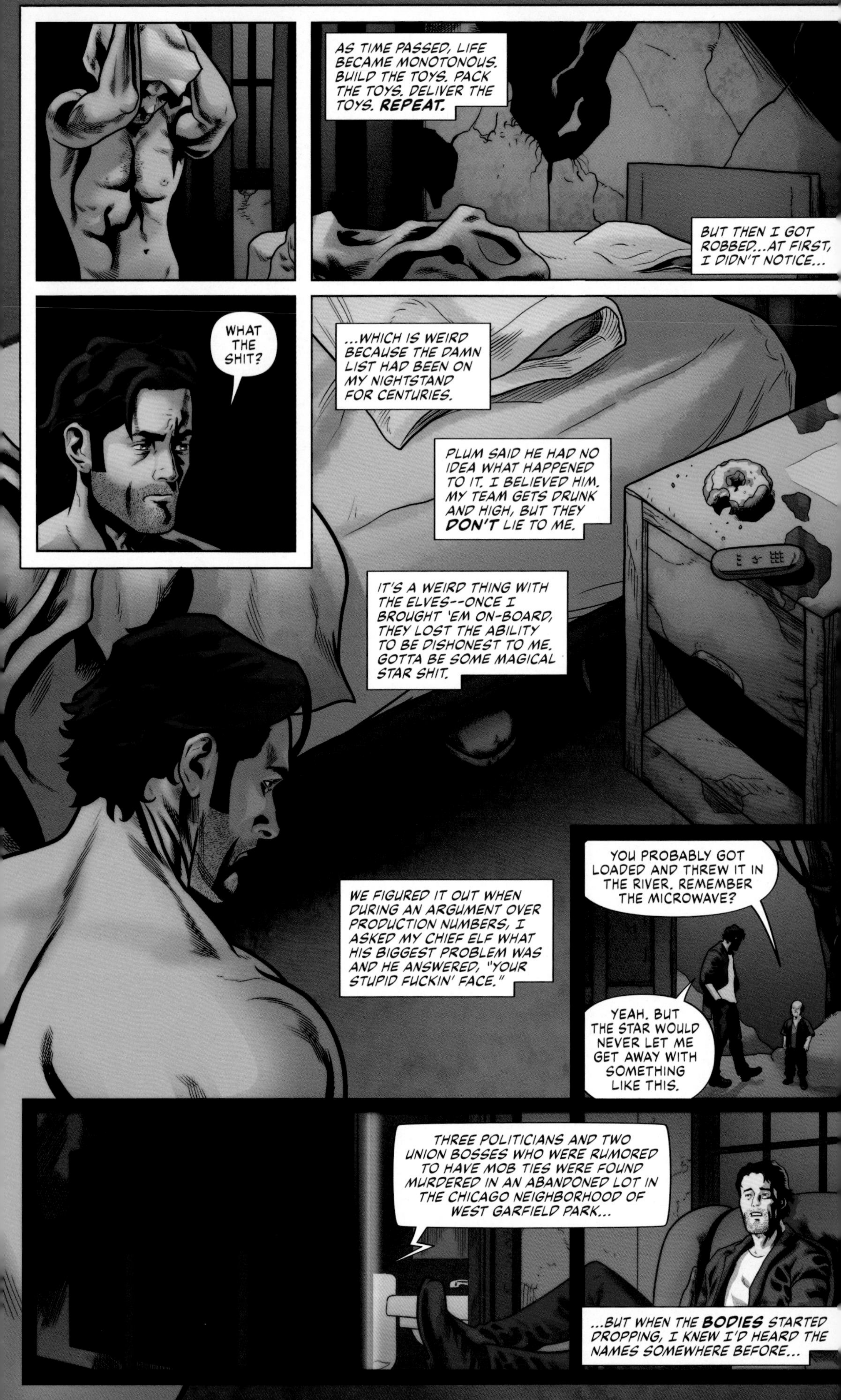
AS TIME PASSED, LIFE BECAME MONOTONOUS. BUILD THE TOYS. PACK THE TOYS. DELIVER THE TOYS. **REPEAT.**
BUT THEN I GOT ROBBED...AT FIRST, I DIDN'T NOTICE...
WHAT THE SHIT?
...WHICH IS WEIRD BECAUSE THE DAMN LIST HAD BEEN ON MY NIGHTSTAND FOR CENTURIES.
PLUM SAID HE HAD NO IDEA WHAT HAPPENED TO IT. I BELIEVED HIM. MY TEAM GETS DRUNK AND HIGH, BUT THEY **DON'T** LIE TO ME.
IT'S A WEIRD THING WITH THE ELVES--ONCE I BROUGHT 'EM ON-BOARD, THEY LOST THE ABILITY TO BE DISHONEST TO ME. GOTTA BE SOME MAGICAL STAR SHIT.
WE FIGURED IT OUT WHEN DURING AN ARGUMENT OVER PRODUCTION NUMBERS, I ASKED MY CHIEF ELF WHAT HIS BIGGEST PROBLEM WAS AND HE ANSWERED, "YOUR STUPID FUCKIN' FACE."
YOU PROBABLY GOT LOADED AND THREW IT IN THE RIVER. REMEMBER THE MICROWAVE?
YEAH. BUT THE STAR WOULD NEVER LET ME GET AWAY WITH SOMETHING LIKE THIS.
THREE POLITICIANS AND TWO UNION BOSSES WHO WERE RUMORED TO HAVE MOB TIES WERE FOUND MURDERED IN AN ABANDONED LOT IN THE CHICAGO NEIGHBORHOOD OF WEST GARFIELD PARK...
...BUT WHEN THE **BODIES** STARTED DROPPING, I KNEW I'D HEARD THE NAMES SOMEWHERE BEFORE...

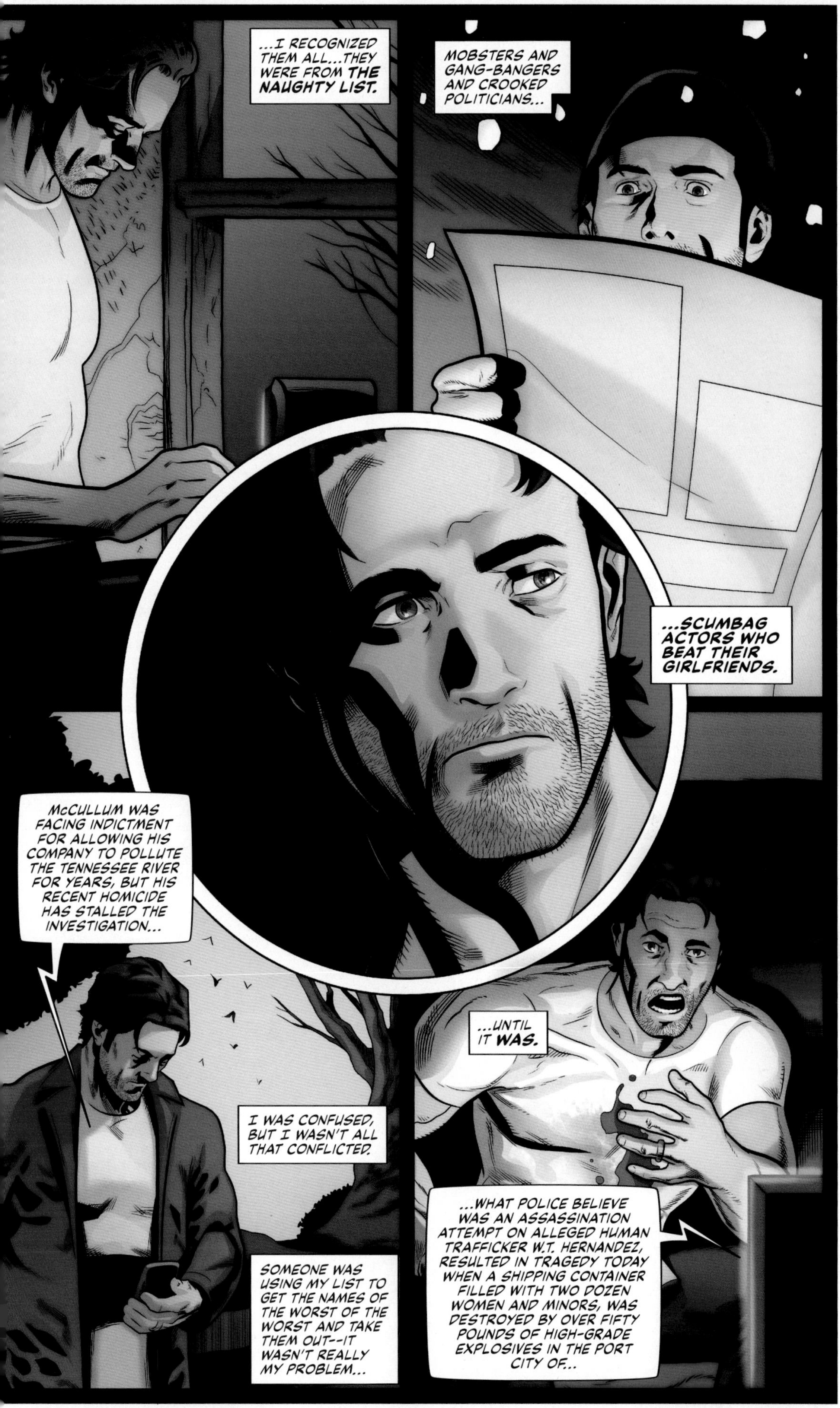
...I RECOGNIZED THEM ALL...THEY WERE FROM THE NAUGHTY LIST.
MOBSTERS AND GANG-BANGERS AND CROOKED POLITICIANS...
...SCUMBAG ACTORS WHO BEAT THEIR GIRLFRIENDS.
McCULLUM WAS FACING INDICTMENT FOR ALLOWING HIS COMPANY TO POLLUTE THE TENNESSEE RIVER FOR YEARS, BUT HIS RECENT HOMICIDE HAS STALLED THE INVESTIGATION...
I WAS CONFUSED, BUT I WASN'T ALL THAT CONFLICTED.
SOMEONE WAS USING MY LIST TO GET THE NAMES OF THE WORST OF THE WORST AND TAKE THEM OUT--IT WASN'T REALLY MY PROBLEM...
...UNTIL IT WAS.
...WHAT POLICE BELIEVE WAS AN ASSASSINATION ATTEMPT ON ALLEGED HUMAN TRAFFICKER W.T. HERNANDEZ, RESULTED IN TRAGEDY TODAY WHEN A SHIPPING CONTAINER FILLED WITH TWO DOZEN WOMEN AND MINORS, WAS DESTROYED BY OVER FIFTY POUNDS OF HIGH-GRADE EXPLOSIVES IN THE PORT CITY OF...

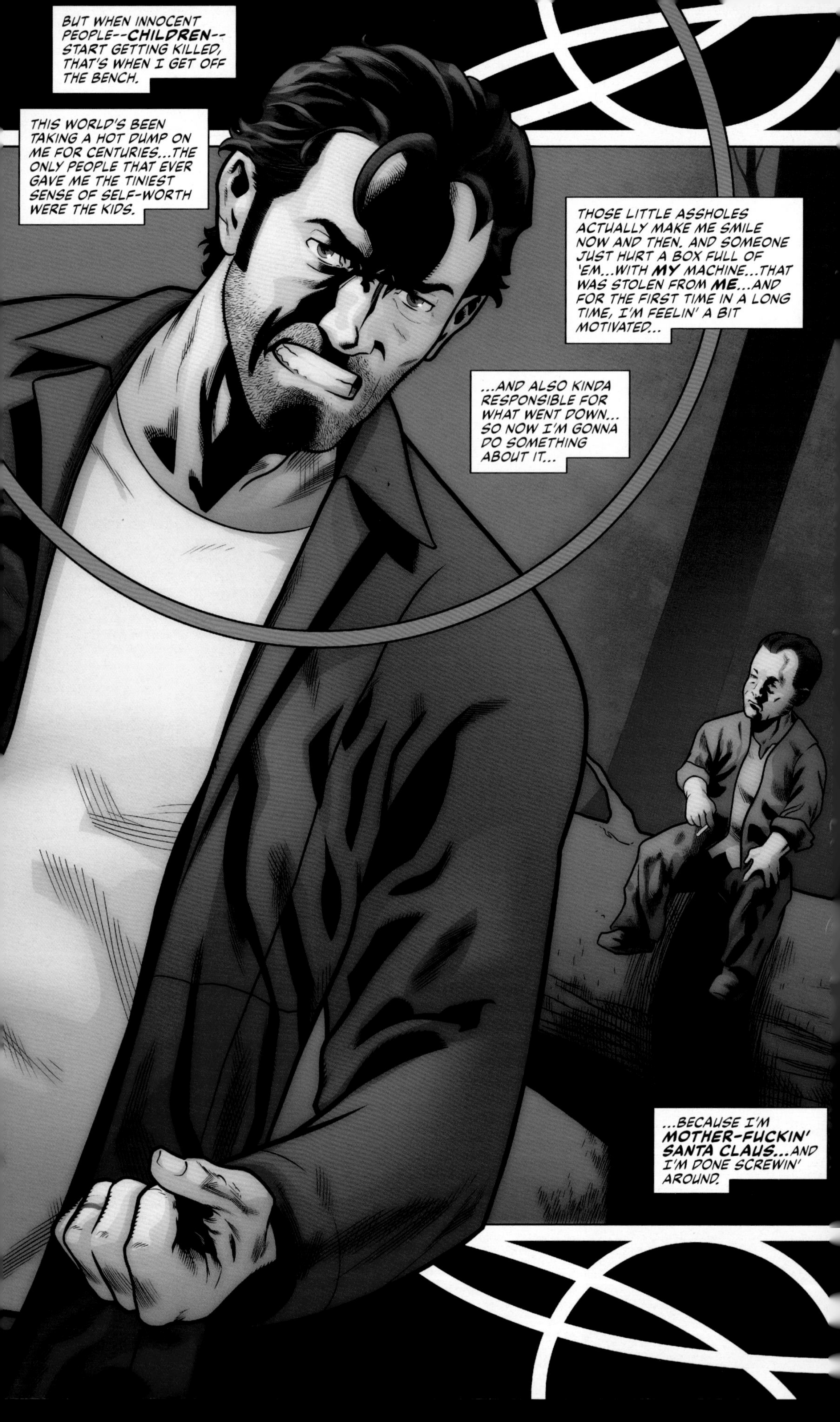
BUT WHEN INNOCENT PEOPLE--CHILDREN--START GETTING KILLED, THAT'S WHEN I GET OFF THE BENCH.
THIS WORLD'S BEEN TAKING A HOT DUMP ON ME FOR CENTURIES...THE ONLY PEOPLE THAT EVER GAVE ME THE TINIEST SENSE OF SELF-WORTH WERE THE KIDS.
THOSE LITTLE ASSHOLES ACTUALLY MAKE ME SMILE NOW AND THEN. AND SOMEONE JUST HURT A BOX FULL OF 'EM...WITH MY MACHINE...THAT WAS STOLEN FROM ME...AND FOR THE FIRST TIME IN A LONG TIME, I'M FEELIN' A BIT MOTIVATED...
...AND ALSO KINDA RESPONSIBLE FOR WHAT WENT DOWN... SO NOW I'M GONNA DO SOMETHING ABOUT IT...
...BECAUSE I'M MOTHER-FUCKIN' SANTA CLAUS...AND I'M DONE SCREWIN' AROUND.

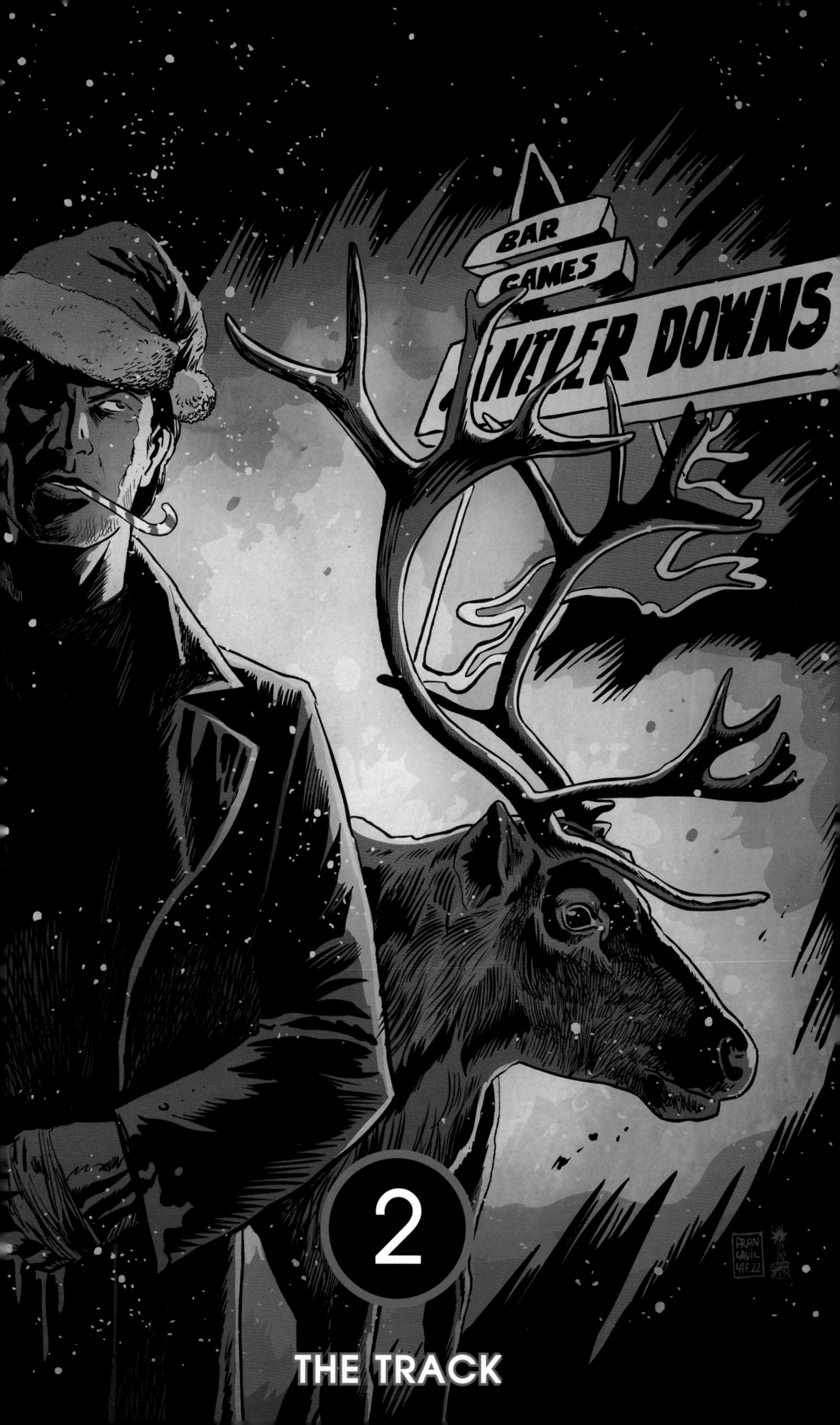
BAR
GAMES
NTLER DOWNS

2

THE TRACK

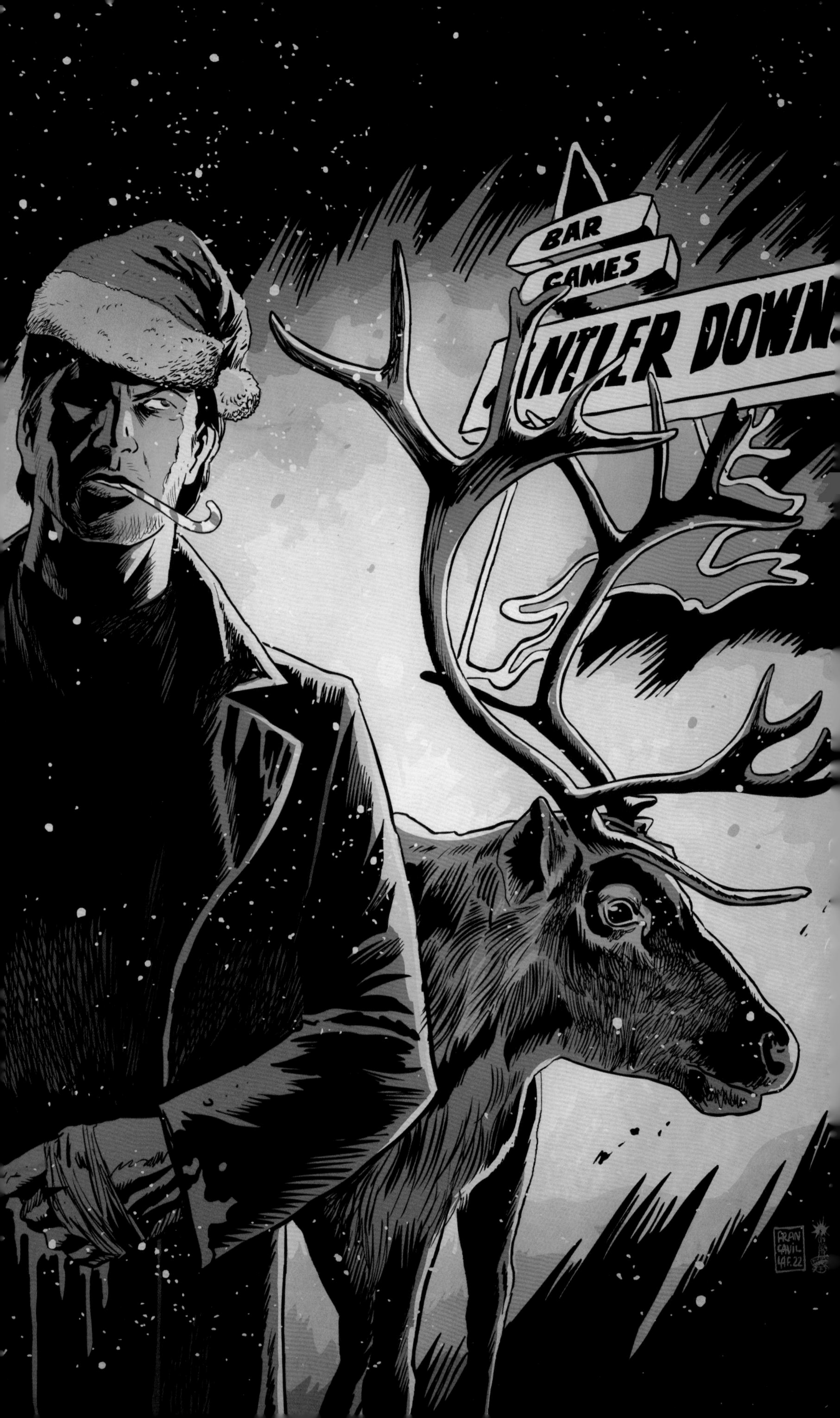
BAR
GAMES
ANTLER DOWN
FRAN GAVIL LAF.22

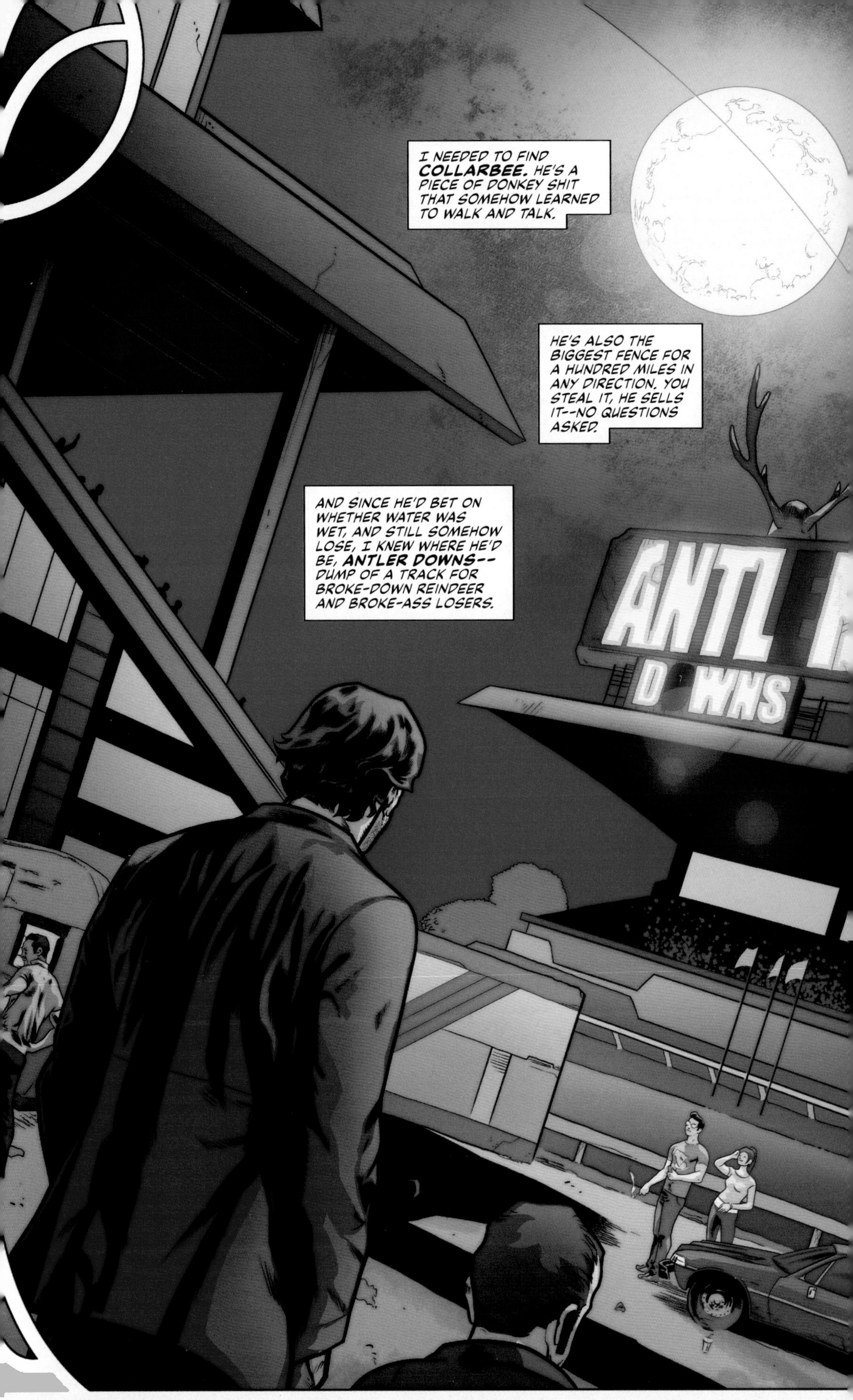
I NEEDED TO FIND COLLARBEE. HE'S A PIECE OF DONKEY SHIT THAT SOMEHOW LEARNED TO WALK AND TALK.
HE'S ALSO THE BIGGEST FENCE FOR A HUNDRED MILES IN ANY DIRECTION. YOU STEAL IT, HE SELLS IT--NO QUESTIONS ASKED.
AND SINCE HE'D BET ON WHETHER WATER WAS WET, AND STILL SOMEHOW LOSE, I KNEW WHERE HE'D BE, ANTLER DOWNS--DUMP OF A TRACK FOR BROKE-DOWN REINDEER AND BROKE-ASS LOSERS.
DOWNS

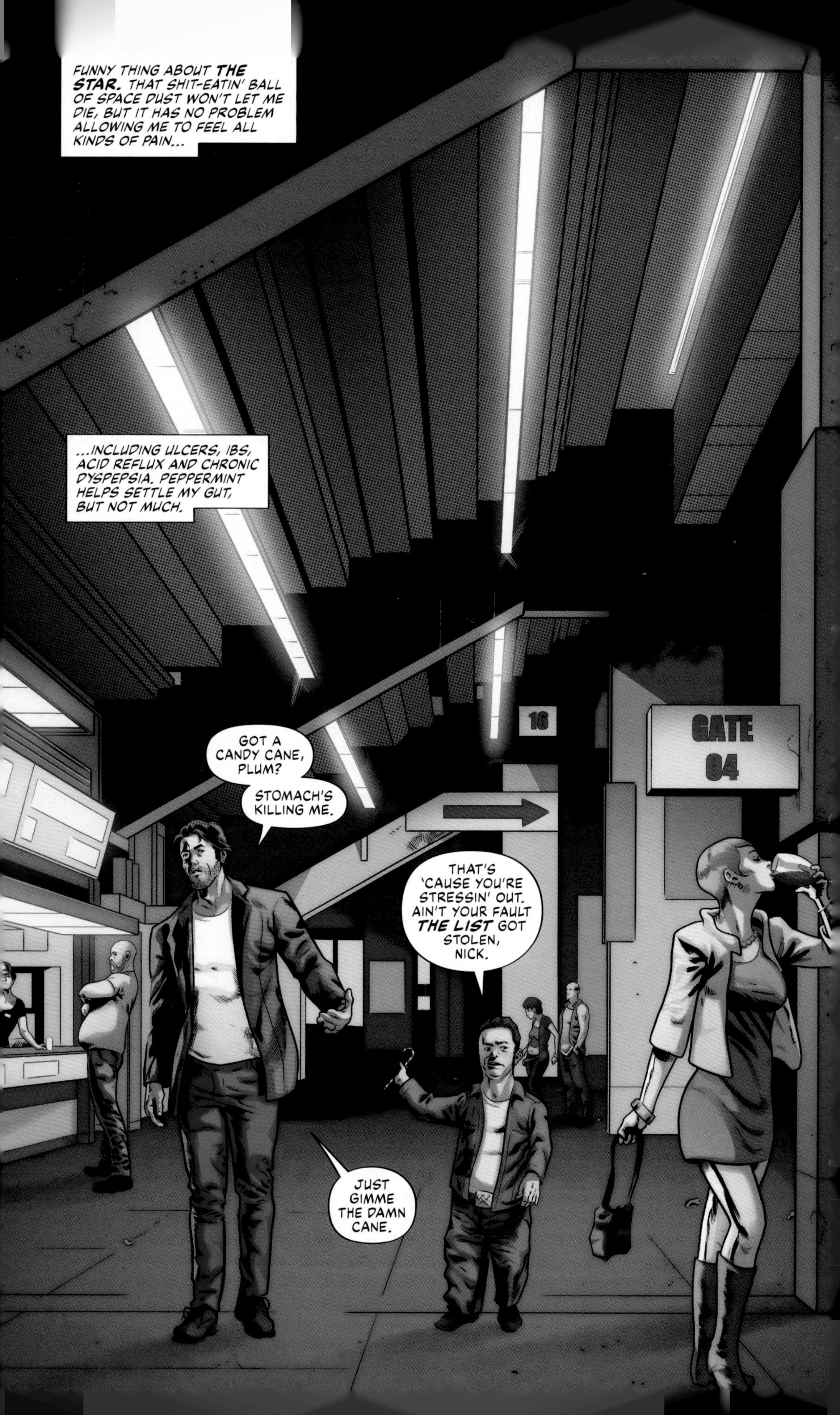
FUNNY THING ABOUT THE STAR. THAT SHIT-EATIN' BALL OF SPACE DUST WON'T LET ME DIE, BUT IT HAS NO PROBLEM ALLOWING ME TO FEEL ALL KINDS OF PAIN...
...INCLUDING ULCERS, IBS, ACID REFLUX AND CHRONIC DYSPEPSIA. PEPPERMINT HELPS SETTLE MY GUT, BUT NOT MUCH.
16
GATE 04
GOT A CANDY CANE, PLUM?
STOMACH'S KILLING ME.
THAT'S 'CAUSE YOU'RE STRESSIN' OUT. AIN'T YOUR FAULT THE LIST GOT STOLEN, NICK.
JUST GIMME THE DAMN CANE.

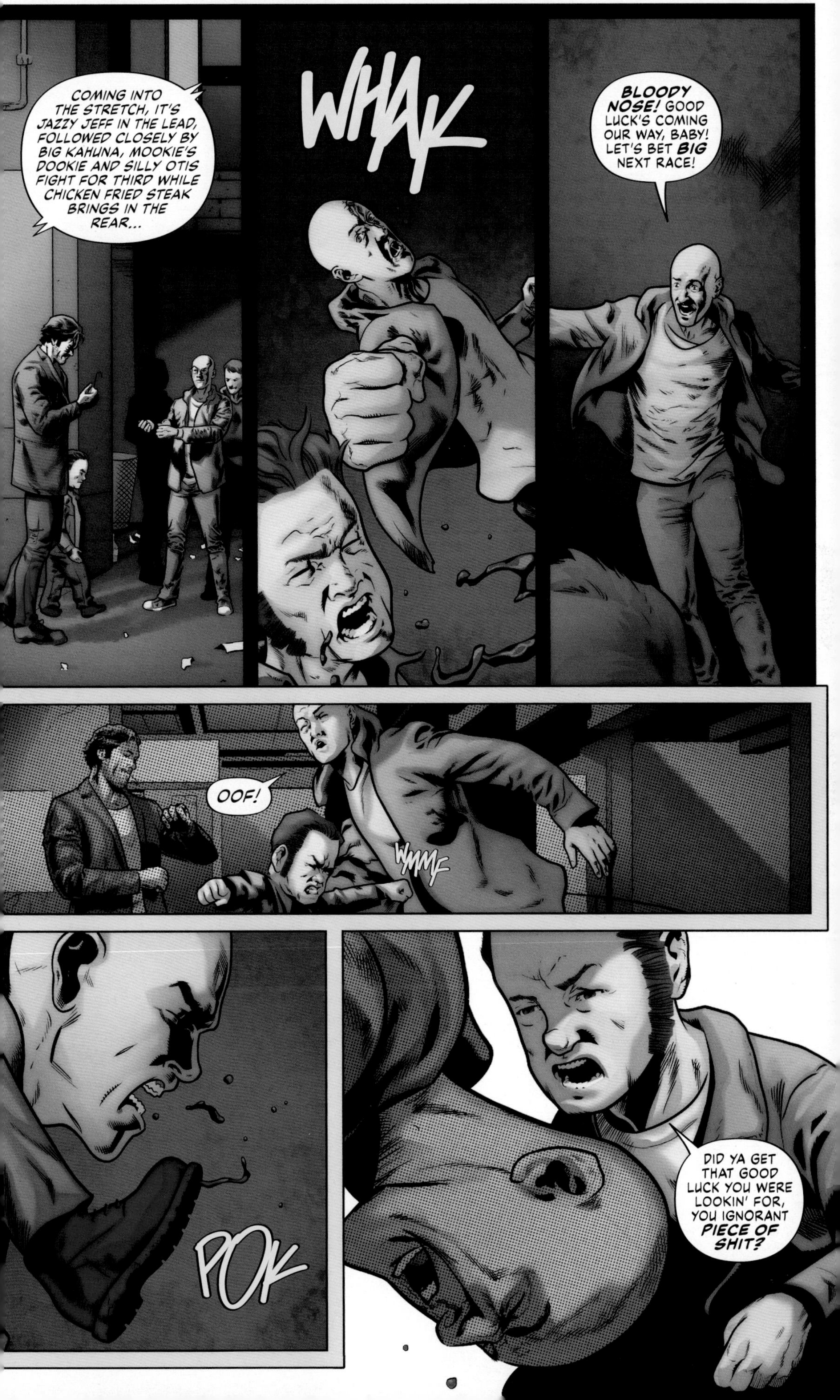
COMING INTO THE STRETCH, IT'S JAZZY JEFF IN THE LEAD, FOLLOWED CLOSELY BY BIG KAHUNA, MOOKIE'S DOOKIE AND SILLY OTIS FIGHT FOR THIRD WHILE CHICKEN FRIED STEAK BRINGS IN THE REAR...
WHAK
BLOODY NOSE! GOOD LUCK'S COMING OUR WAY, BABY! LET'S BET BIG NEXT RACE!
OOF!
WMMF
POK
DID YA GET THAT GOOD LUCK YOU WERE LOOKIN' FOR, YOU IGNORANT PIECE OF SHIT?

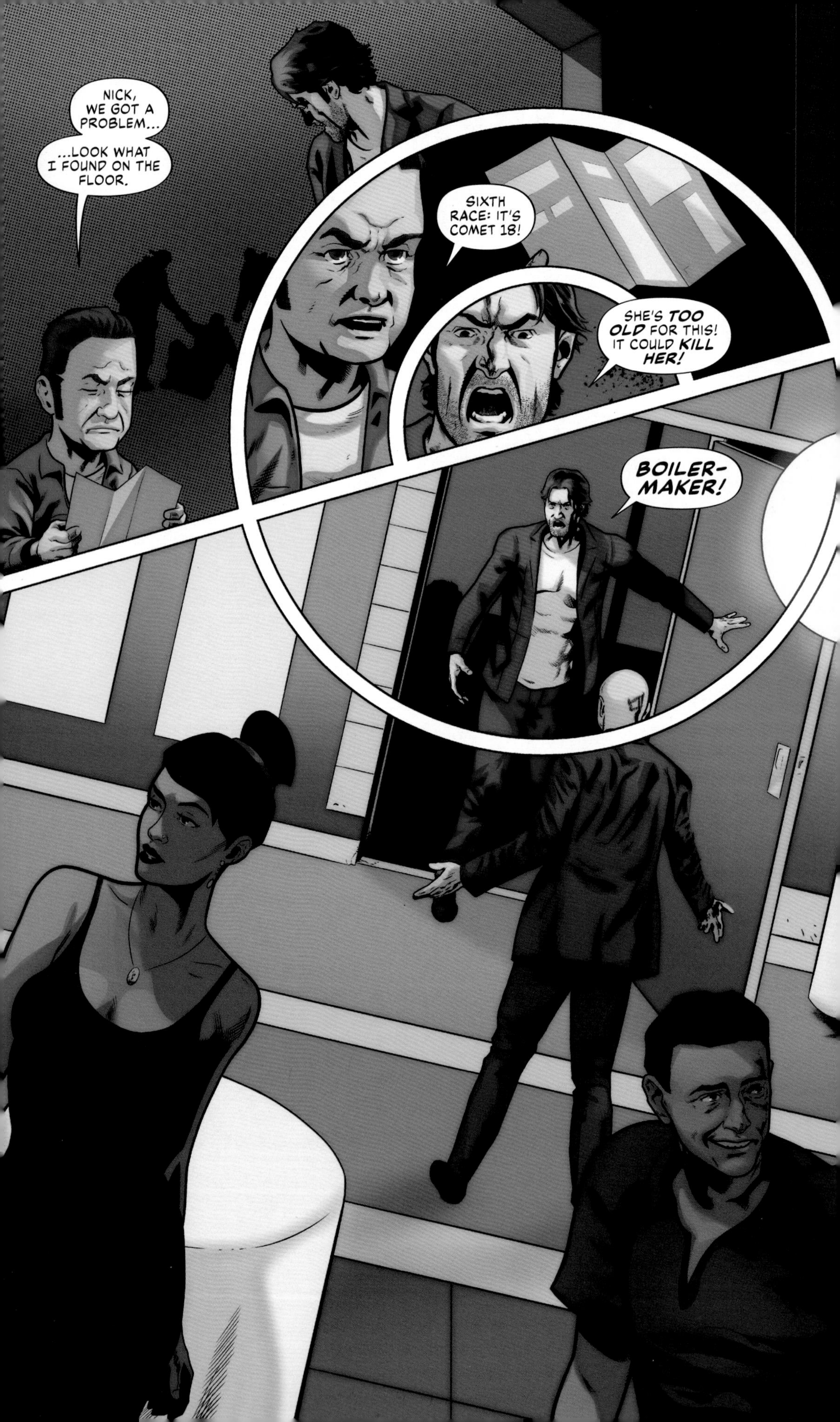
NICK, WE GOT A PROBLEM...
...LOOK WHAT I FOUND ON THE FLOOR.
SIXTH RACE: IT'S COMET 18!
SHE'S TOO OLD FOR THIS! IT COULD KILL HER!
BOILER-MAKER!

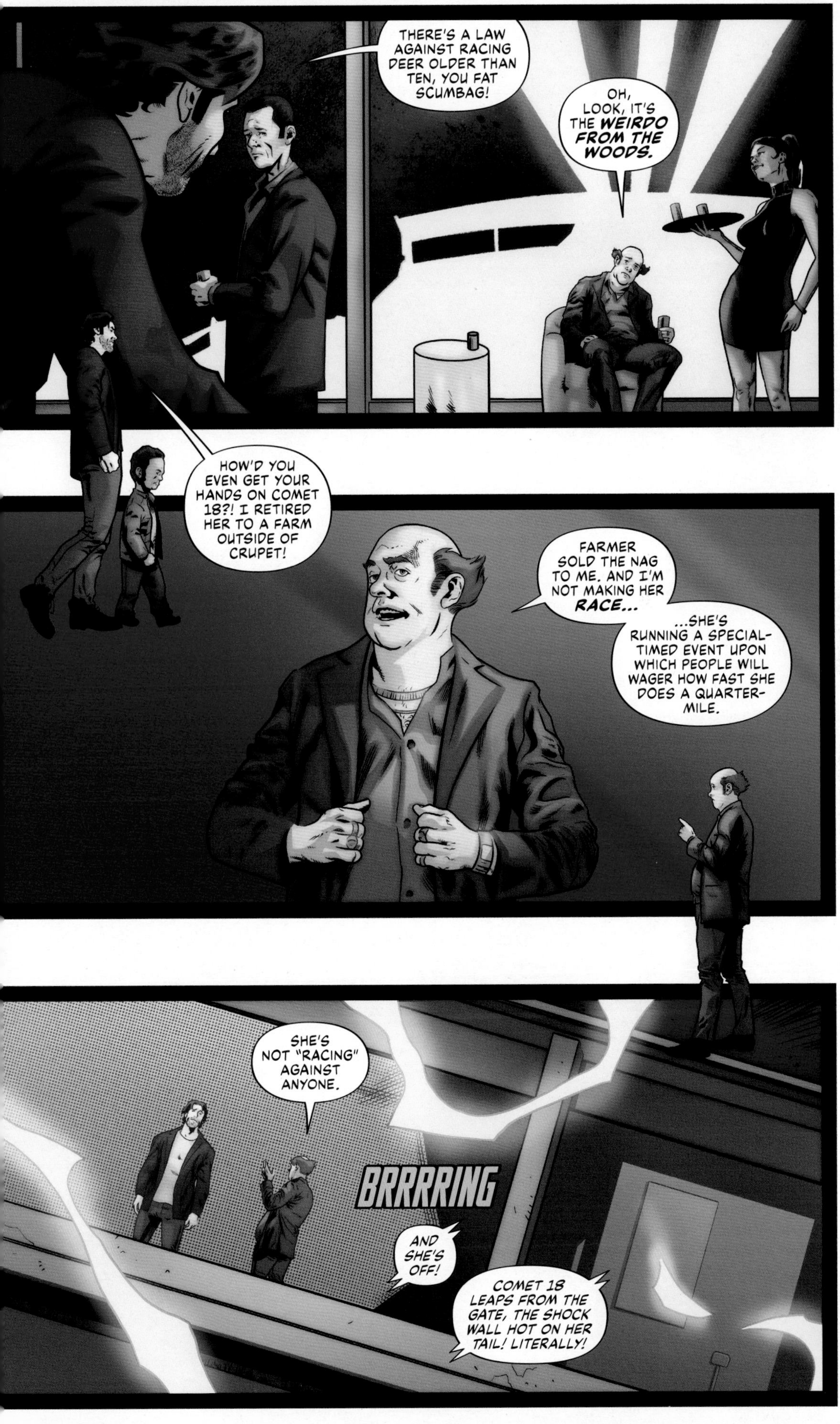
THERE'S A LAW AGAINST RACING DEER OLDER THAN TEN, YOU FAT SCUMBAG!
OH, LOOK, IT'S THE WEIRDO FROM THE WOODS.
HOW'D YOU EVEN GET YOUR HANDS ON COMET 18?! I RETIRED HER TO A FARM OUTSIDE OF CRUPET!
FARMER SOLD THE NAG TO ME. AND I'M NOT MAKING HER RACE...
...SHE'S RUNNING A SPECIAL-TIMED EVENT UPON WHICH PEOPLE WILL WAGER HOW FAST SHE DOES A QUARTER-MILE.
SHE'S NOT "RACING" AGAINST ANYONE.
BRRRRING
AND SHE'S OFF!
COMET 18 LEAPS FROM THE GATE, THE SHOCK WALL HOT ON HER TAIL! LITERALLY!

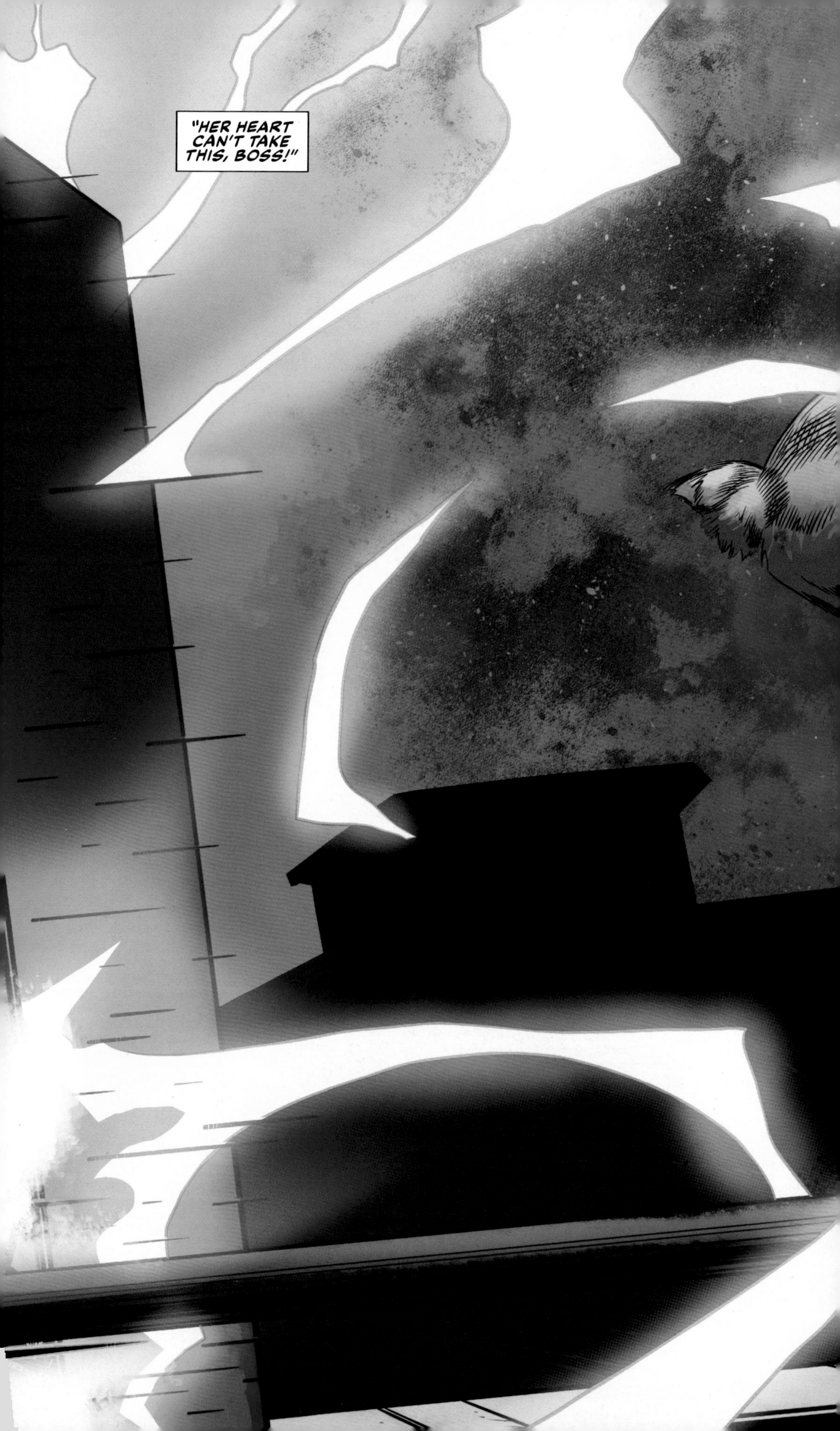
"HER HEART CAN'T TAKE THIS, BOSS!"

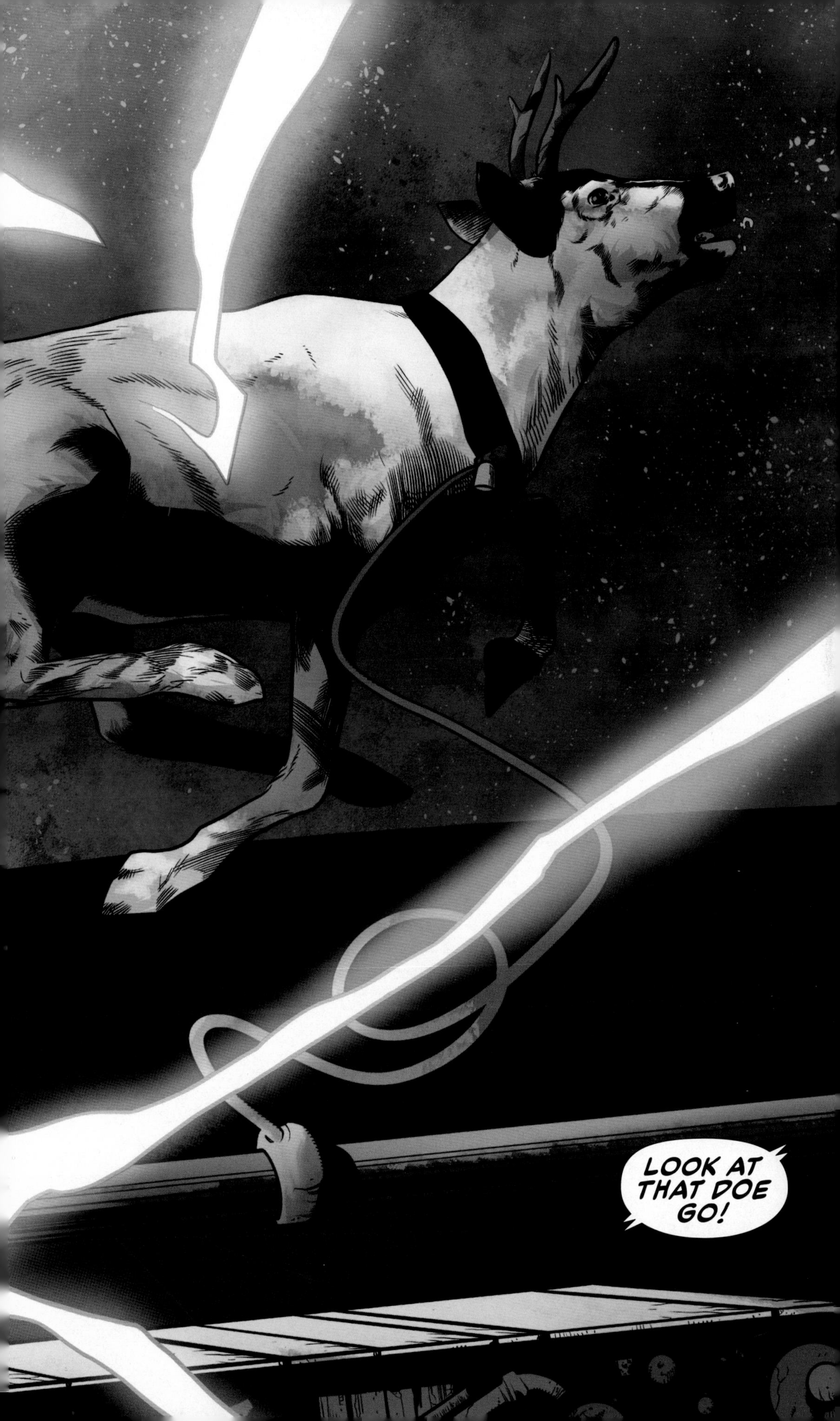
LOOK AT THAT DOE GO!

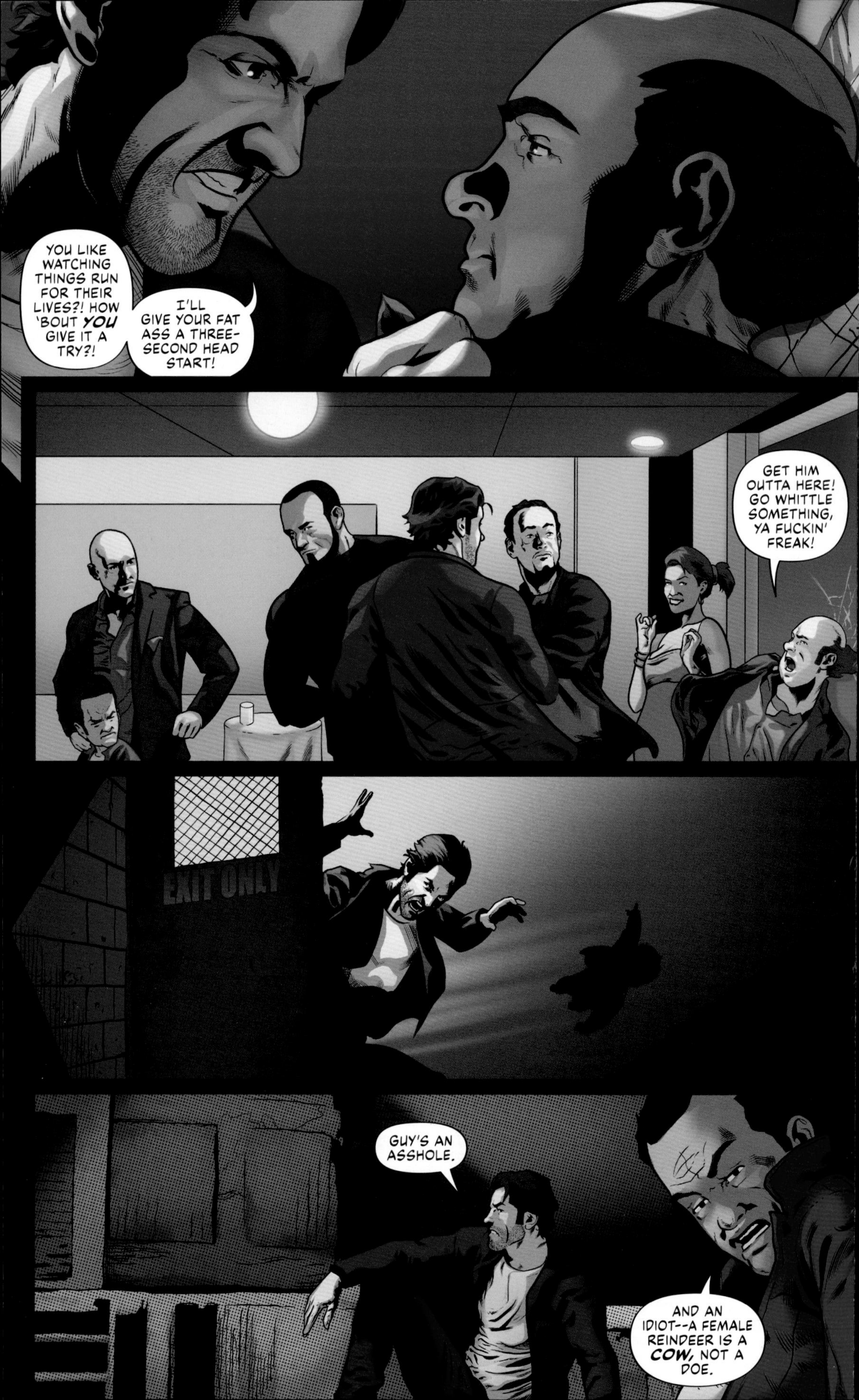
YOU LIKE WATCHING THINGS RUN FOR THEIR LIVES?! HOW 'BOUT *YOU* GIVE IT A TRY?!
I'LL GIVE YOUR FAT ASS A THREE-SECOND HEAD START!
GET HIM OUTTA HERE! GO WHITTLE SOMETHING, YA FUCKIN' FREAK!
EXIT ONLY
GUY'S AN ASSHOLE.
AND AN IDIOT--A FEMALE REINDEER IS A *COW,* NOT A DOE.

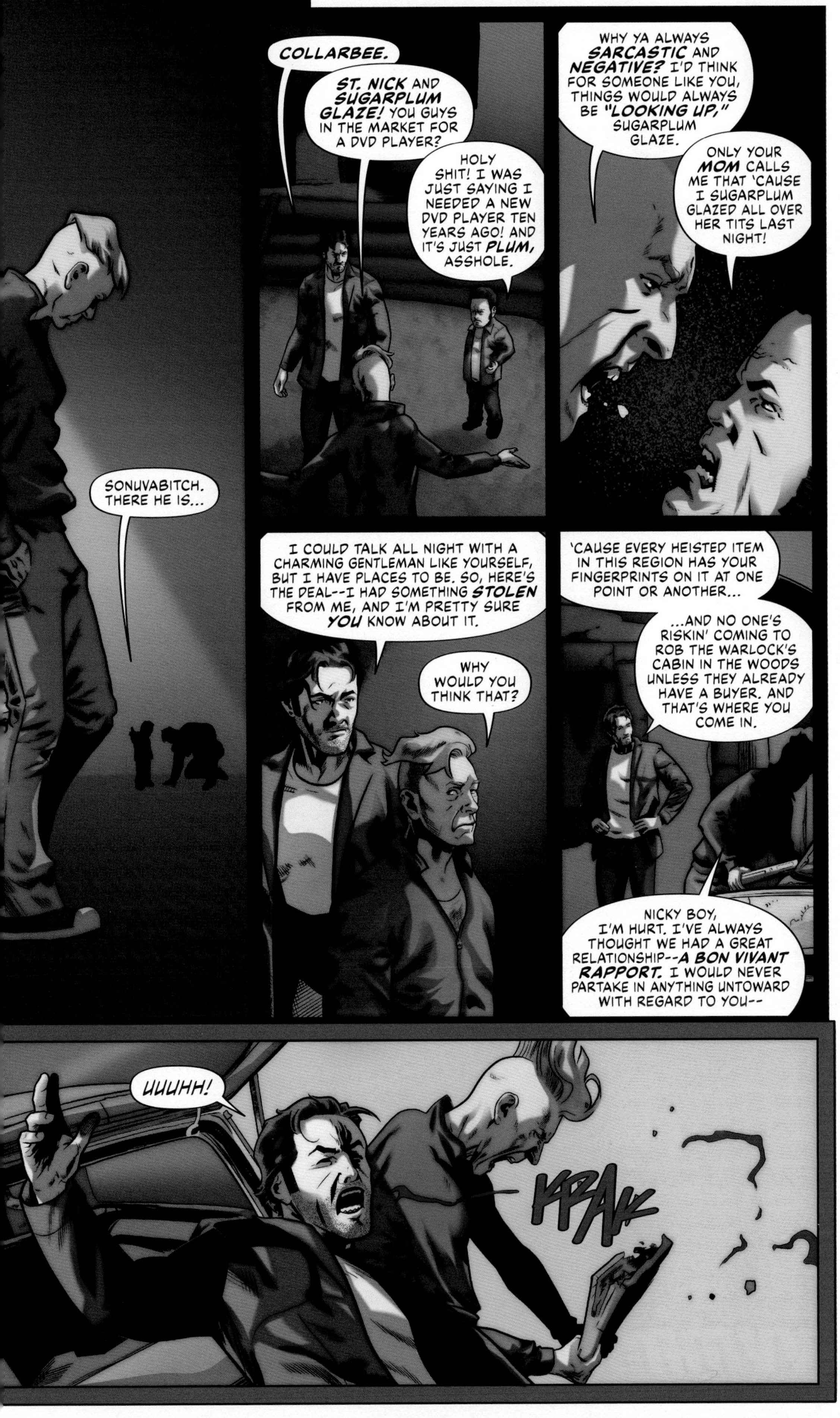
SONUVABITCH. THERE HE IS...
COLLARBEE.
ST. NICK AND SUGARPLUM GLAZE! YOU GUYS IN THE MARKET FOR A DVD PLAYER?
HOLY SHIT! I WAS JUST SAYING I NEEDED A NEW DVD PLAYER TEN YEARS AGO! AND IT'S JUST PLUM, ASSHOLE.
WHY YA ALWAYS SARCASTIC AND NEGATIVE? I'D THINK FOR SOMEONE LIKE YOU, THINGS WOULD ALWAYS BE "LOOKING UP," SUGARPLUM GLAZE.
ONLY YOUR MOM CALLS ME THAT 'CAUSE I SUGARPLUM GLAZED ALL OVER HER TITS LAST NIGHT!
I COULD TALK ALL NIGHT WITH A CHARMING GENTLEMAN LIKE YOURSELF, BUT I HAVE PLACES TO BE. SO, HERE'S THE DEAL--I HAD SOMETHING STOLEN FROM ME, AND I'M PRETTY SURE YOU KNOW ABOUT IT.
WHY WOULD YOU THINK THAT?
'CAUSE EVERY HEISTED ITEM IN THIS REGION HAS YOUR FINGERPRINTS ON IT AT ONE POINT OR ANOTHER...
...AND NO ONE'S RISKIN' COMING TO ROB THE WARLOCK'S CABIN IN THE WOODS UNLESS THEY ALREADY HAVE A BUYER. AND THAT'S WHERE YOU COME IN.
NICKY BOY, I'M HURT. I'VE ALWAYS THOUGHT WE HAD A GREAT RELATIONSHIP--A BON VIVANT RAPPORT. I WOULD NEVER PARTAKE IN ANYTHING UNTOWARD WITH REGARD TO YOU--
UUUHH!
KRAK

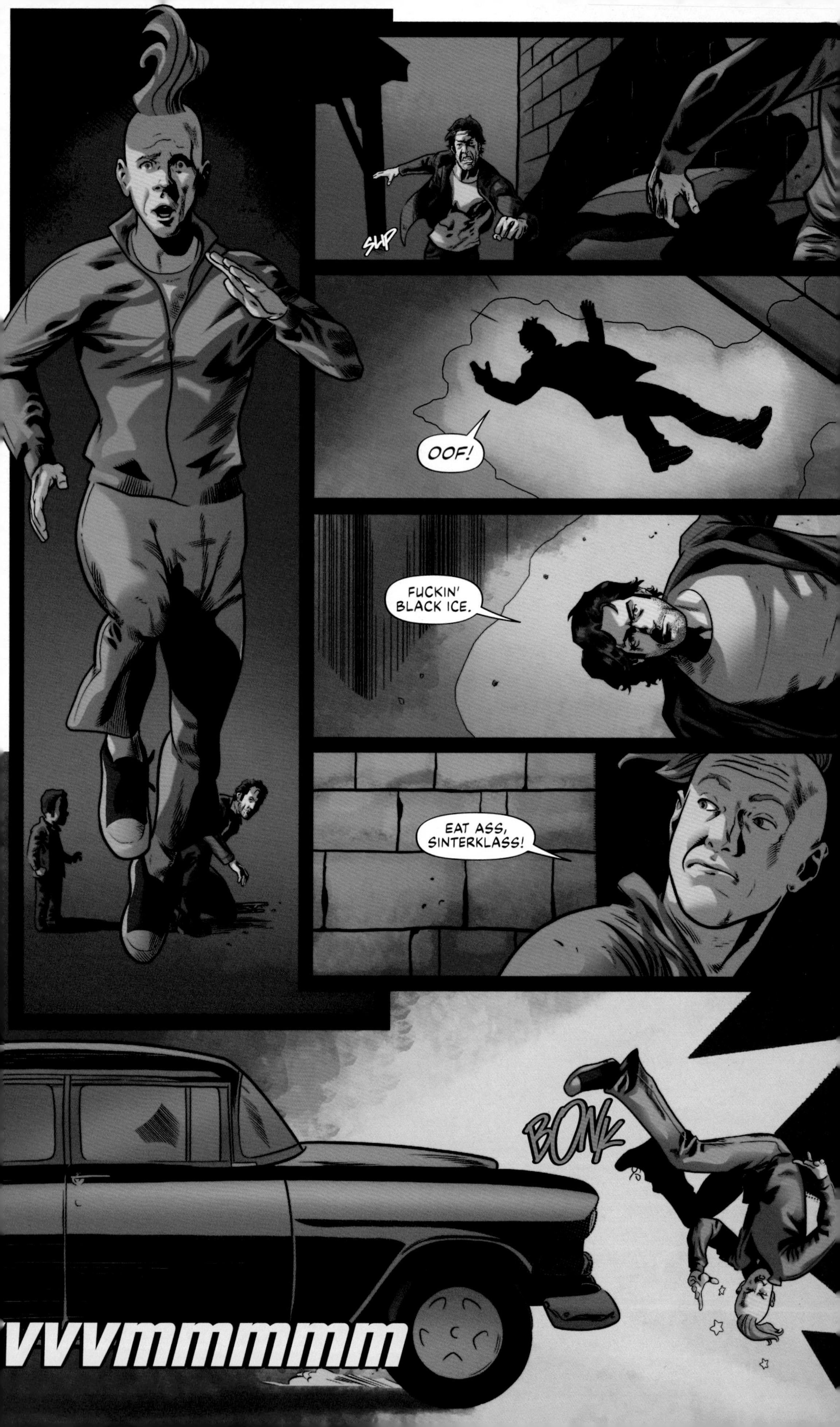
SLIP
OOF!
FUCKIN' BLACK ICE.
EAT ASS, SINTERKLASS!
BONK
VVVMMMMMMM

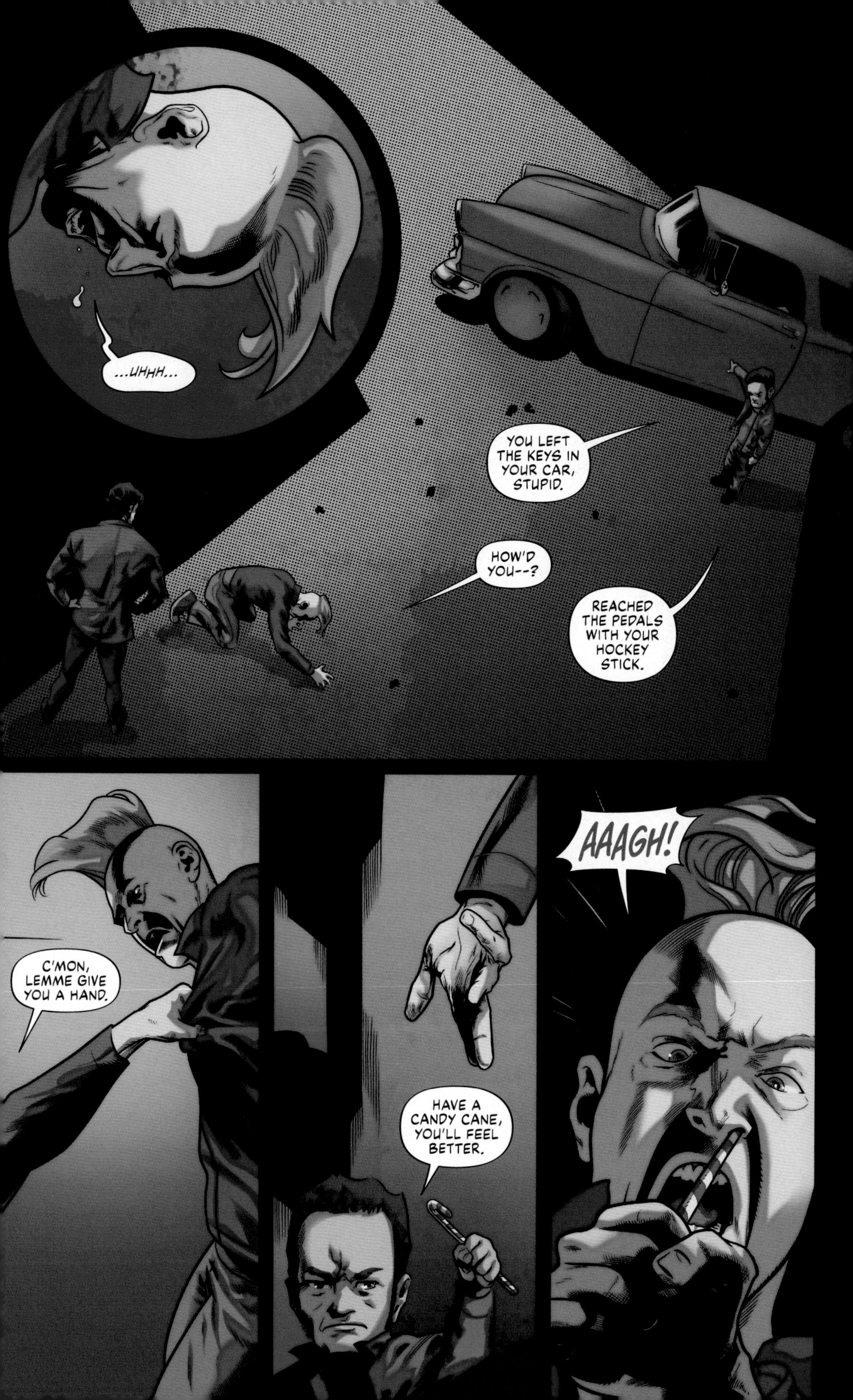
...UHHH...
YOU LEFT THE KEYS IN YOUR CAR, STUPID.
HOW'D YOU--?
REACHED THE PEDALS WITH YOUR HOCKEY STICK.
C'MON, LEMME GIVE YOU A HAND.
HAVE A CANDY CANE, YOU'LL FEEL BETTER.
AAAGH!

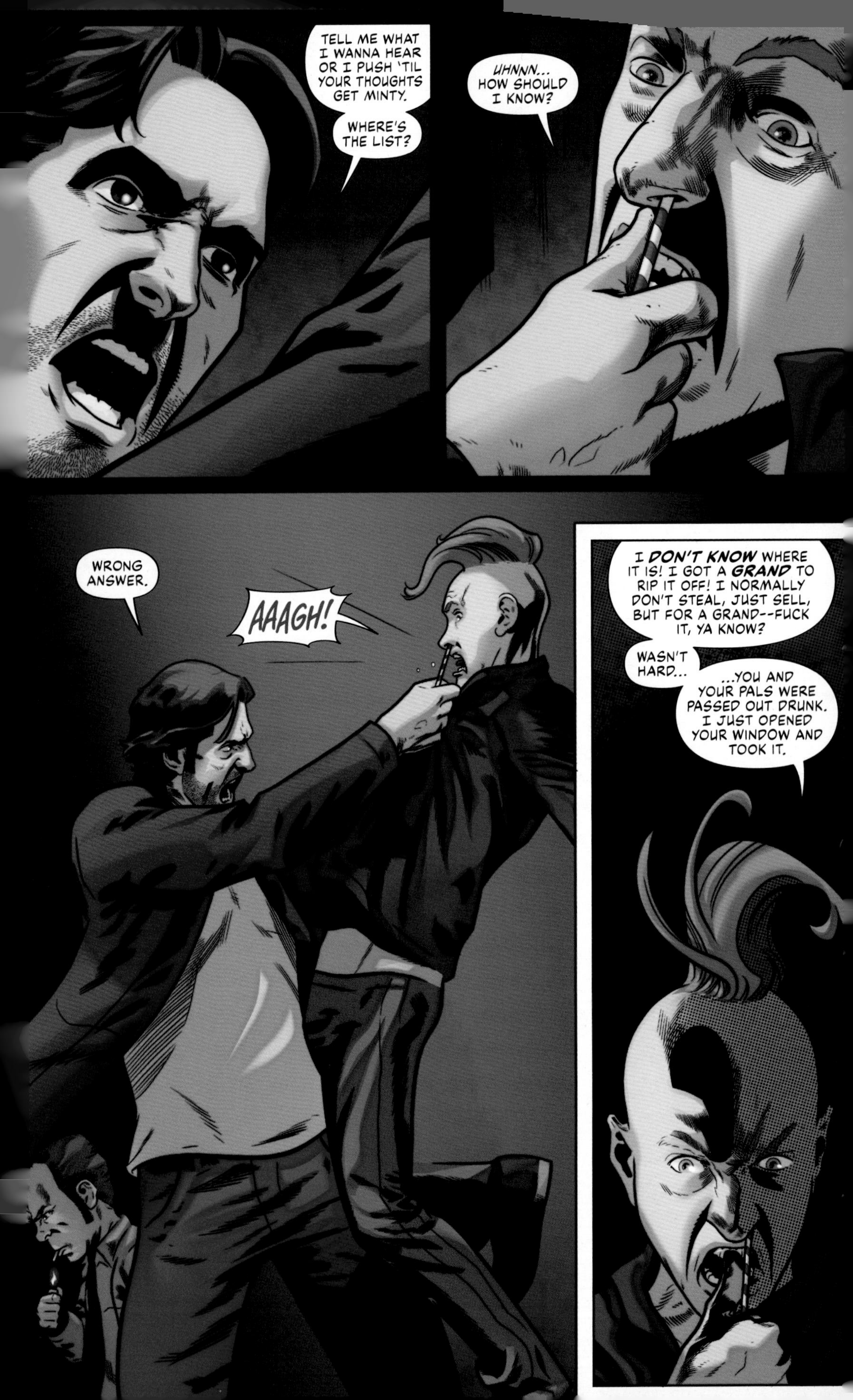
TELL ME WHAT I WANNA HEAR OR I PUSH 'TIL YOUR THOUGHTS GET MINTY.
WHERE'S THE LIST?
UHNNN... HOW SHOULD I KNOW?
WRONG ANSWER.
AAAGH!
I DON'T KNOW WHERE IT IS! I GOT A GRAND TO RIP IT OFF! I NORMALLY DON'T STEAL, JUST SELL, BUT FOR A GRAND--FUCK IT, YA KNOW?
WASN'T HARD...
...YOU AND YOUR PALS WERE PASSED OUT DRUNK. I JUST OPENED YOUR WINDOW AND TOOK IT.

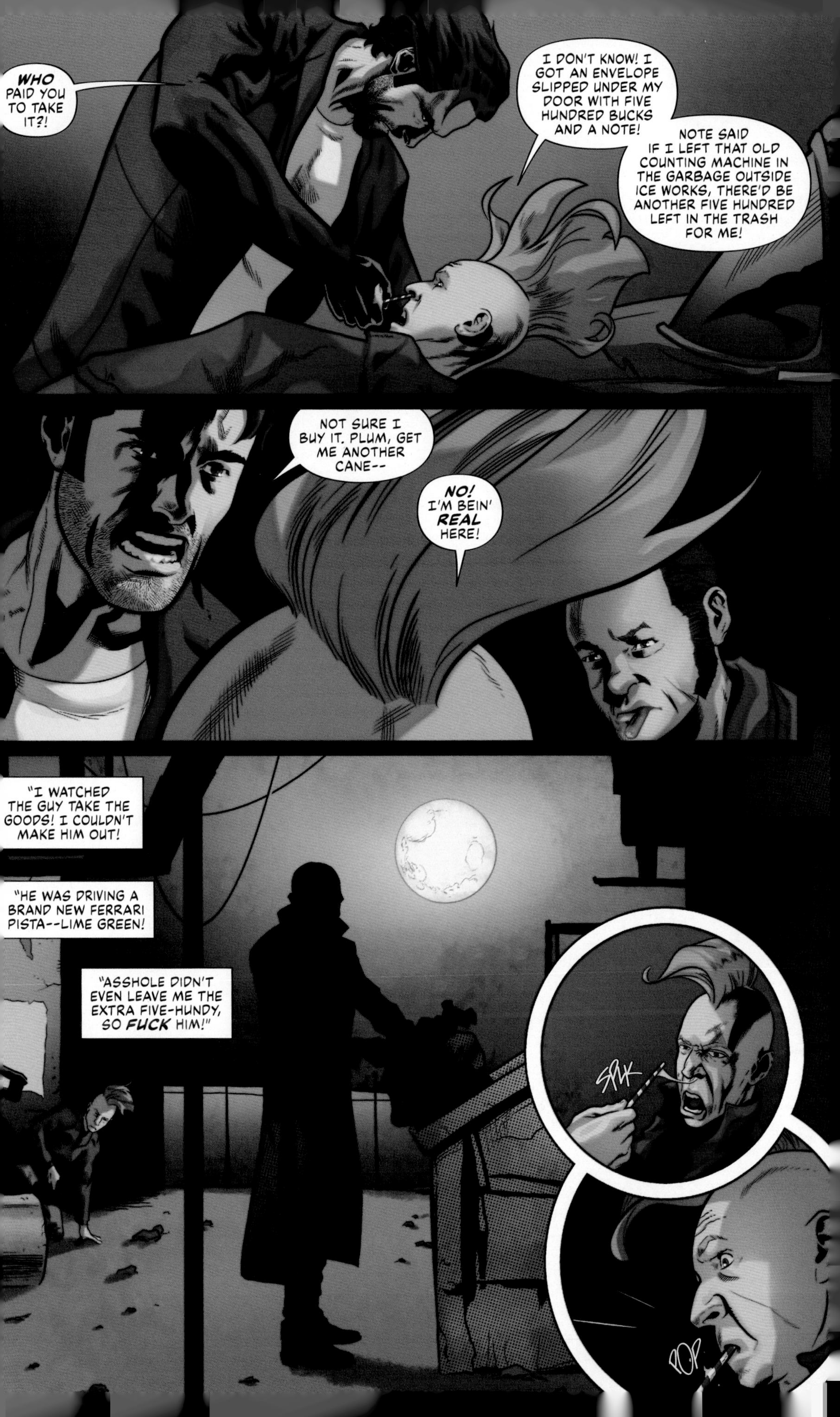
WHO PAID YOU TO TAKE IT?!
I DON'T KNOW! I GOT AN ENVELOPE SLIPPED UNDER MY DOOR WITH FIVE HUNDRED BUCKS AND A NOTE!
NOTE SAID IF I LEFT THAT OLD COUNTING MACHINE IN THE GARBAGE OUTSIDE ICE WORKS, THERE'D BE ANOTHER FIVE HUNDRED LEFT IN THE TRASH FOR ME!
NOT SURE I BUY IT. PLUM, GET ME ANOTHER CANE--
NO! I'M BEIN' REAL HERE!
"I WATCHED THE GUY TAKE THE GOODS! I COULDN'T MAKE HIM OUT!
"HE WAS DRIVING A BRAND NEW FERRARI PISTA--LIME GREEN!
"ASSHOLE DIDN'T EVEN LEAVE ME THE EXTRA FIVE-HUNDY, SO FUCK HIM!"
SPLK
POP

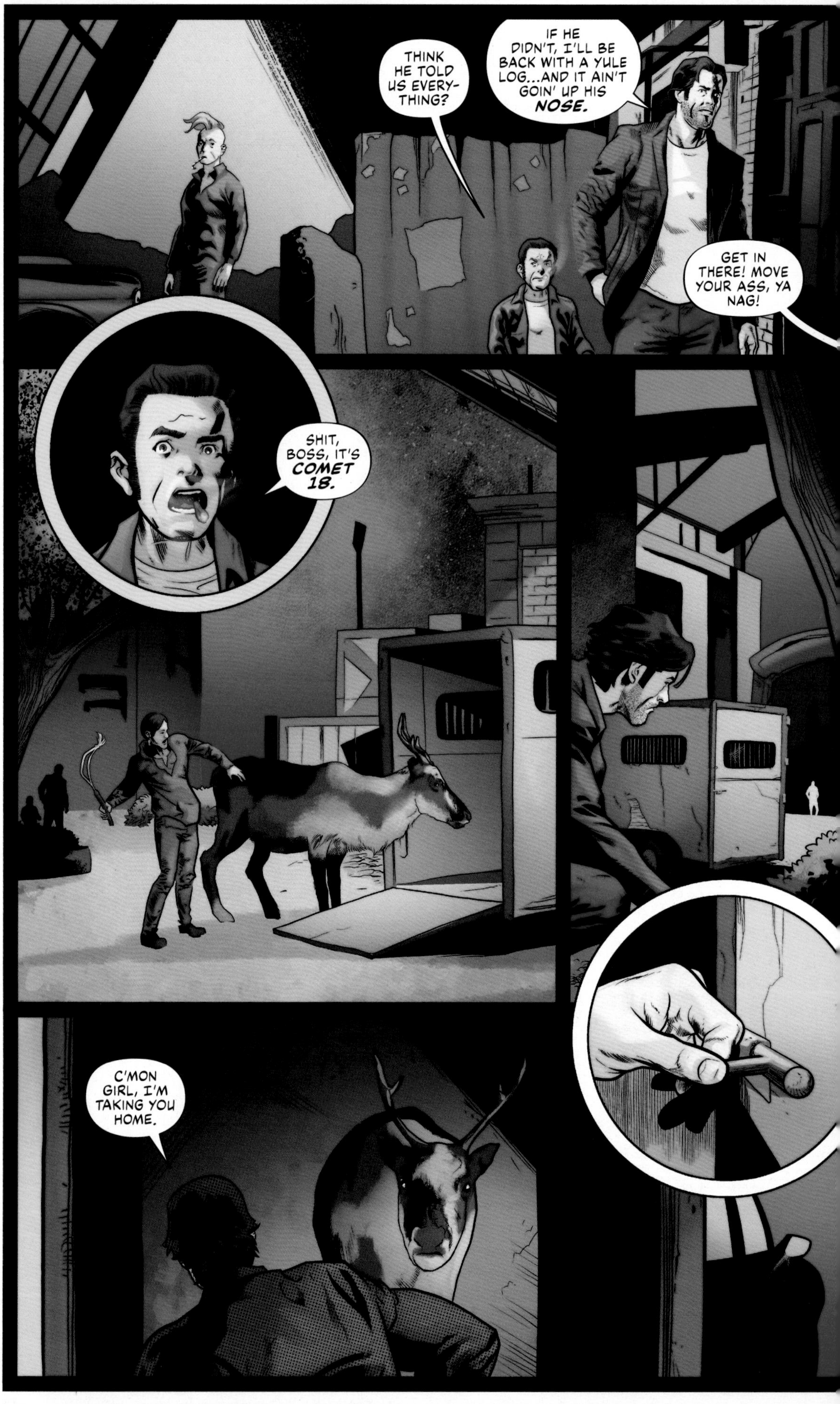
THINK HE TOLD US EVERY-THING?
IF HE DIDN'T, I'LL BE BACK WITH A YULE LOG...AND IT AIN'T GOIN' UP HIS NOSE.
GET IN THERE! MOVE YOUR ASS, YA NAG!
SHIT, BOSS, IT'S COMET 18.
C'MON GIRL, I'M TAKING YOU HOME.

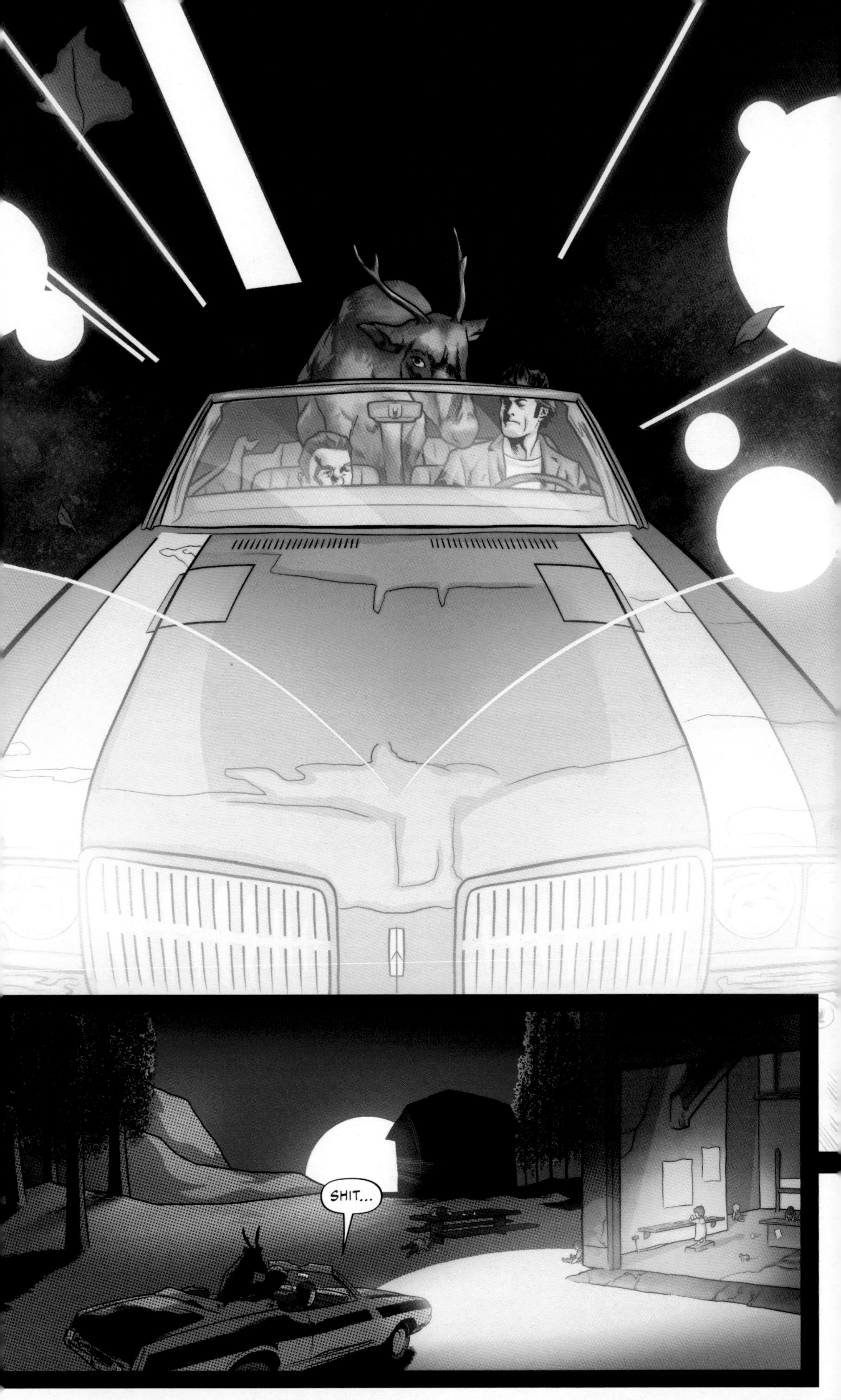
SHIT...

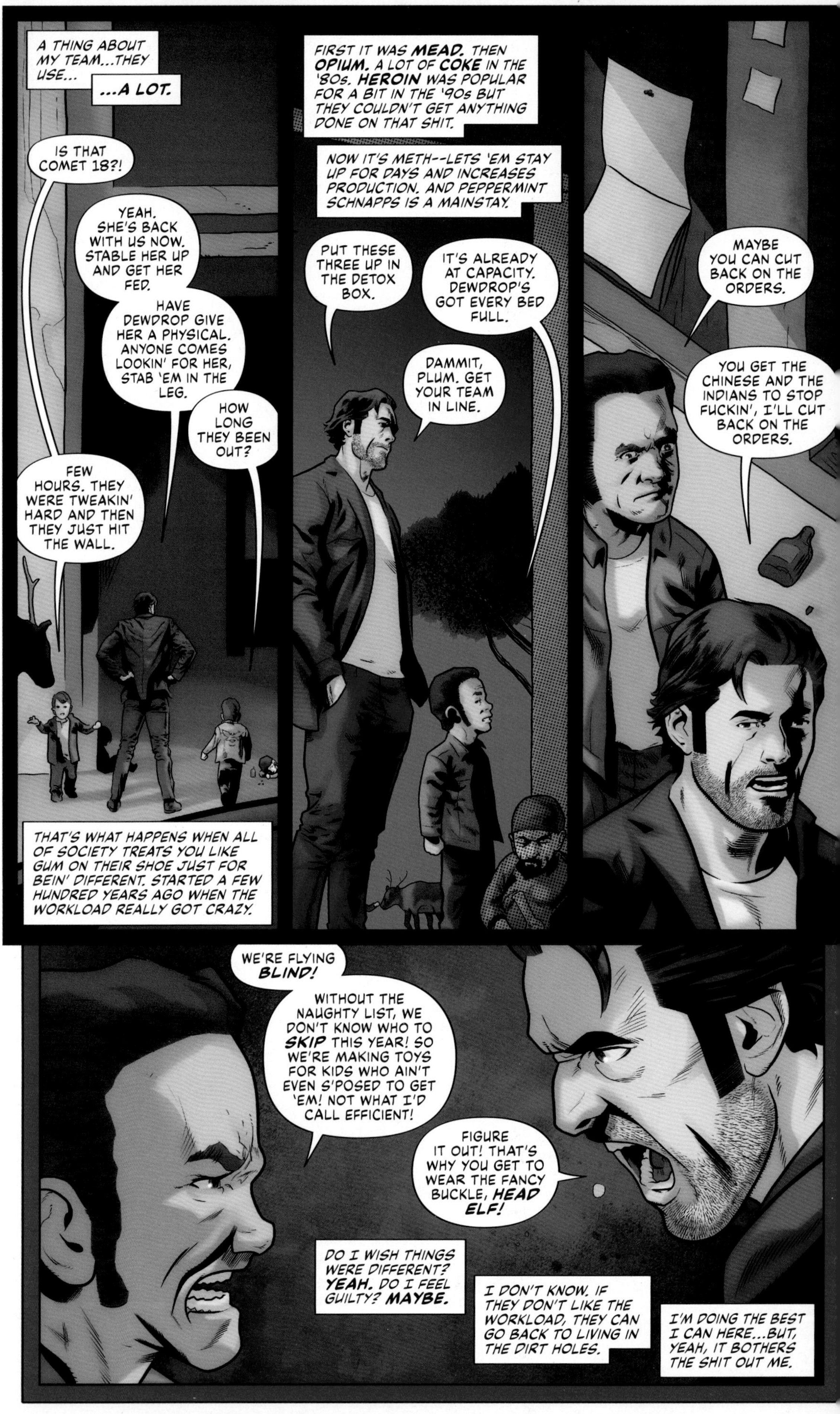

A THING ABOUT MY TEAM...THEY USE...
...A LOT.
IS THAT COMET 18?!
YEAH. SHE'S BACK WITH US NOW. STABLE HER UP AND GET HER FED.
HAVE DEWDROP GIVE HER A PHYSICAL. ANYONE COMES LOOKIN' FOR HER, STAB 'EM IN THE LEG.
HOW LONG THEY BEEN OUT?
FEW HOURS. THEY WERE TWEAKIN' HARD AND THEN THEY JUST HIT THE WALL.
THAT'S WHAT HAPPENS WHEN ALL OF SOCIETY TREATS YOU LIKE GUM ON THEIR SHOE JUST FOR BEIN' DIFFERENT. STARTED A FEW HUNDRED YEARS AGO WHEN THE WORKLOAD REALLY GOT CRAZY.
FIRST IT WAS MEAD. THEN OPIUM. A LOT OF COKE IN THE '80s. HEROIN WAS POPULAR FOR A BIT IN THE '90s BUT THEY COULDN'T GET ANYTHING DONE ON THAT SHIT.
NOW IT'S METH--LETS 'EM STAY UP FOR DAYS AND INCREASES PRODUCTION. AND PEPPERMINT SCHNAPPS IS A MAINSTAY.
PUT THESE THREE UP IN THE DETOX BOX.
IT'S ALREADY AT CAPACITY. DEWDROP'S GOT EVERY BED FULL.
DAMMIT, PLUM. GET YOUR TEAM IN LINE.
MAYBE YOU CAN CUT BACK ON THE ORDERS.
YOU GET THE CHINESE AND THE INDIANS TO STOP FUCKIN', I'LL CUT BACK ON THE ORDERS.
WE'RE FLYING BLIND!
WITHOUT THE NAUGHTY LIST, WE DON'T KNOW WHO TO SKIP THIS YEAR! SO WE'RE MAKING TOYS FOR KIDS WHO AIN'T EVEN S'POSED TO GET 'EM! NOT WHAT I'D CALL EFFICIENT!
FIGURE IT OUT! THAT'S WHY YOU GET TO WEAR THE FANCY BUCKLE, HEAD ELF!
DO I WISH THINGS WERE DIFFERENT? YEAH. DO I FEEL GUILTY? MAYBE.
I DON'T KNOW. IF THEY DON'T LIKE THE WORKLOAD, THEY CAN GO BACK TO LIVING IN THE DIRT HOLES.
I'M DOING THE BEST I CAN HERE...BUT, YEAH, IT BOTHERS THE SHIT OUT ME.

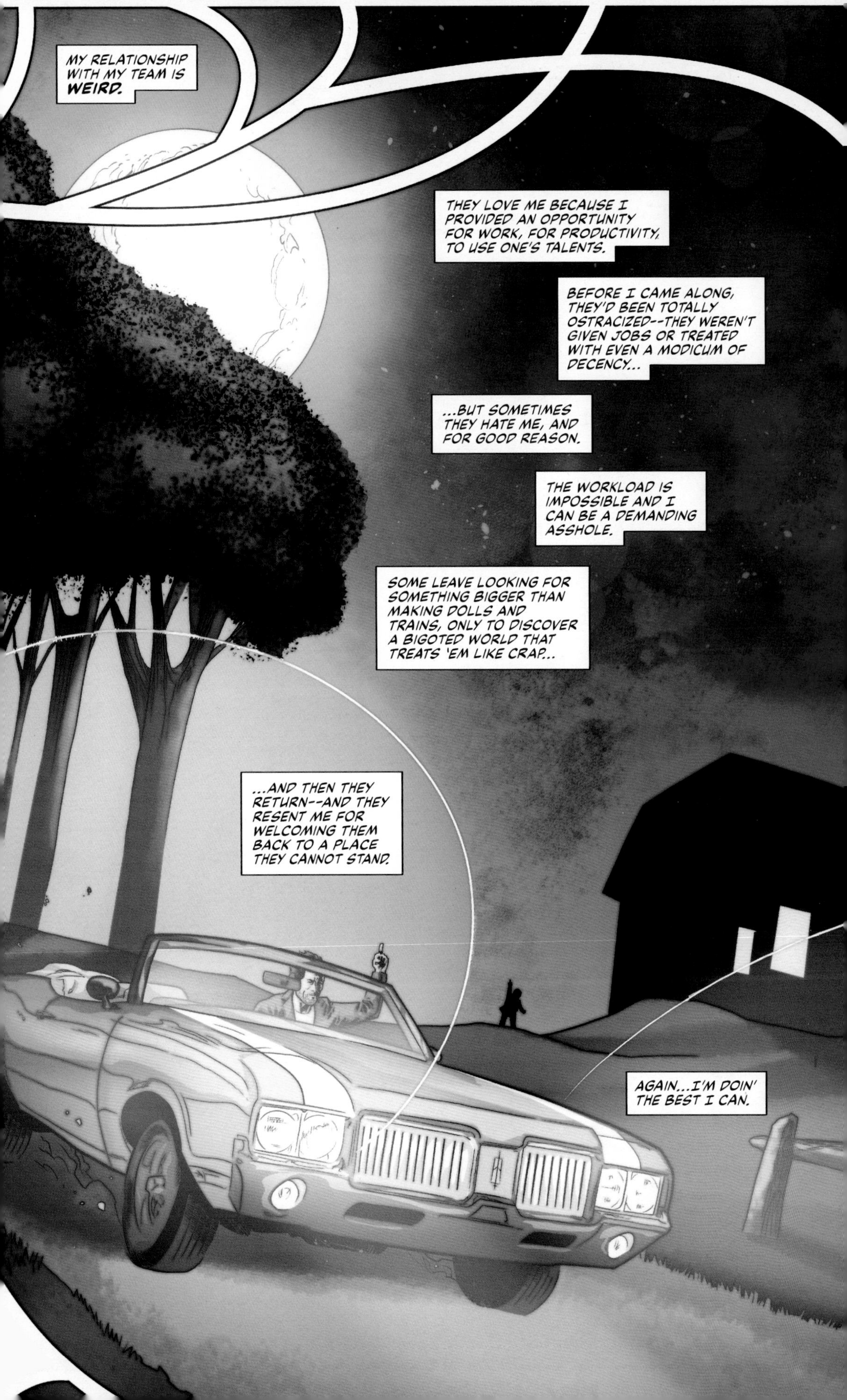
MY RELATIONSHIP WITH MY TEAM IS **WEIRD.**
THEY LOVE ME BECAUSE I PROVIDED AN OPPORTUNITY FOR WORK, FOR PRODUCTIVITY, TO USE ONE'S TALENTS.
BEFORE I CAME ALONG, THEY'D BEEN TOTALLY OSTRACIZED--THEY WEREN'T GIVEN JOBS OR TREATED WITH EVEN A MODICUM OF DECENCY...
...BUT SOMETIMES THEY HATE ME, AND FOR GOOD REASON.
THE WORKLOAD IS IMPOSSIBLE AND I CAN BE A DEMANDING ASSHOLE.
SOME LEAVE LOOKING FOR SOMETHING BIGGER THAN MAKING DOLLS AND TRAINS, ONLY TO DISCOVER A BIGOTED WORLD THAT TREATS 'EM LIKE CRAP...
...AND THEN THEY RETURN--AND THEY RESENT ME FOR WELCOMING THEM BACK TO A PLACE THEY CANNOT STAND.
AGAIN...I'M DOIN' THE BEST I CAN.

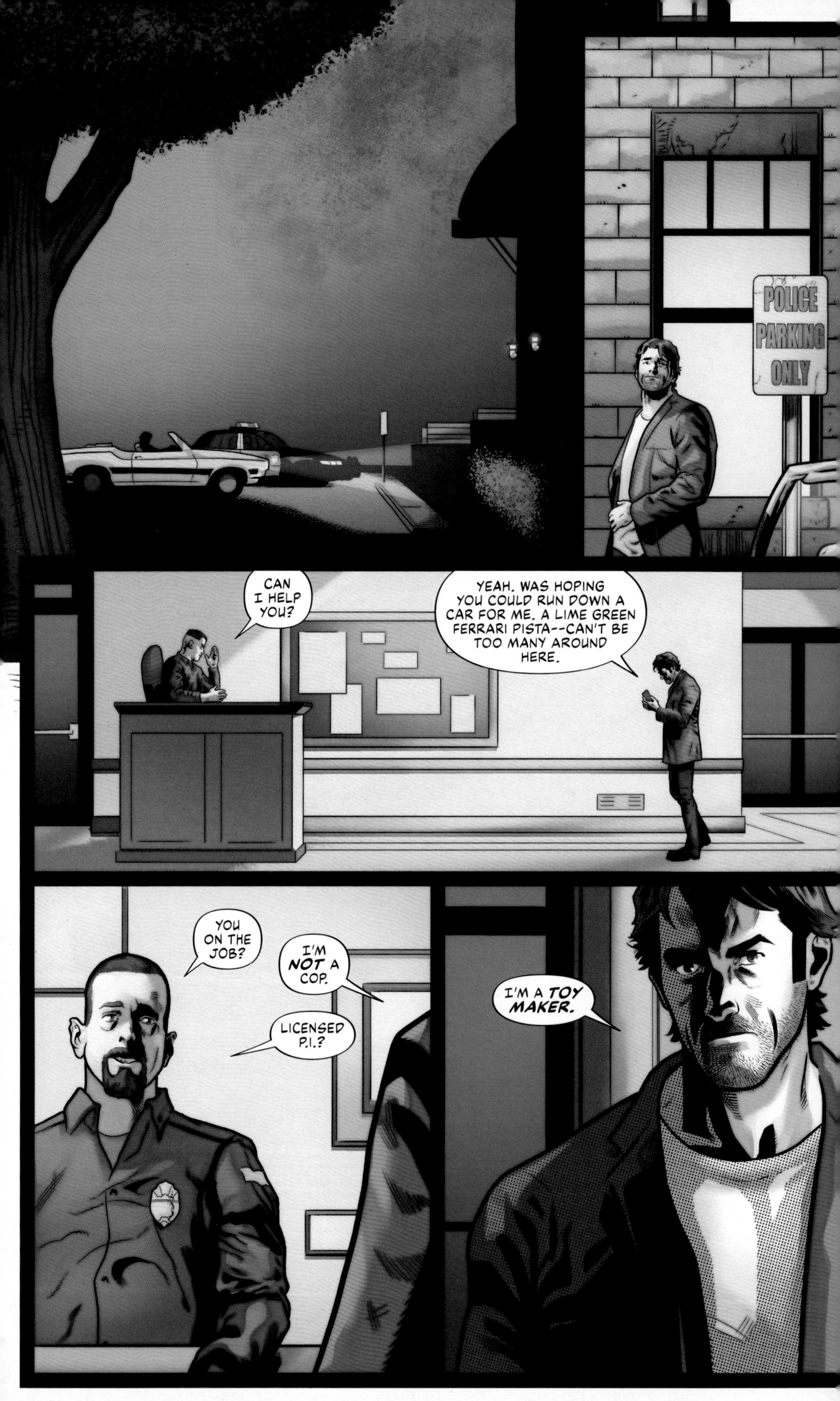
POLICE PARKING ONLY
CAN I HELP YOU?
YEAH. WAS HOPING YOU COULD RUN DOWN A CAR FOR ME. A LIME GREEN FERRARI PISTA--CAN'T BE TOO MANY AROUND HERE.
YOU ON THE JOB?
I'M *NOT* A COP.
LICENSED P.I.?
I'M A *TOY MAKER.*

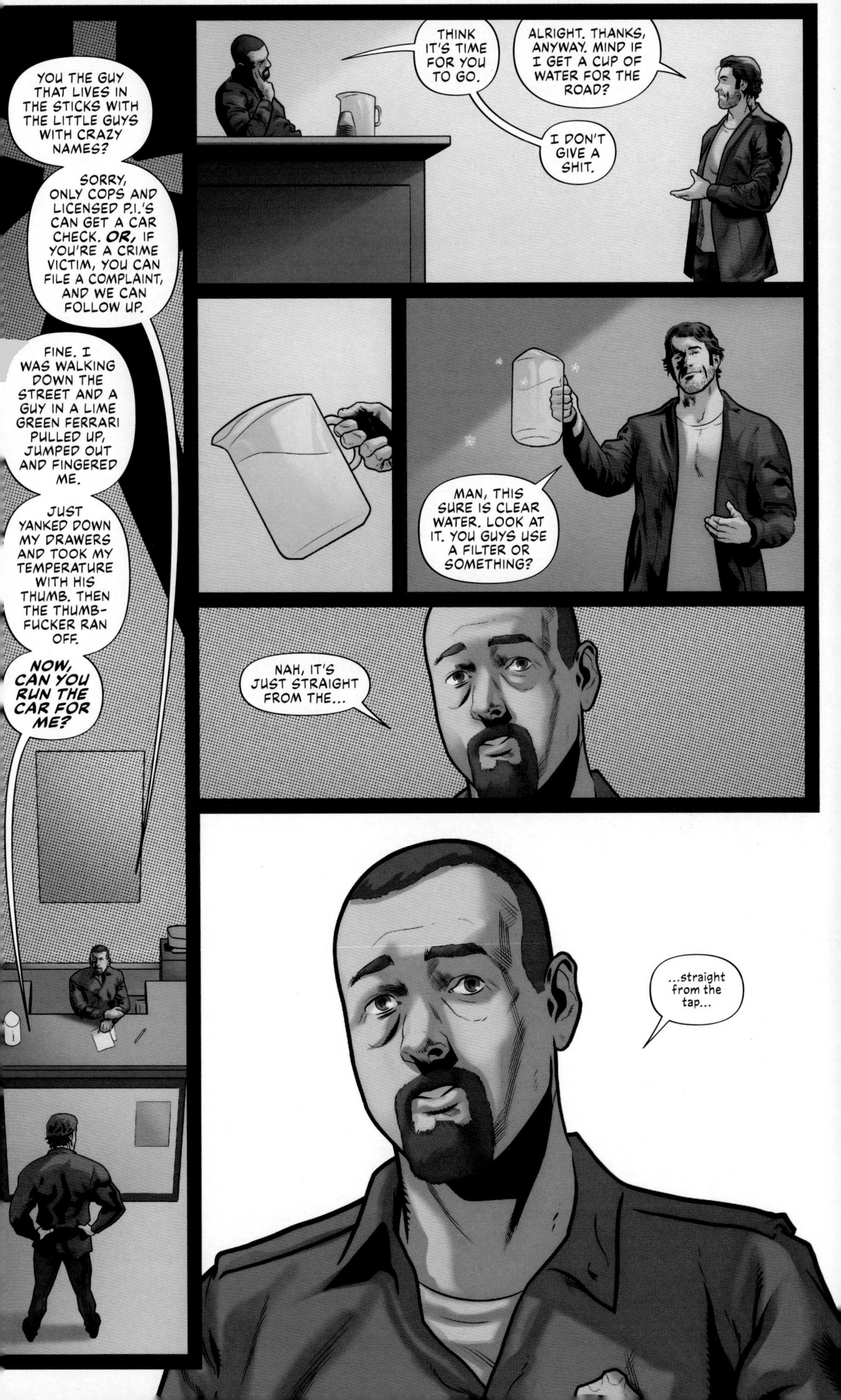
YOU THE GUY THAT LIVES IN THE STICKS WITH THE LITTLE GUYS WITH CRAZY NAMES?
SORRY, ONLY COPS AND LICENSED P.I.'S CAN GET A CAR CHECK. OR, IF YOU'RE A CRIME VICTIM, YOU CAN FILE A COMPLAINT, AND WE CAN FOLLOW UP.
FINE. I WAS WALKING DOWN THE STREET AND A GUY IN A LIME GREEN FERRARI PULLED UP, JUMPED OUT AND FINGERED ME.
JUST YANKED DOWN MY DRAWERS AND TOOK MY TEMPERATURE WITH HIS THUMB. THEN THE THUMB-FUCKER RAN OFF.
NOW, CAN YOU RUN THE CAR FOR ME?
THINK IT'S TIME FOR YOU TO GO.
ALRIGHT. THANKS, ANYWAY. MIND IF I GET A CUP OF WATER FOR THE ROAD?
I DON'T GIVE A SHIT.
MAN, THIS SURE IS CLEAR WATER. LOOK AT IT. YOU GUYS USE A FILTER OR SOMETHING?
NAH, IT'S JUST STRAIGHT FROM THE...
...straight from the tap...

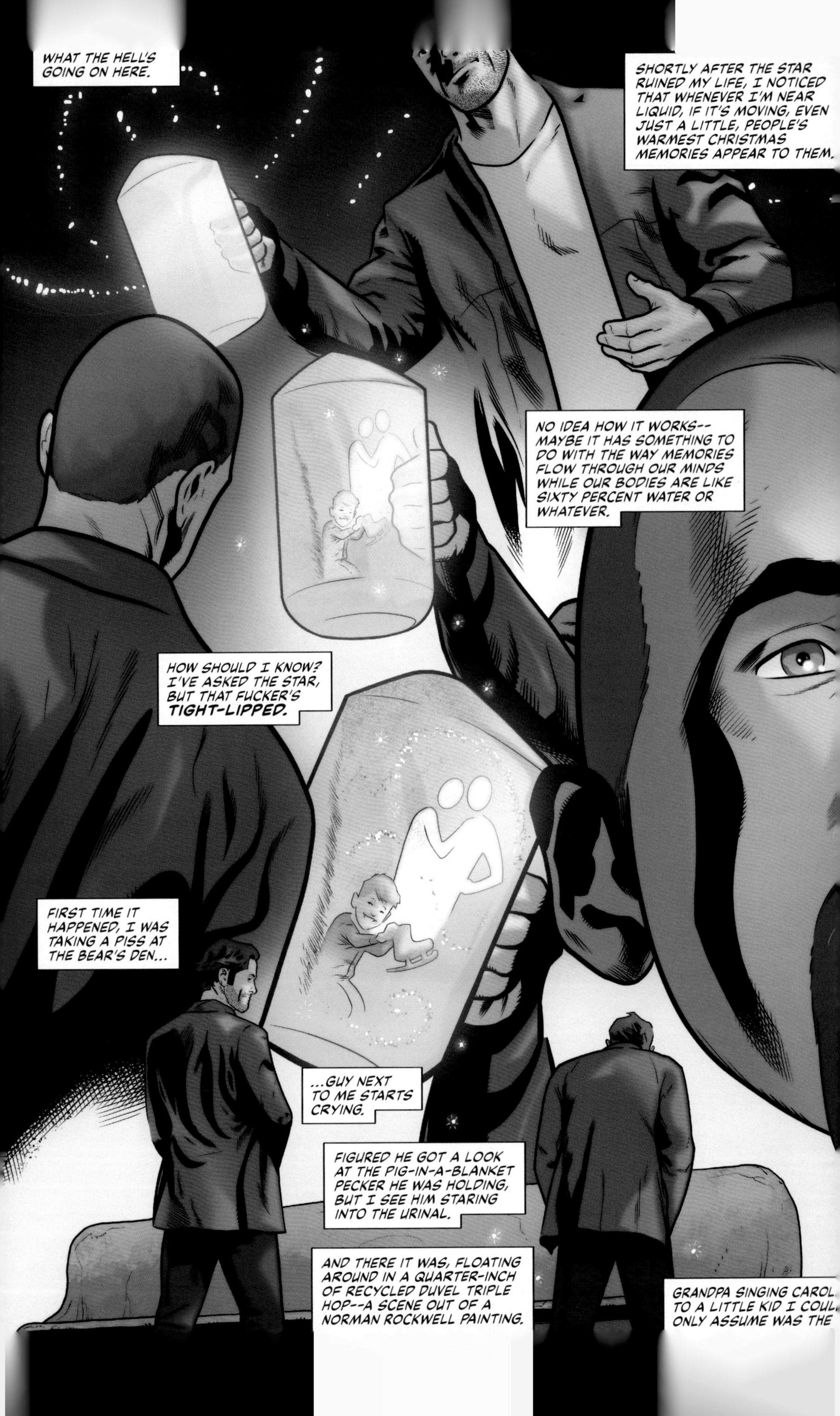
WHAT THE HELL'S GOING ON HERE.
SHORTLY AFTER THE STAR RUINED MY LIFE, I NOTICED THAT WHENEVER I'M NEAR LIQUID, IF IT'S MOVING, EVEN JUST A LITTLE, PEOPLE'S WARMEST CHRISTMAS MEMORIES APPEAR TO THEM.
NO IDEA HOW IT WORKS--MAYBE IT HAS SOMETHING TO DO WITH THE WAY MEMORIES FLOW THROUGH OUR MINDS WHILE OUR BODIES ARE LIKE SIXTY PERCENT WATER OR WHATEVER.
HOW SHOULD I KNOW? I'VE ASKED THE STAR, BUT THAT FUCKER'S **TIGHT-LIPPED.**
FIRST TIME IT HAPPENED, I WAS TAKING A PISS AT THE BEAR'S DEN...
...GUY NEXT TO ME STARTS CRYING.
FIGURED HE GOT A LOOK AT THE PIG-IN-A-BLANKET PECKER HE WAS HOLDING, BUT I SEE HIM STARING INTO THE URINAL.
AND THERE IT WAS, FLOATING AROUND IN A QUARTER-INCH OF RECYCLED DUVEL TRIPLE HOP--A SCENE OUT OF A NORMAN ROCKWELL PAINTING.
GRANDPA SINGING CAROL TO A LITTLE KID I COUL ONLY ASSUME WAS THE

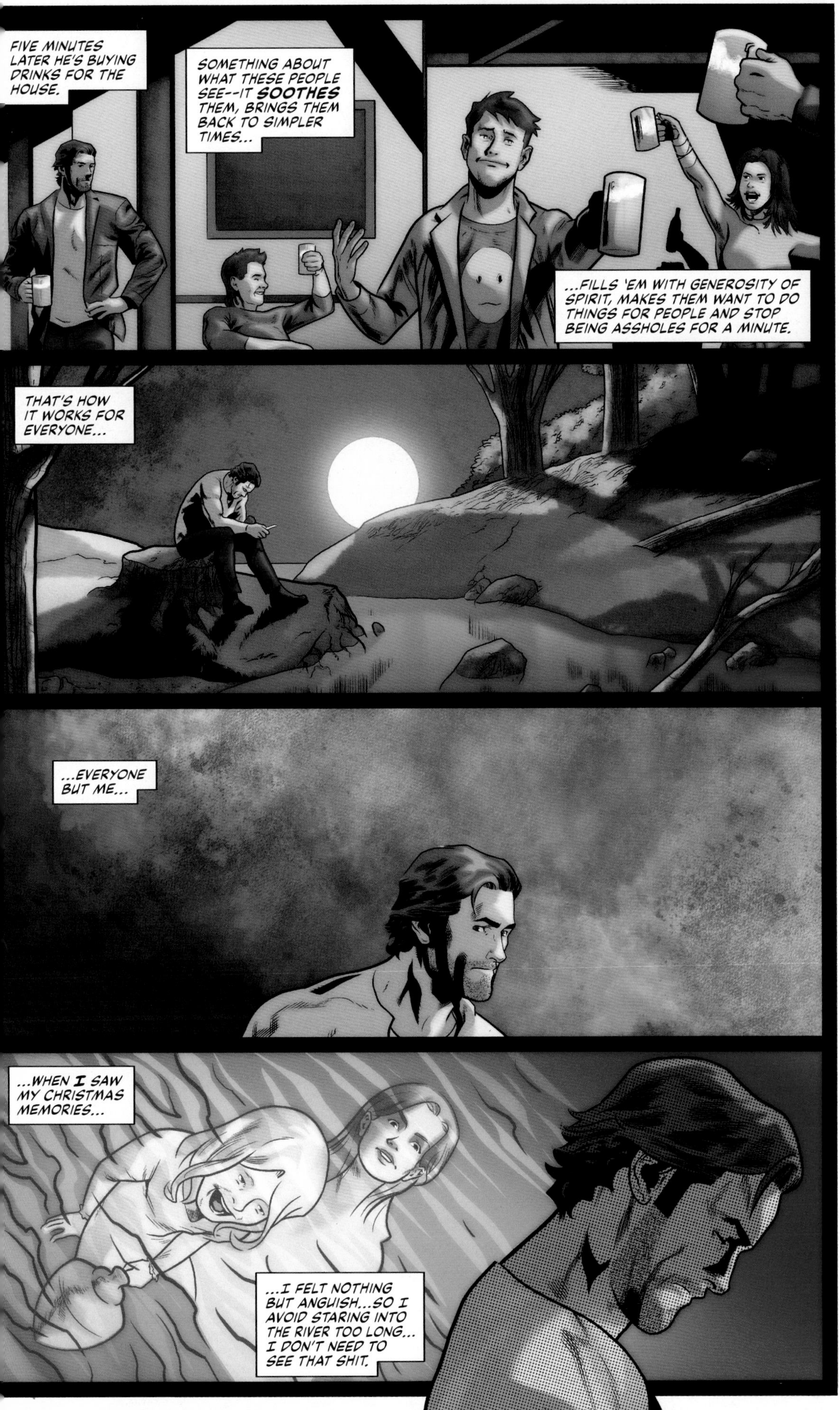
FIVE MINUTES LATER HE'S BUYING DRINKS FOR THE HOUSE.
SOMETHING ABOUT WHAT THESE PEOPLE SEE--IT SOOTHES THEM, BRINGS THEM BACK TO SIMPLER TIMES...
...FILLS 'EM WITH GENEROSITY OF SPIRIT, MAKES THEM WANT TO DO THINGS FOR PEOPLE AND STOP BEING ASSHOLES FOR A MINUTE.
THAT'S HOW IT WORKS FOR EVERYONE...
...EVERYONE BUT ME...
...WHEN I SAW MY CHRISTMAS MEMORIES...
...I FELT NOTHING BUT ANGUISH...SO I AVOID STARING INTO THE RIVER TOO LONG... I DON'T NEED TO SEE THAT SHIT.

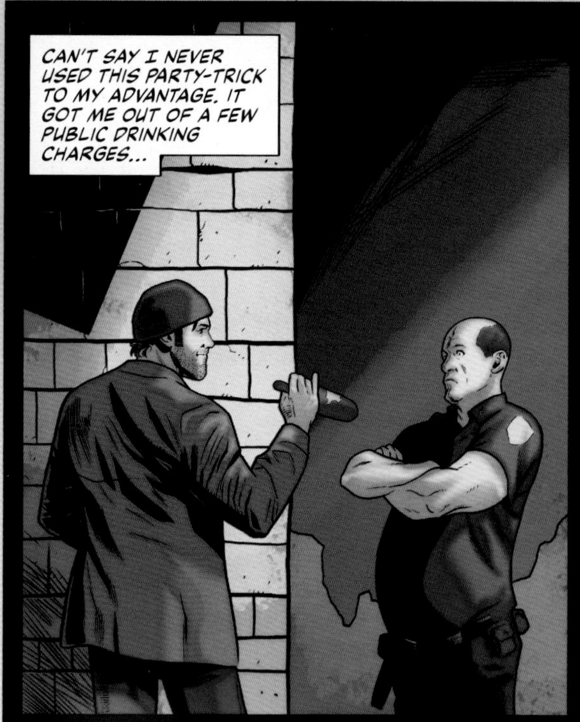
CAN'T SAY I NEVER USED THIS PARTY-TRICK TO MY ADVANTAGE. IT GOT ME OUT OF A FEW PUBLIC DRINKING CHARGES...

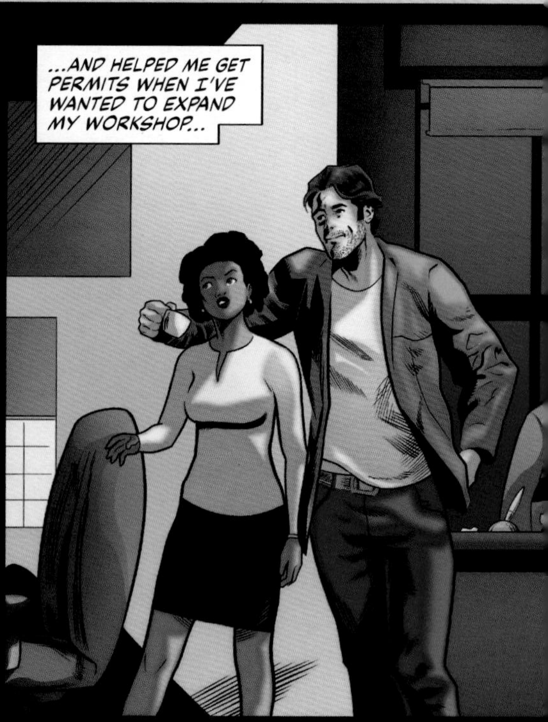
...AND HELPED ME GET PERMITS WHEN I'VE WANTED TO EXPAND MY WORKSHOP...

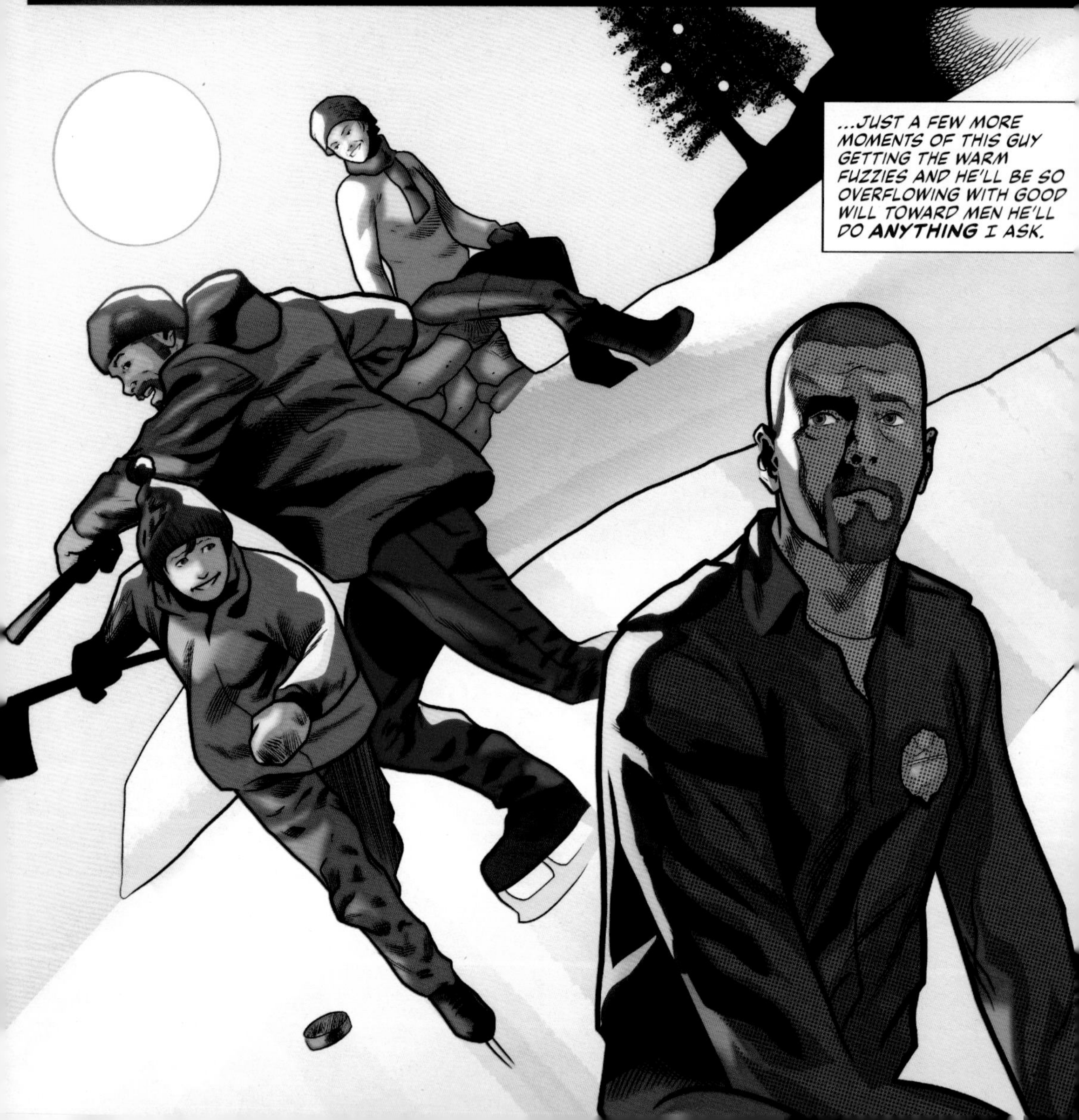
...JUST A FEW MORE MOMENTS OF THIS GUY GETTING THE WARM FUZZIES AND HE'LL BE SO OVERFLOWING WITH GOOD WILL TOWARD MEN HE'LL DO **ANYTHING** I ASK.

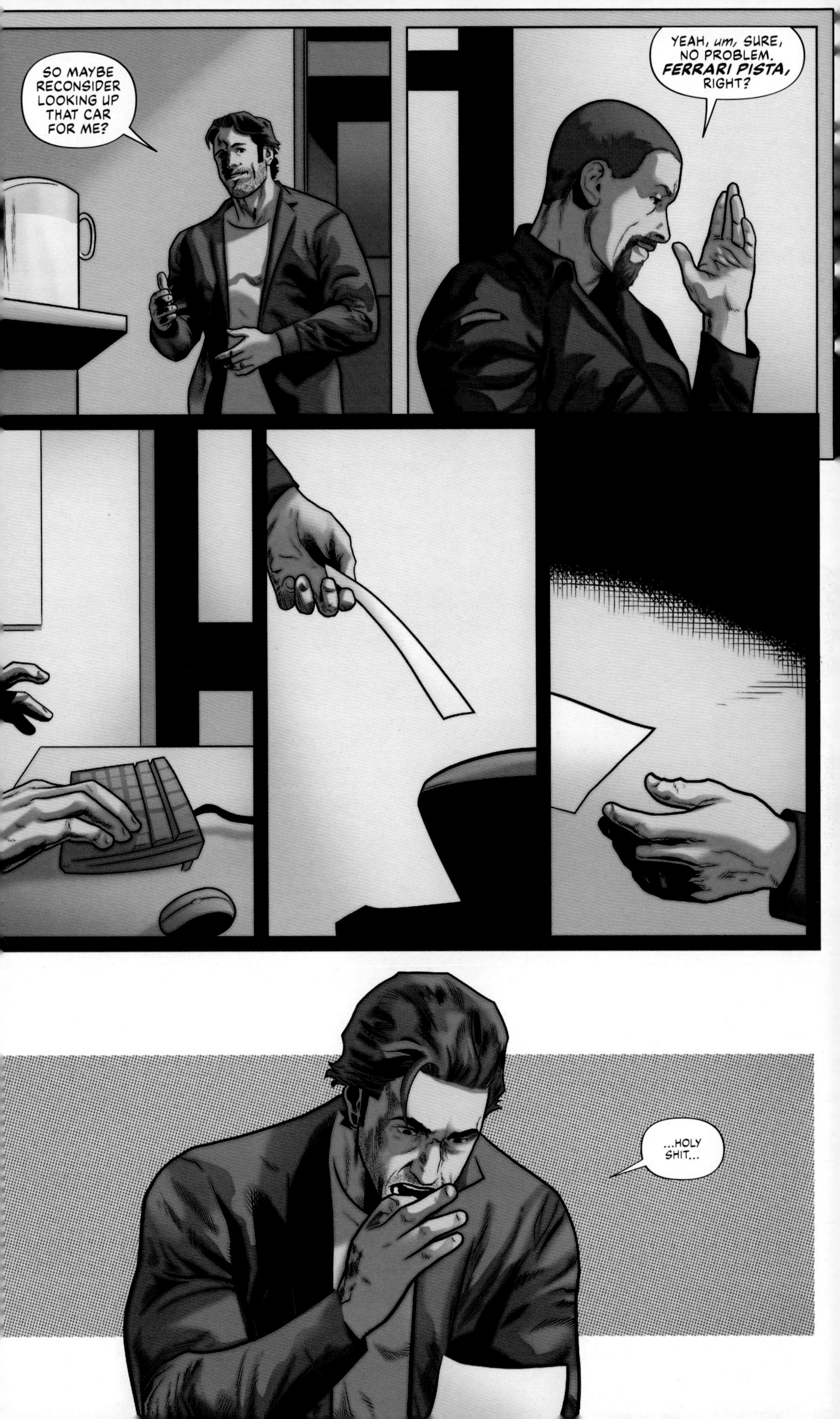
SO MAYBE RECONSIDER LOOKING UP THAT CAR FOR ME?
YEAH, *um,* SURE, NO PROBLEM. ***FERRARI PISTA,*** RIGHT?
...HOLY SHIT...

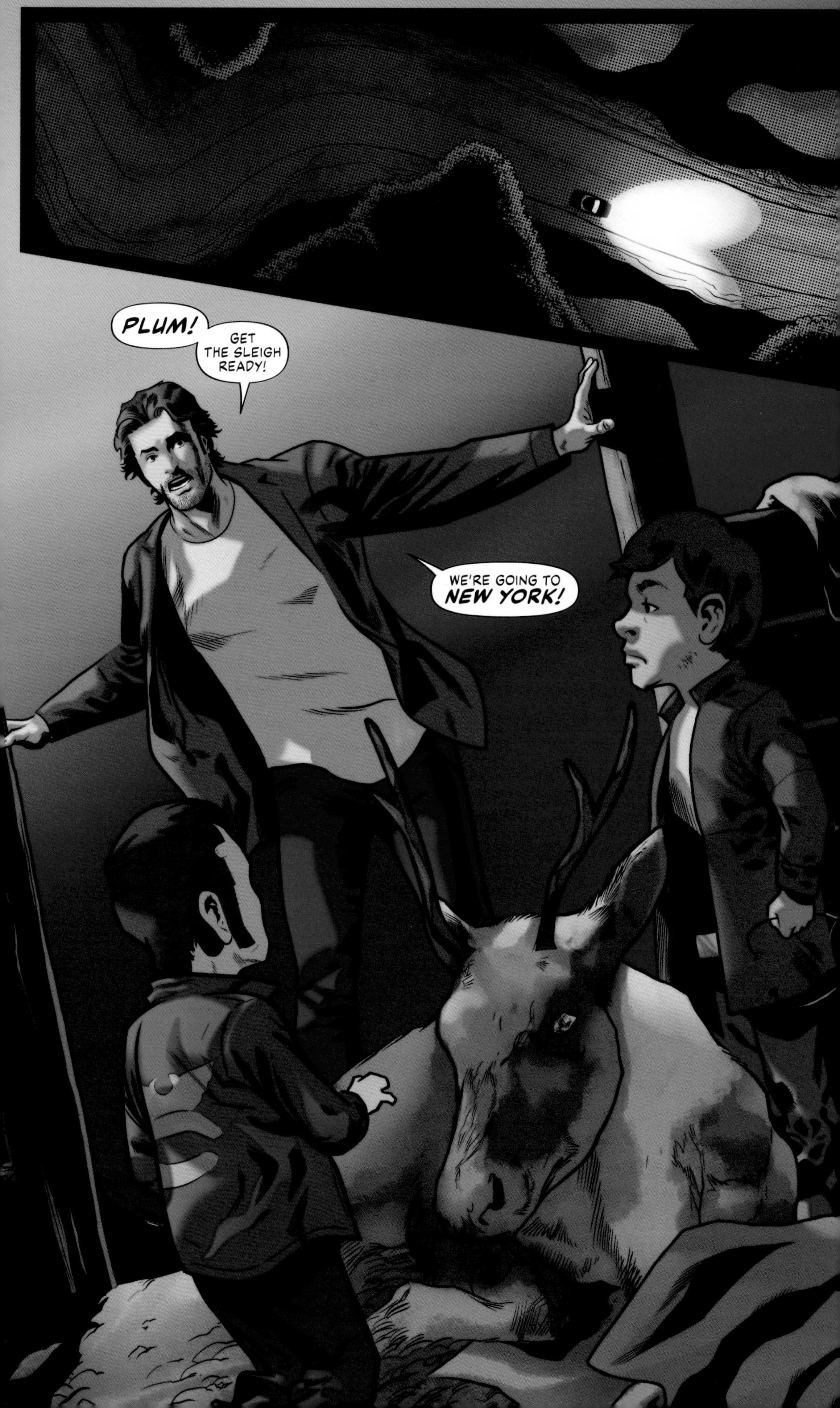
PLUM!
GET THE SLEIGH READY!
WE'RE GOING TO NEW YORK!

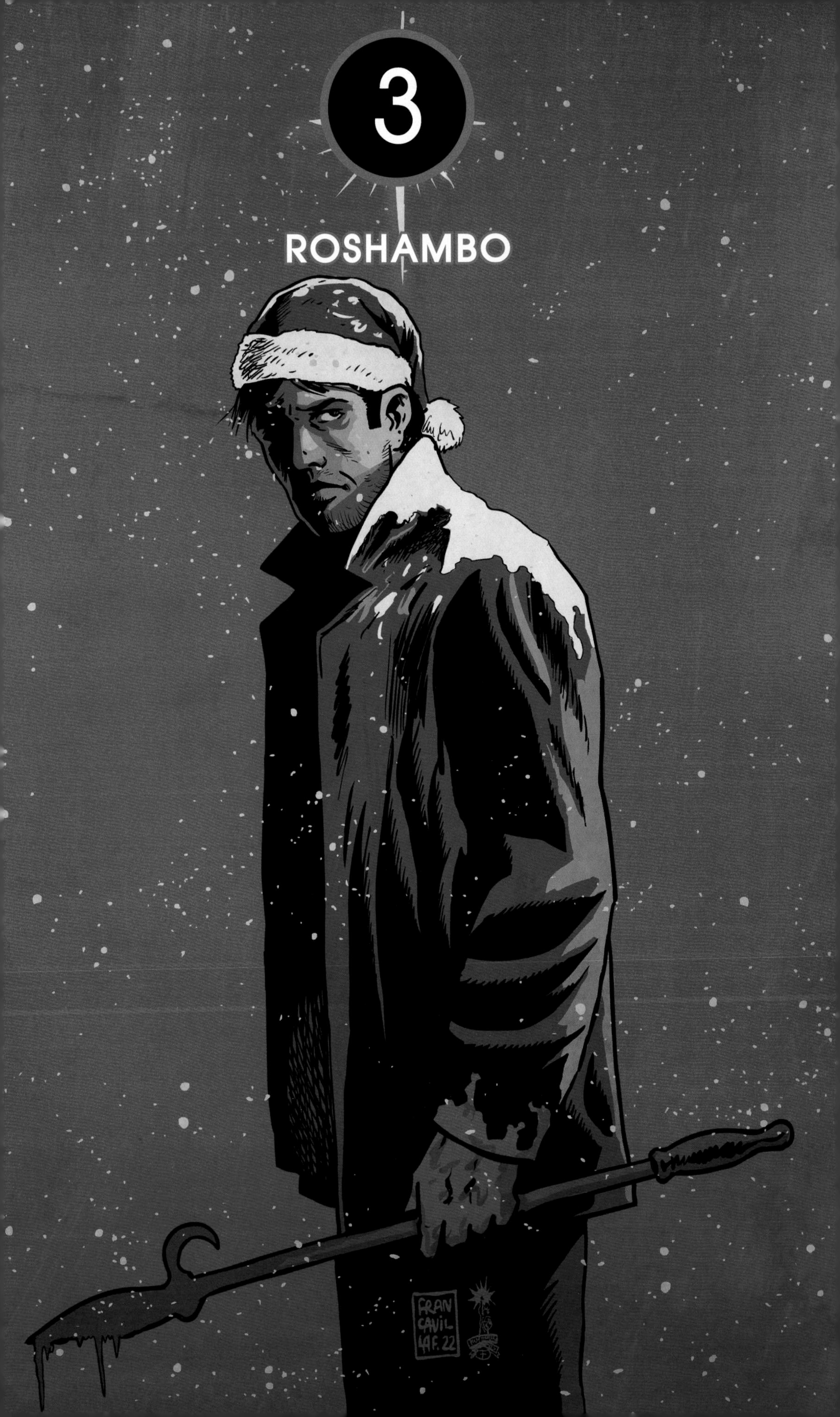
3
ROSHAMBO

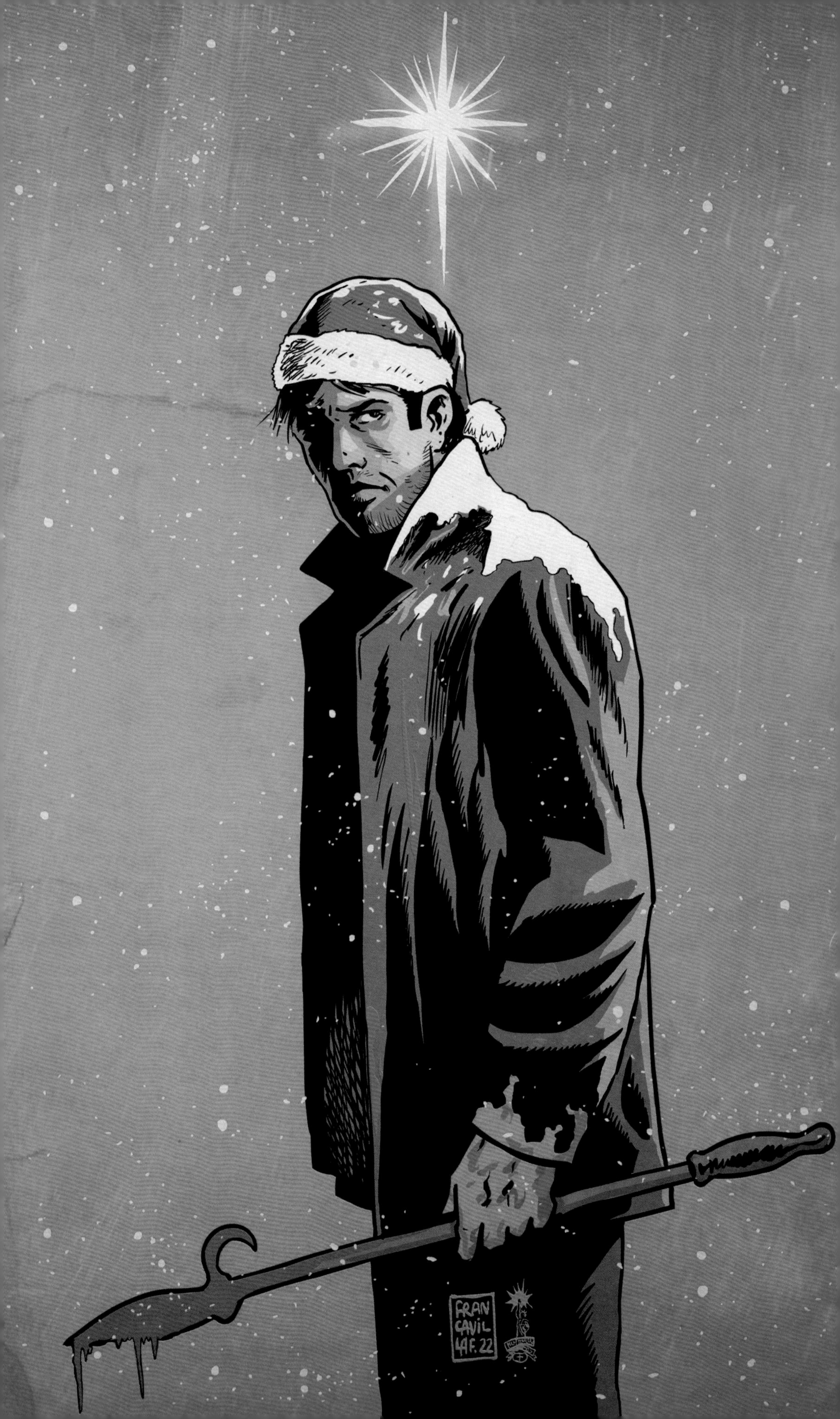
FRAN
CAVIL
44F.22

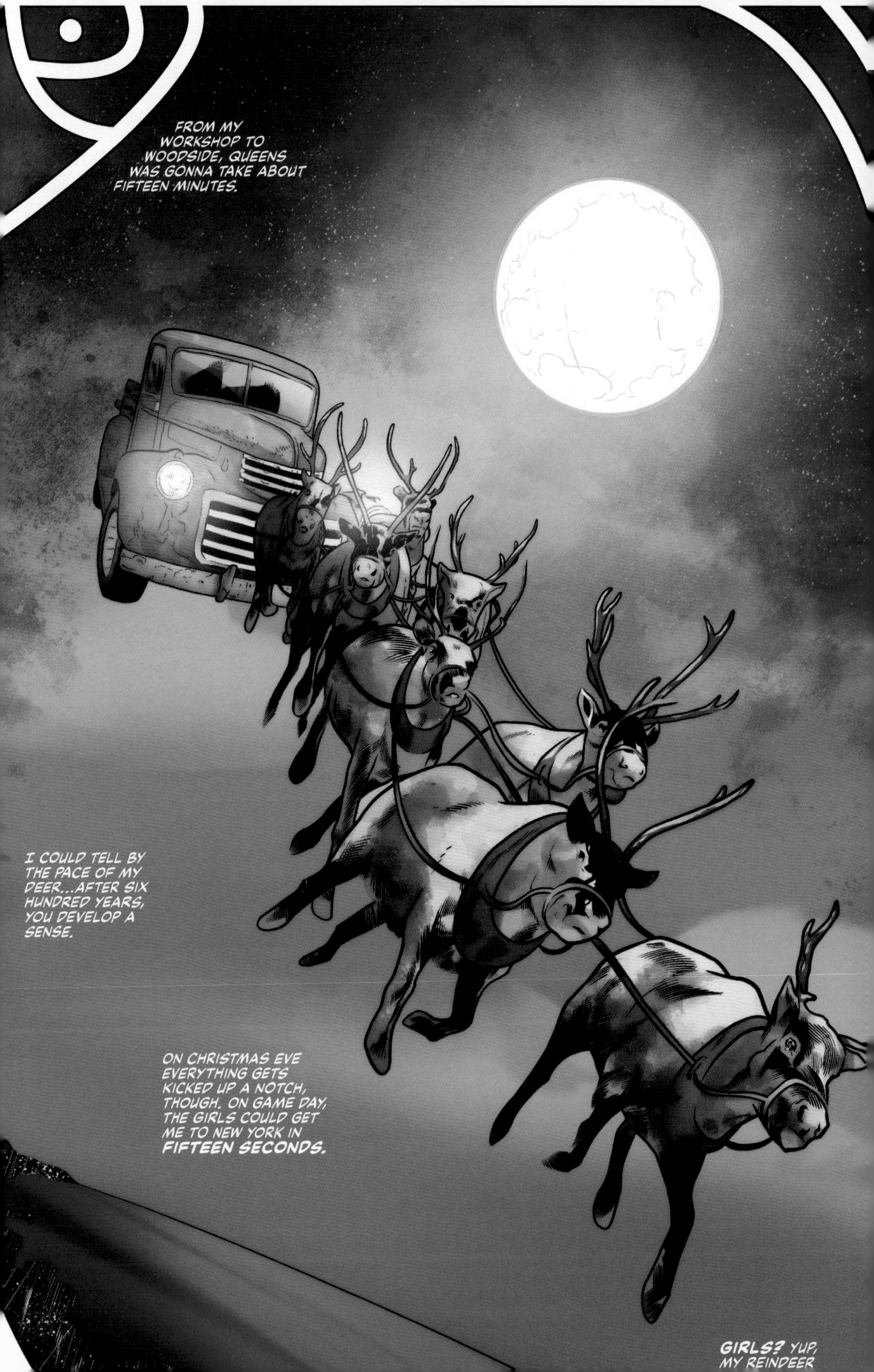
FROM MY WORKSHOP TO WOODSIDE, QUEENS WAS GONNA TAKE ABOUT FIFTEEN MINUTES.
I COULD TELL BY THE PACE OF MY DEER...AFTER SIX HUNDRED YEARS, YOU DEVELOP A SENSE.
ON CHRISTMAS EVE EVERYTHING GETS KICKED UP A NOTCH, THOUGH. ON GAME DAY, THE GIRLS COULD GET ME TO NEW YORK IN FIFTEEN SECONDS.
GIRLS? YUP, MY REINDEER

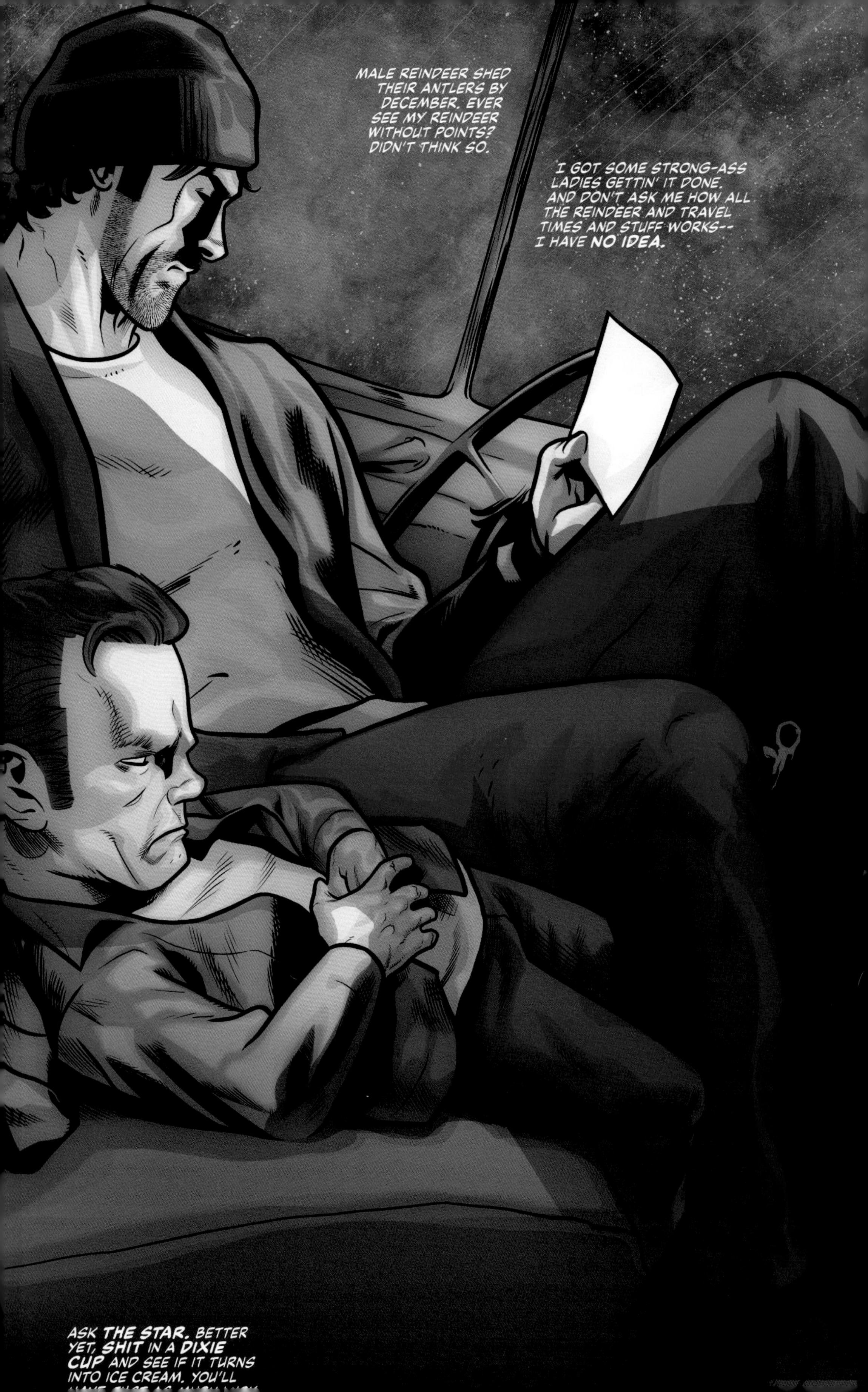
MALE REINDEER SHED THEIR ANTLERS BY DECEMBER. EVER SEE MY REINDEER WITHOUT POINTS? DIDN'T THINK SO.
I GOT SOME STRONG-ASS LADIES GETTIN' IT DONE. AND DON'T ASK ME HOW ALL THE REINDEER AND TRAVEL TIMES AND STUFF WORKS-- I HAVE NO IDEA.
ASK THE STAR. BETTER YET, SHIT IN A DIXIE CUP AND SEE IF IT TURNS INTO ICE CREAM. YOU'LL

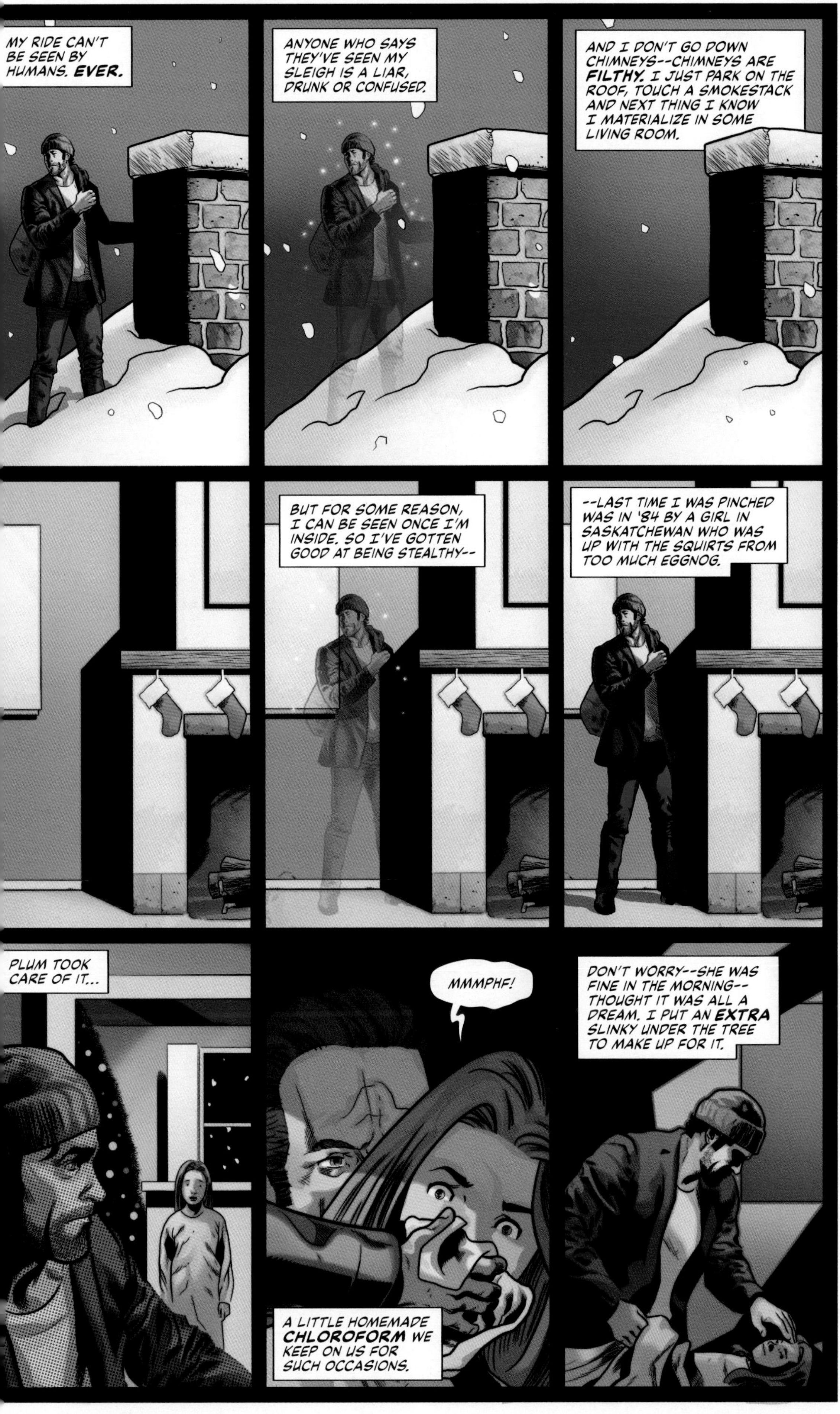

MY RIDE CAN'T BE SEEN BY HUMANS. EVER.
ANYONE WHO SAYS THEY'VE SEEN MY SLEIGH IS A LIAR, DRUNK OR CONFUSED.
AND I DON'T GO DOWN CHIMNEYS--CHIMNEYS ARE FILTHY. I JUST PARK ON THE ROOF, TOUCH A SMOKESTACK AND NEXT THING I KNOW I MATERIALIZE IN SOME LIVING ROOM.
BUT FOR SOME REASON, I CAN BE SEEN ONCE I'M INSIDE. SO I'VE GOTTEN GOOD AT BEING STEALTHY--
--LAST TIME I WAS PINCHED WAS IN '84 BY A GIRL IN SASKATCHEWAN WHO WAS UP WITH THE SQUIRTS FROM TOO MUCH EGGNOG.
PLUM TOOK CARE OF IT...
MMMPHF!
A LITTLE HOMEMADE CHLOROFORM WE KEEP ON US FOR SUCH OCCASIONS.
DON'T WORRY--SHE WAS FINE IN THE MORNING--THOUGHT IT WAS ALL A DREAM. I PUT AN EXTRA SLINKY UNDER THE TREE TO MAKE UP FOR IT.

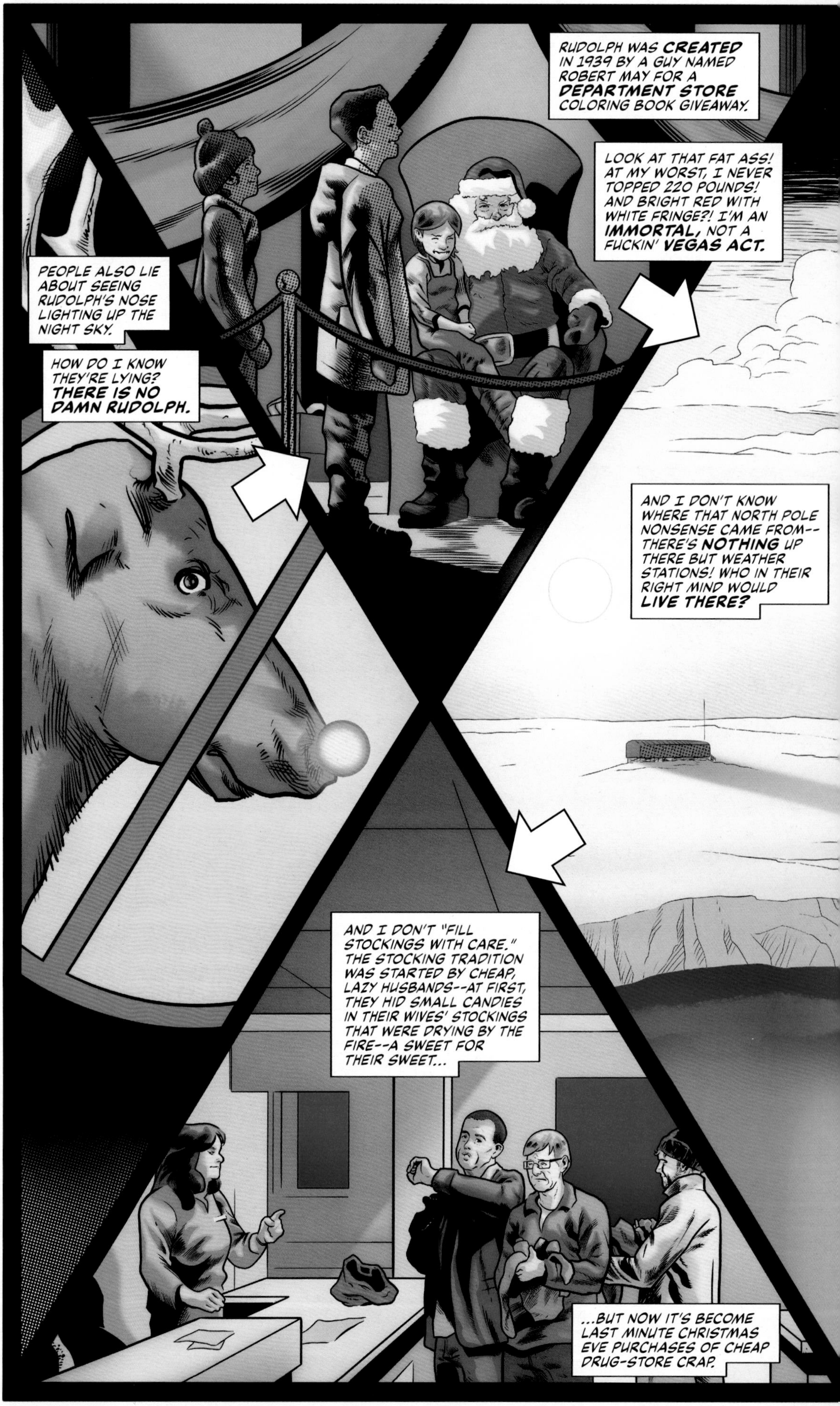
RUDOLPH WAS CREATED IN 1939 BY A GUY NAMED ROBERT MAY FOR A DEPARTMENT STORE COLORING BOOK GIVEAWAY.
LOOK AT THAT FAT ASS! AT MY WORST, I NEVER TOPPED 220 POUNDS! AND BRIGHT RED WITH WHITE FRINGE?! I'M AN IMMORTAL, NOT A FUCKIN' VEGAS ACT.
PEOPLE ALSO LIE ABOUT SEEING RUDOLPH'S NOSE LIGHTING UP THE NIGHT SKY.
HOW DO I KNOW THEY'RE LYING? THERE IS NO DAMN RUDOLPH.
AND I DON'T KNOW WHERE THAT NORTH POLE NONSENSE CAME FROM--THERE'S NOTHING UP THERE BUT WEATHER STATIONS! WHO IN THEIR RIGHT MIND WOULD LIVE THERE?
AND I DON'T "FILL STOCKINGS WITH CARE." THE STOCKING TRADITION WAS STARTED BY CHEAP, LAZY HUSBANDS--AT FIRST, THEY HID SMALL CANDIES IN THEIR WIVES' STOCKINGS THAT WERE DRYING BY THE FIRE--A SWEET FOR THEIR SWEET...
...BUT NOW IT'S BECOME LAST MINUTE CHRISTMAS EVE PURCHASES OF CHEAP DRUG-STORE CRAP.

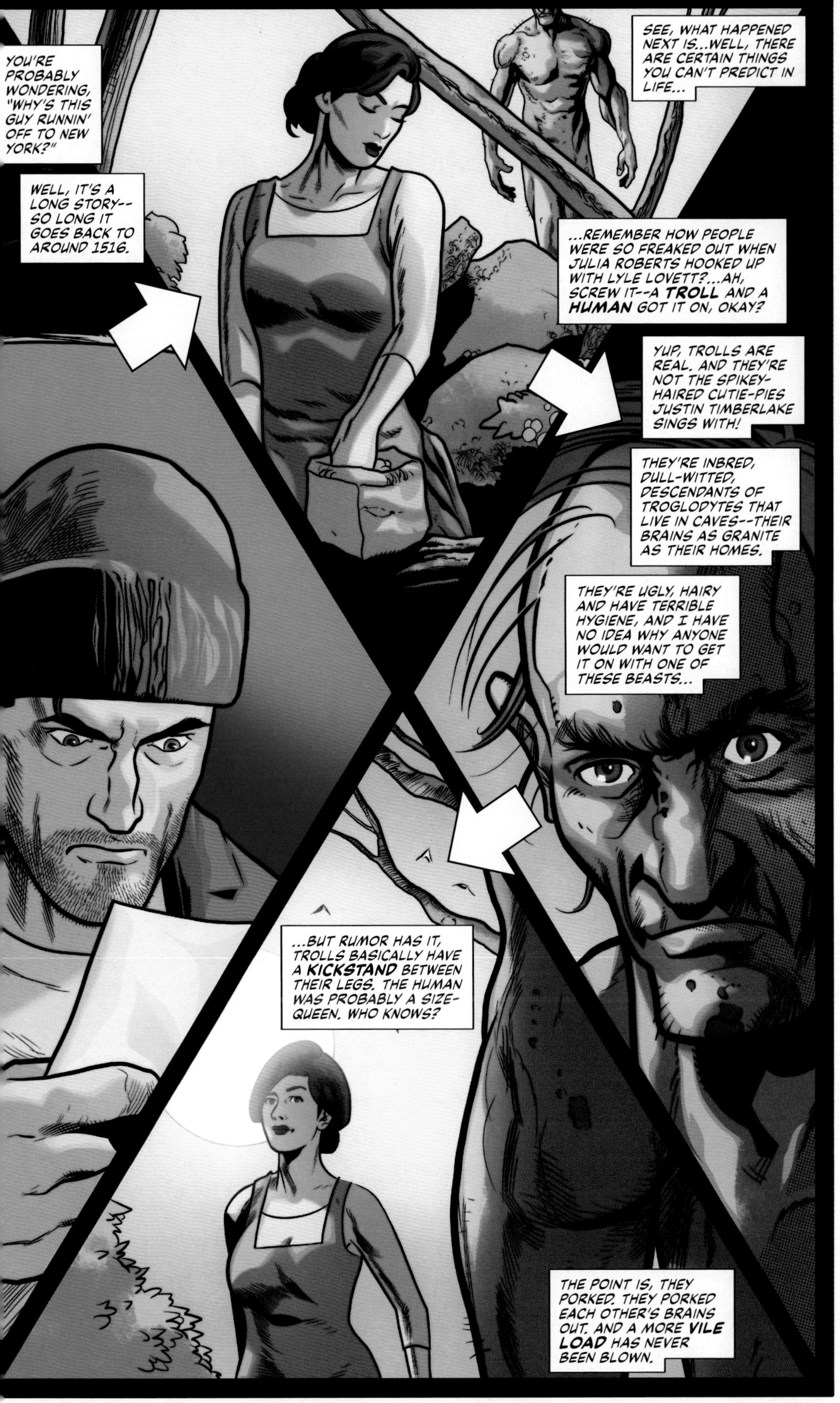
YOU'RE PROBABLY WONDERING, "WHY'S THIS GUY RUNNIN' OFF TO NEW YORK?"
WELL, IT'S A LONG STORY-- SO LONG IT GOES BACK TO AROUND 1516.
SEE, WHAT HAPPENED NEXT IS...WELL, THERE ARE CERTAIN THINGS YOU CAN'T PREDICT IN LIFE...
...REMEMBER HOW PEOPLE WERE SO FREAKED OUT WHEN JULIA ROBERTS HOOKED UP WITH LYLE LOVETT?...AH, SCREW IT--A TROLL AND A HUMAN GOT IT ON, OKAY?
YUP, TROLLS ARE REAL. AND THEY'RE NOT THE SPIKEY-HAIRED CUTIE-PIES JUSTIN TIMBERLAKE SINGS WITH!
THEY'RE INBRED, DULL-WITTED, DESCENDANTS OF TROGLODYTES THAT LIVE IN CAVES--THEIR BRAINS AS GRANITE AS THEIR HOMES.
THEY'RE UGLY, HAIRY AND HAVE TERRIBLE HYGIENE, AND I HAVE NO IDEA WHY ANYONE WOULD WANT TO GET IT ON WITH ONE OF THESE BEASTS...
...BUT RUMOR HAS IT, TROLLS BASICALLY HAVE A KICKSTAND BETWEEN THEIR LEGS. THE HUMAN WAS PROBABLY A SIZE-QUEEN. WHO KNOWS?
THE POINT IS, THEY PORKED. THEY PORKED EACH OTHER'S BRAINS OUT. AND A MORE VILE LOAD HAS NEVER BEEN BLOWN.

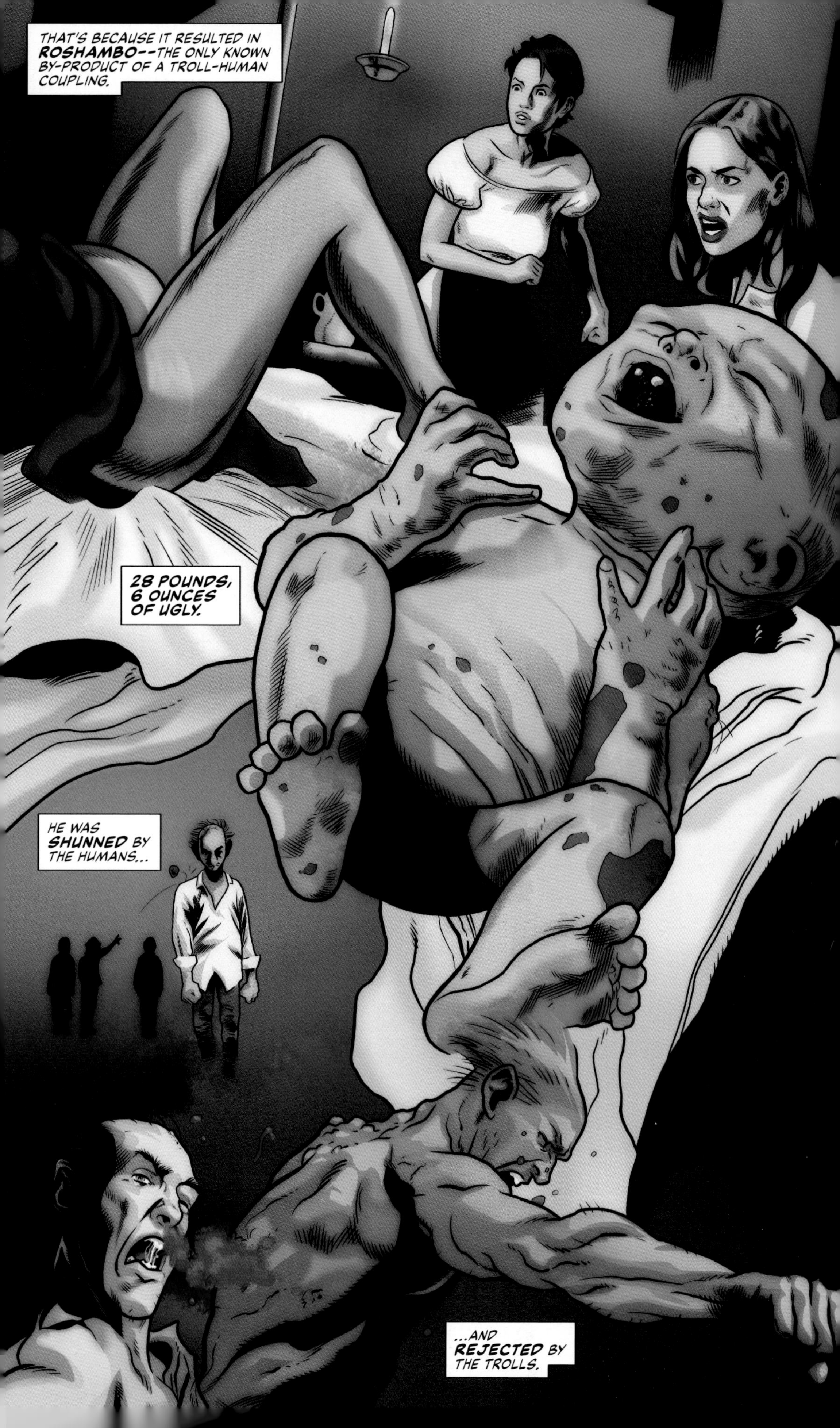
THAT'S BECAUSE IT RESULTED IN ROSHAMBO--THE ONLY KNOWN BY-PRODUCT OF A TROLL-HUMAN COUPLING.
28 POUNDS, 6 OUNCES OF UGLY.
HE WAS SHUNNED BY THE HUMANS...
...AND REJECTED BY THE TROLLS.

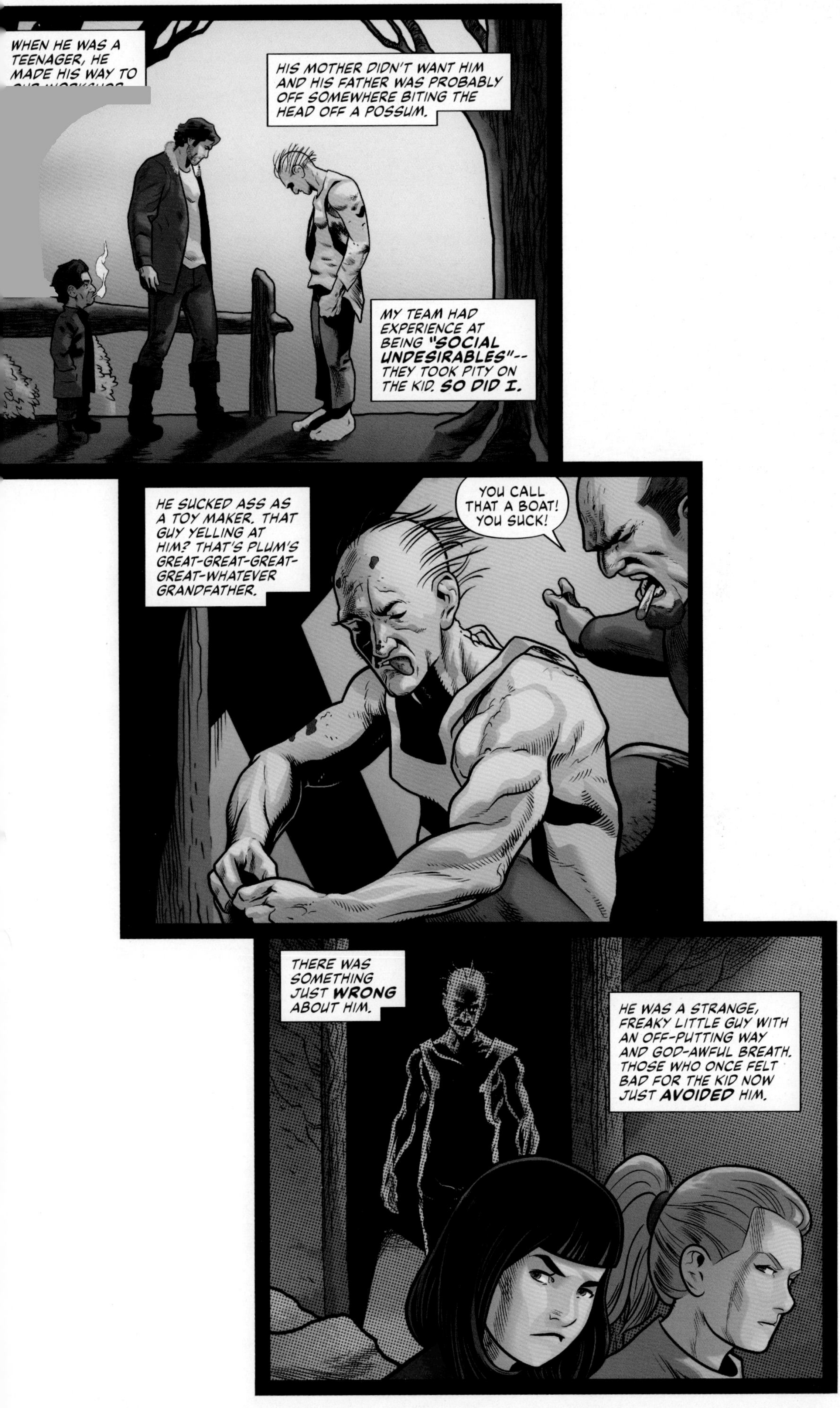
WHEN HE WAS A TEENAGER, HE MADE HIS WAY TO
HIS MOTHER DIDN'T WANT HIM AND HIS FATHER WAS PROBABLY OFF SOMEWHERE BITING THE HEAD OFF A POSSUM.
MY TEAM HAD EXPERIENCE AT BEING "SOCIAL UNDESIRABLES"-- THEY TOOK PITY ON THE KID. SO DID I.
HE SUCKED ASS AS A TOY MAKER. THAT GUY YELLING AT HIM? THAT'S PLUM'S GREAT-GREAT-GREAT-GREAT-WHATEVER GRANDFATHER.
YOU CALL THAT A BOAT! YOU SUCK!
THERE WAS SOMETHING JUST WRONG ABOUT HIM.
HE WAS A STRANGE, FREAKY LITTLE GUY WITH AN OFF-PUTTING WAY AND GOD-AWFUL BREATH. THOSE WHO ONCE FELT BAD FOR THE KID NOW JUST AVOIDED HIM.

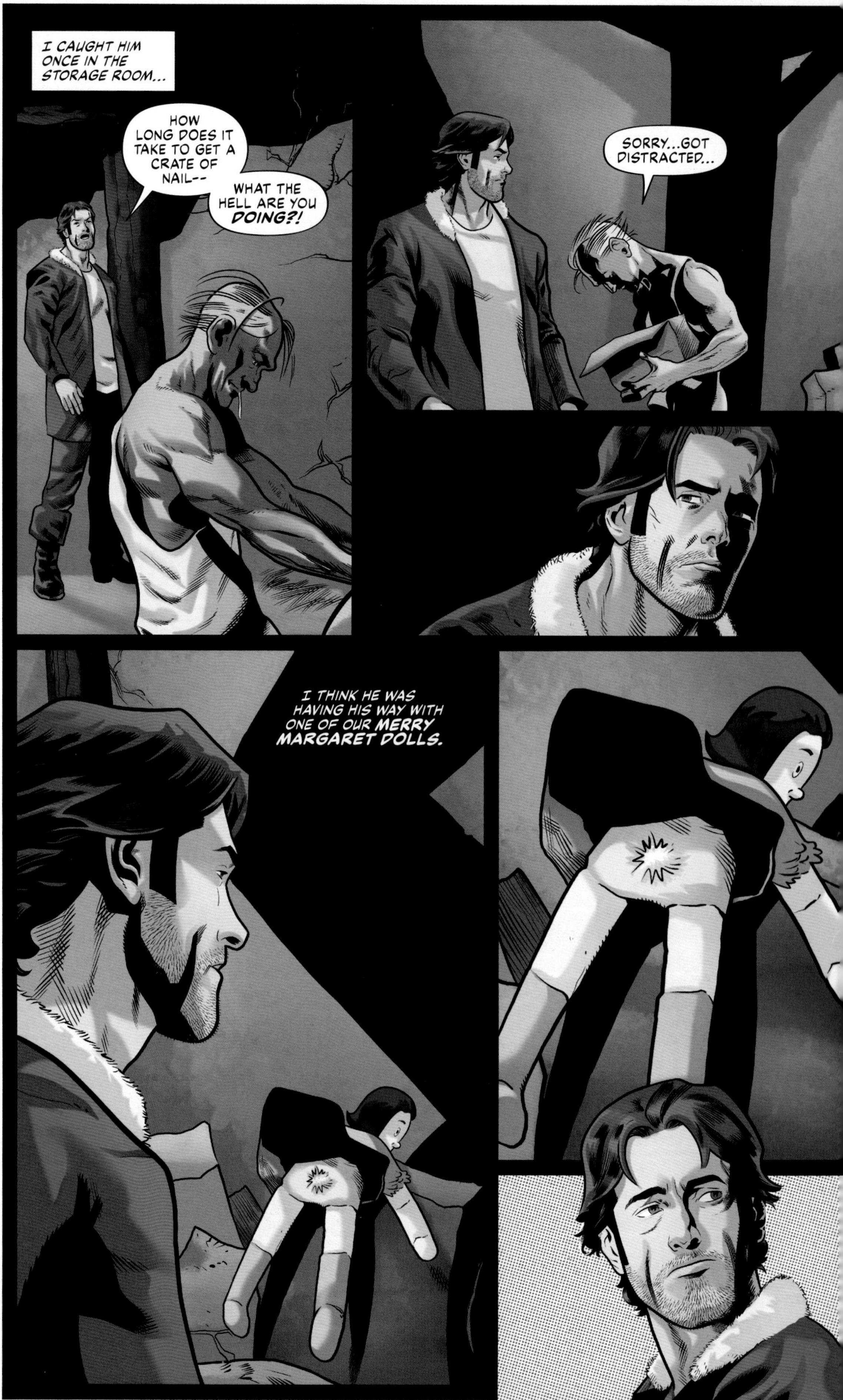
I CAUGHT HIM ONCE IN THE STORAGE ROOM...
HOW LONG DOES IT TAKE TO GET A CRATE OF NAIL--
WHAT THE HELL ARE YOU DOING?!
SORRY...GOT DISTRACTED...
I THINK HE WAS HAVING HIS WAY WITH ONE OF OUR MERRY MARGARET DOLLS.

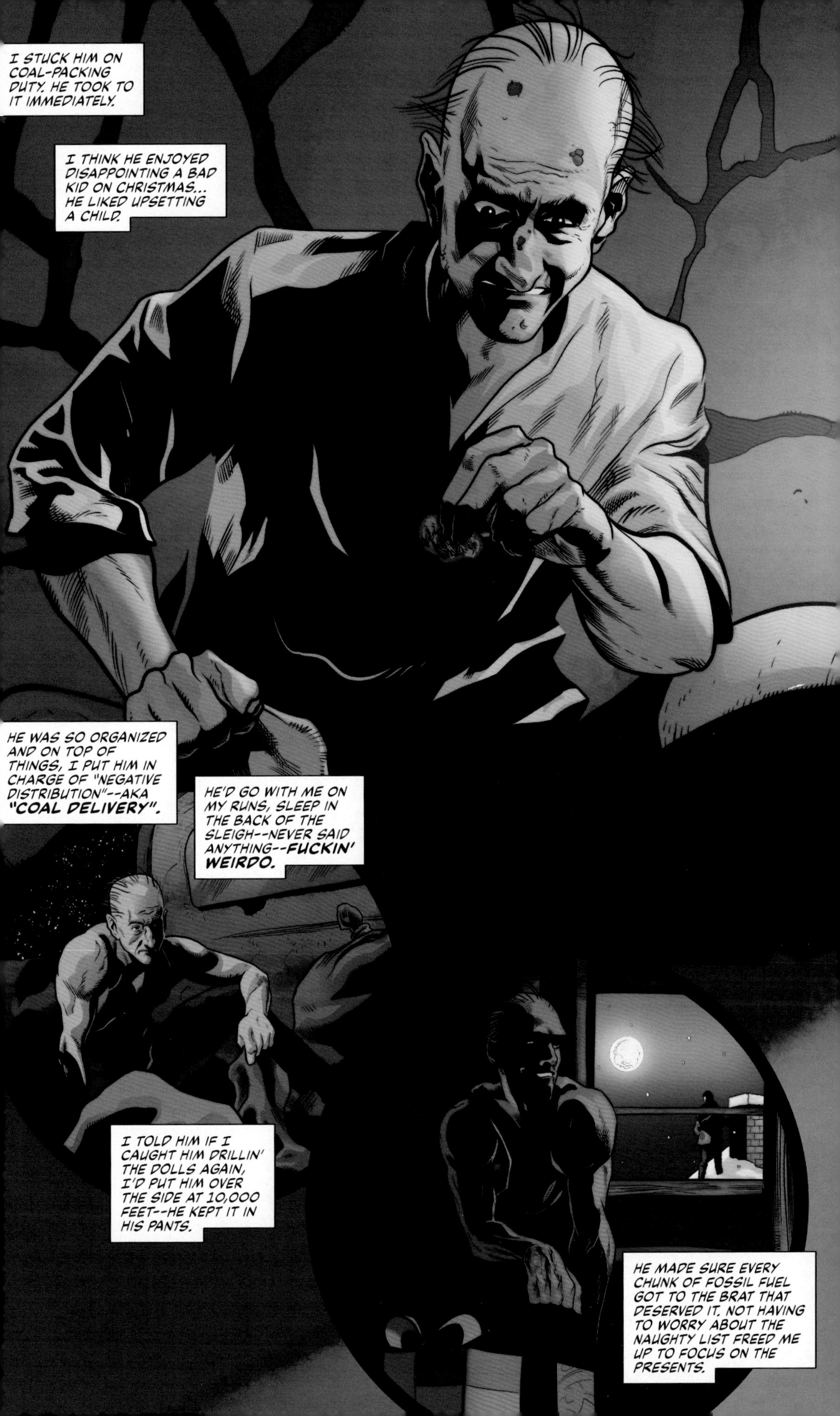
I STUCK HIM ON COAL-PACKING DUTY. HE TOOK TO IT IMMEDIATELY.
I THINK HE ENJOYED DISAPPOINTING A BAD KID ON CHRISTMAS... HE LIKED UPSETTING A CHILD.
HE WAS SO ORGANIZED AND ON TOP OF THINGS, I PUT HIM IN CHARGE OF "NEGATIVE DISTRIBUTION"--AKA **"COAL DELIVERY".**
HE'D GO WITH ME ON MY RUNS, SLEEP IN THE BACK OF THE SLEIGH--NEVER SAID ANYTHING--**FUCKIN' WEIRDO.**
I TOLD HIM IF I CAUGHT HIM DRILLIN' THE DOLLS AGAIN, I'D PUT HIM OVER THE SIDE AT 10,000 FEET--HE KEPT IT IN HIS PANTS.
HE MADE SURE EVERY CHUNK OF FOSSIL FUEL GOT TO THE BRAT THAT DESERVED IT. NOT HAVING TO WORRY ABOUT THE NAUGHTY LIST FREED ME UP TO FOCUS ON THE PRESENTS.

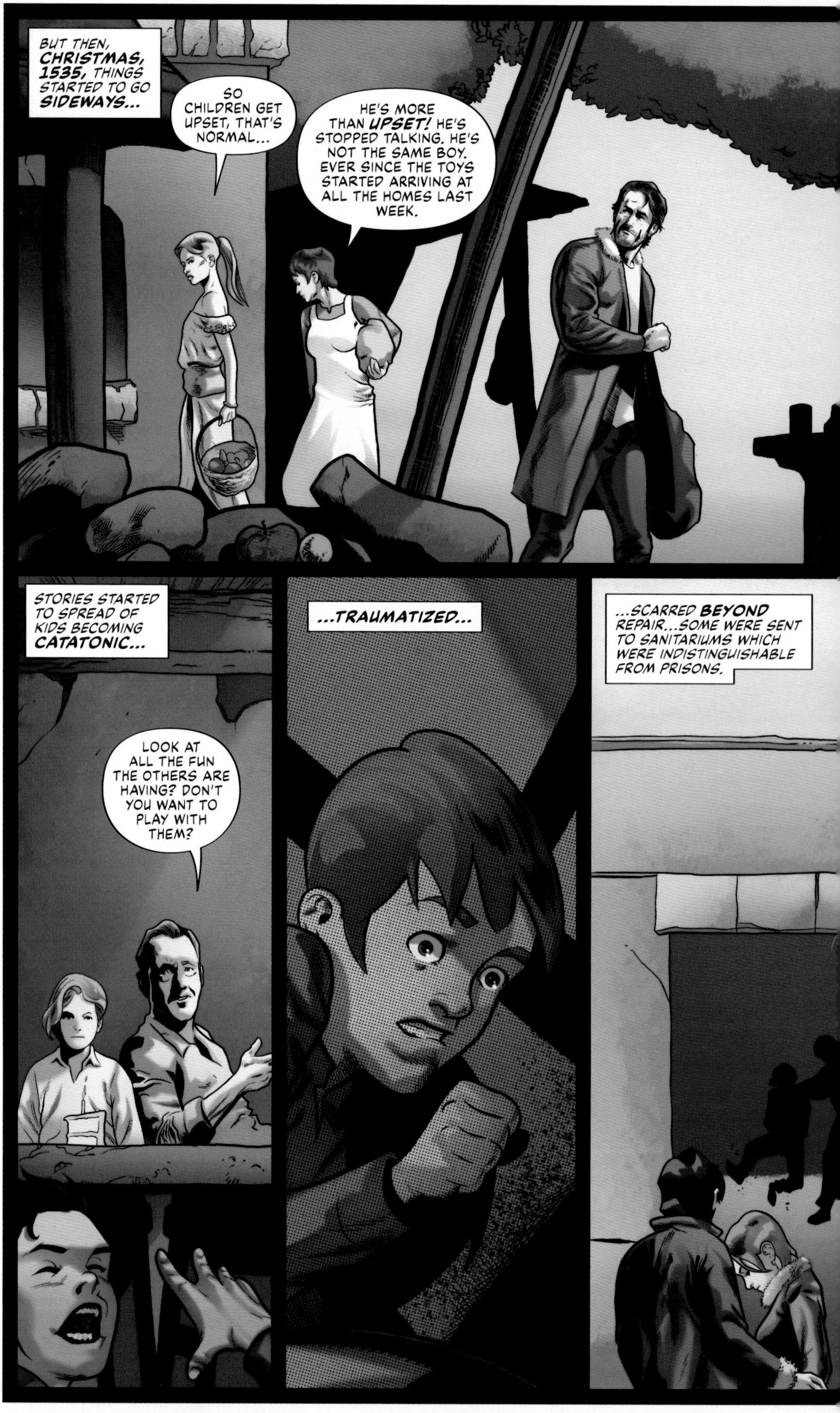
BUT THEN, CHRISTMAS, 1535, THINGS STARTED TO GO SIDEWAYS...
SO CHILDREN GET UPSET, THAT'S NORMAL...
HE'S MORE THAN UPSET! HE'S STOPPED TALKING. HE'S NOT THE SAME BOY. EVER SINCE THE TOYS STARTED ARRIVING AT ALL THE HOMES LAST WEEK.
STORIES STARTED TO SPREAD OF KIDS BECOMING CATATONIC...
LOOK AT ALL THE FUN THE OTHERS ARE HAVING? DON'T YOU WANT TO PLAY WITH THEM?
...TRAUMATIZED...
...SCARRED BEYOND REPAIR...SOME WERE SENT TO SANITARIUMS WHICH WERE INDISTINGUISHABLE FROM PRISONS.

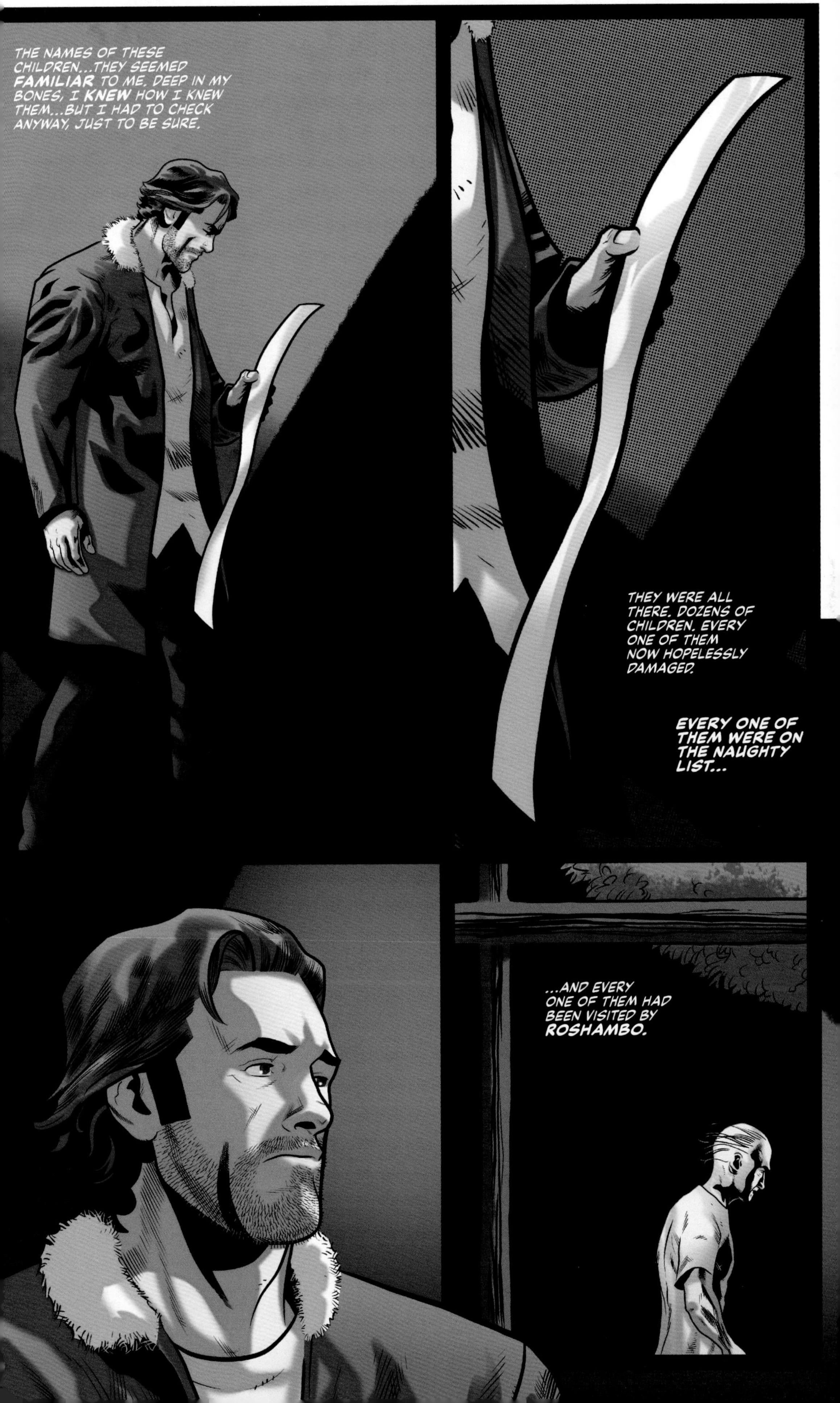
THE NAMES OF THESE CHILDREN...THEY SEEMED **FAMILIAR** TO ME. DEEP IN MY BONES, I **KNEW** HOW I KNEW THEM...BUT I HAD TO CHECK ANYWAY, JUST TO BE SURE.
THEY WERE ALL THERE. DOZENS OF CHILDREN. EVERY ONE OF THEM NOW HOPELESSLY DAMAGED.
EVERY ONE OF THEM WERE ON THE NAUGHTY LIST...
...AND EVERY ONE OF THEM HAD BEEN VISITED BY **ROSHAMBO.**

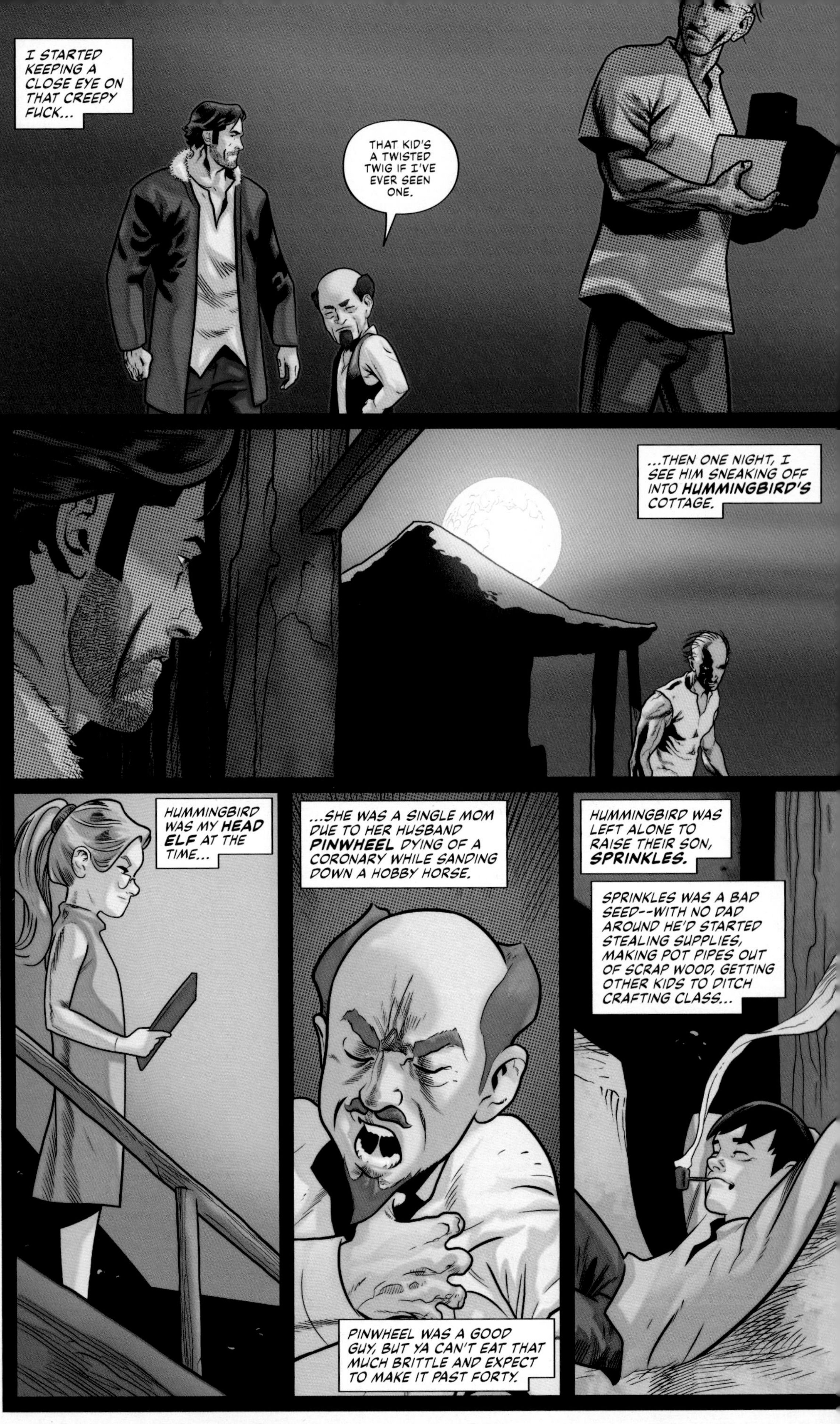

I STARTED KEEPING A CLOSE EYE ON THAT CREEPY FUCK...
THAT KID'S A TWISTED TWIG IF I'VE EVER SEEN ONE.
...THEN ONE NIGHT, I SEE HIM SNEAKING OFF INTO HUMMINGBIRD'S COTTAGE.
HUMMINGBIRD WAS MY HEAD ELF AT THE TIME...
...SHE WAS A SINGLE MOM DUE TO HER HUSBAND PINWHEEL DYING OF A CORONARY WHILE SANDING DOWN A HOBBY HORSE.
PINWHEEL WAS A GOOD GUY, BUT YA CAN'T EAT THAT MUCH BRITTLE AND EXPECT TO MAKE IT PAST FORTY.
HUMMINGBIRD WAS LEFT ALONE TO RAISE THEIR SON, SPRINKLES.
SPRINKLES WAS A BAD SEED--WITH NO DAD AROUND HE'D STARTED STEALING SUPPLIES, MAKING POT PIPES OUT OF SCRAP WOOD, GETTING OTHER KIDS TO DITCH CRAFTING CLASS...

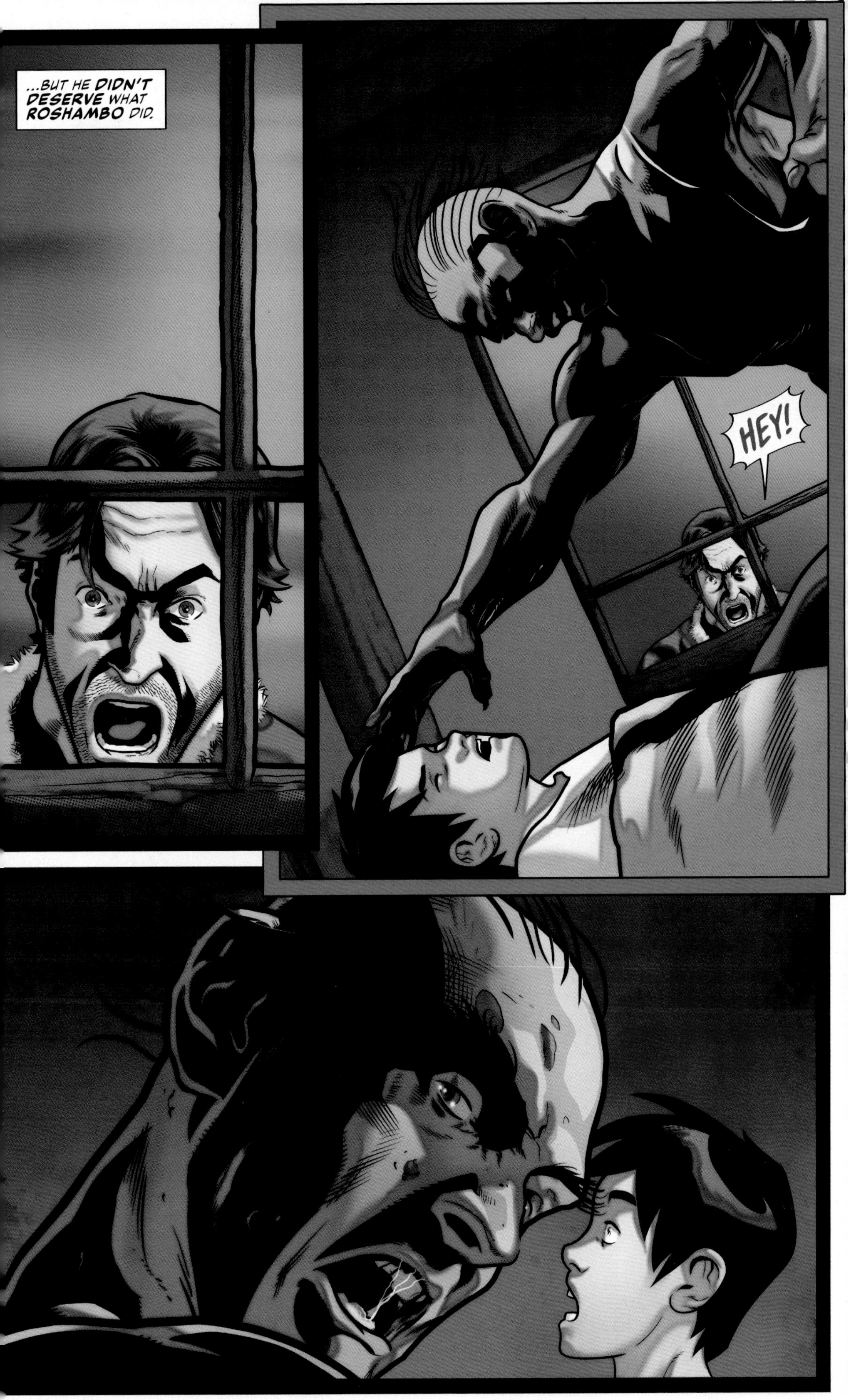
...BUT HE DIDN'T DESERVE WHAT ROSHAMBO DID.
HEY!

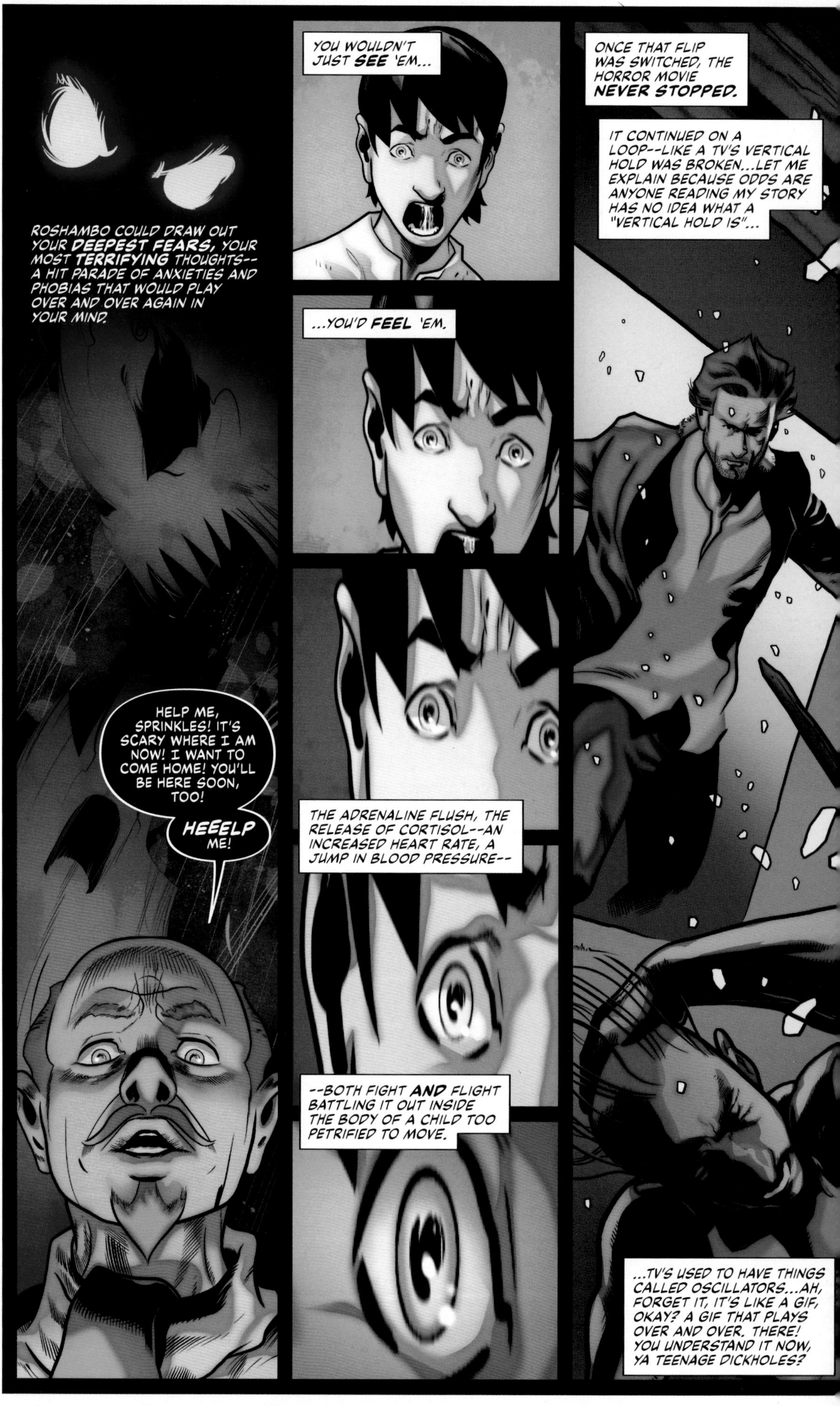
ROSHAMBO COULD DRAW OUT YOUR DEEPEST FEARS, YOUR MOST TERRIFYING THOUGHTS-- A HIT PARADE OF ANXIETIES AND PHOBIAS THAT WOULD PLAY OVER AND OVER AGAIN IN YOUR MIND.
HELP ME, SPRINKLES! IT'S SCARY WHERE I AM NOW! I WANT TO COME HOME! YOU'LL BE HERE SOON, TOO!
HEEELP ME!
YOU WOULDN'T JUST SEE 'EM...
...YOU'D FEEL 'EM.
THE ADRENALINE FLUSH, THE RELEASE OF CORTISOL--AN INCREASED HEART RATE, A JUMP IN BLOOD PRESSURE--
--BOTH FIGHT AND FLIGHT BATTLING IT OUT INSIDE THE BODY OF A CHILD TOO PETRIFIED TO MOVE.
ONCE THAT FLIP WAS SWITCHED, THE HORROR MOVIE NEVER STOPPED.
IT CONTINUED ON A LOOP--LIKE A TV'S VERTICAL HOLD WAS BROKEN...LET ME EXPLAIN BECAUSE ODDS ARE ANYONE READING MY STORY HAS NO IDEA WHAT A "VERTICAL HOLD IS"...
...TV'S USED TO HAVE THINGS CALLED OSCILLATORS...AH, FORGET IT, IT'S LIKE A GIF, OKAY? A GIF THAT PLAYS OVER AND OVER. THERE! YOU UNDERSTAND IT NOW, YA TEENAGE DICKHOLES?

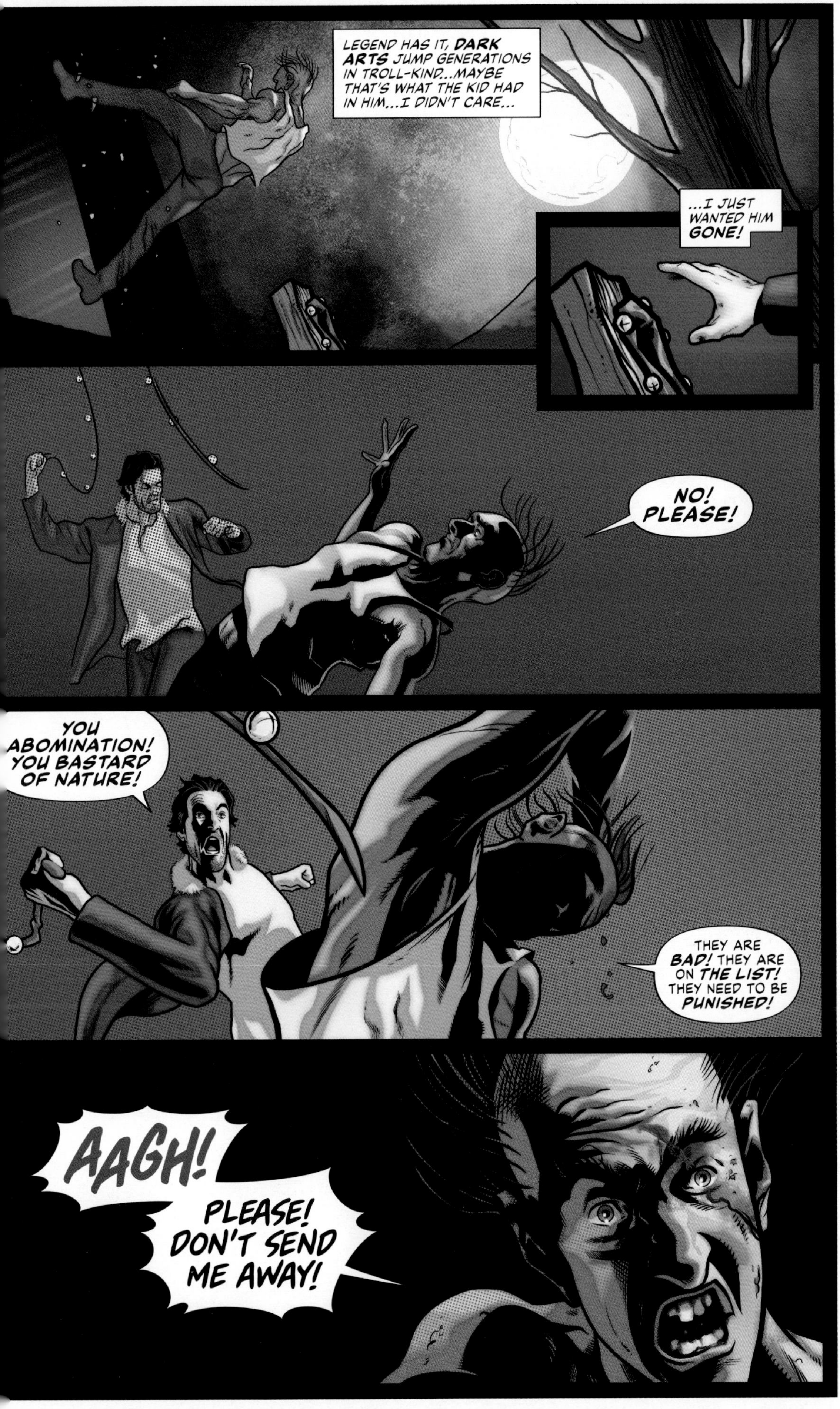
LEGEND HAS IT, DARK ARTS JUMP GENERATIONS IN TROLL-KIND...MAYBE THAT'S WHAT THE KID HAD IN HIM...I DIDN'T CARE...
...I JUST WANTED HIM GONE!
NO! PLEASE!
YOU ABOMINATION! YOU BASTARD OF NATURE!
THEY ARE BAD! THEY ARE ON THE LIST! THEY NEED TO BE PUNISHED!
AAGH!
PLEASE! DON'T SEND ME AWAY!

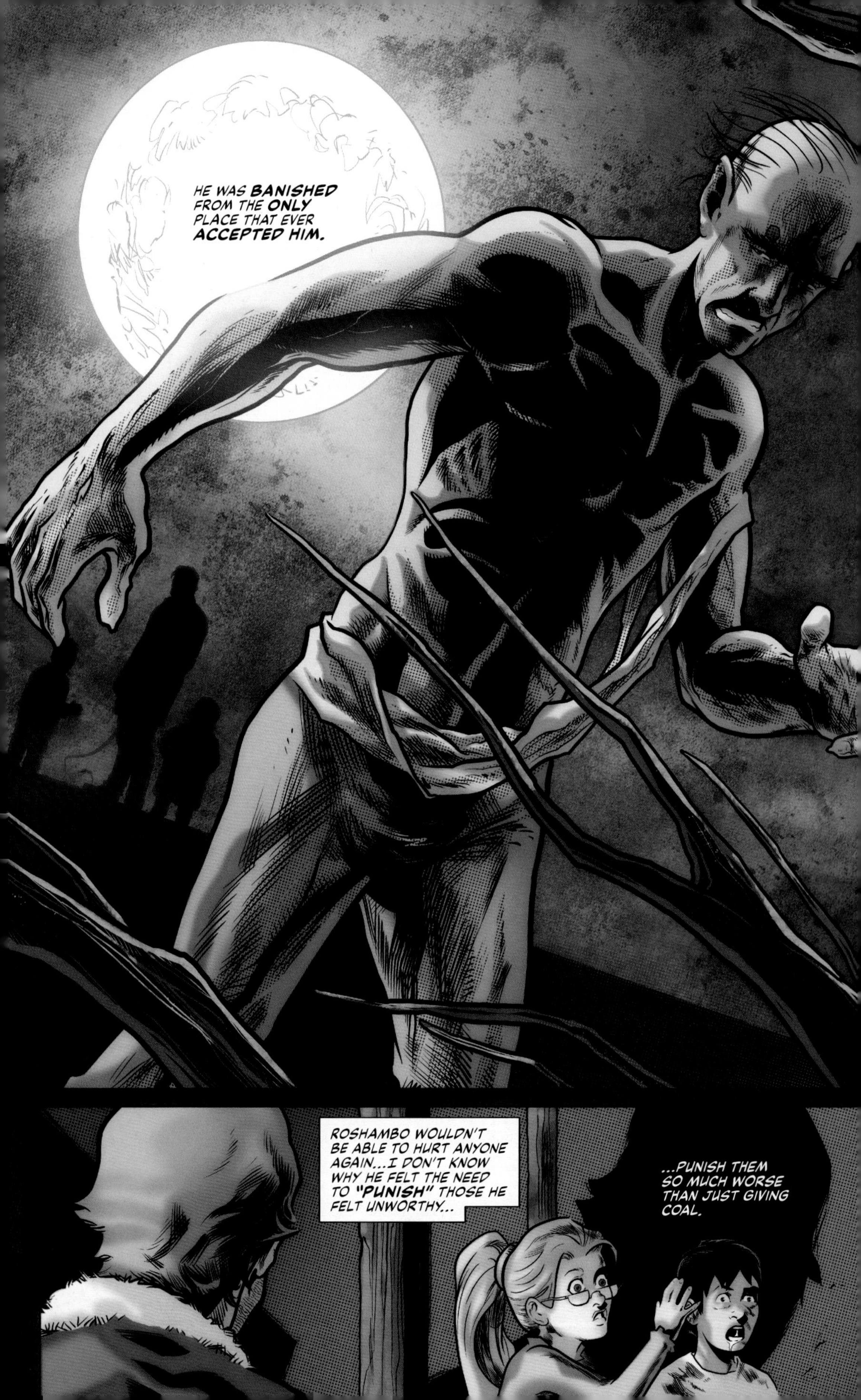
HE WAS BANISHED FROM THE ONLY PLACE THAT EVER ACCEPTED HIM.
ROSHAMBO WOULDN'T BE ABLE TO HURT ANYONE AGAIN...I DON'T KNOW WHY HE FELT THE NEED TO "PUNISH" THOSE HE FELT UNWORTHY...
...PUNISH THEM SO MUCH WORSE THAN JUST GIVING COAL.

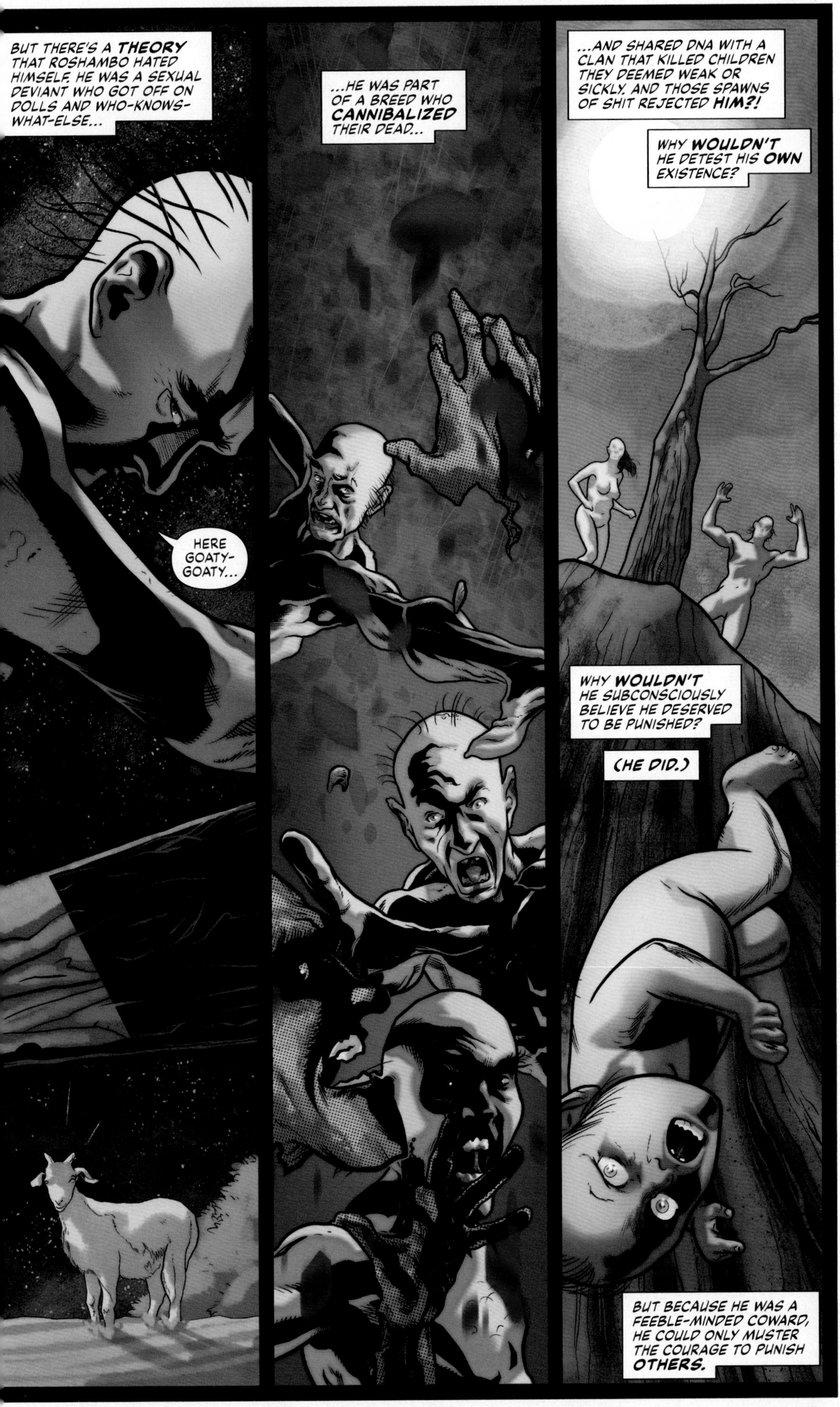

BUT THERE'S A THEORY THAT ROSHAMBO HATED HIMSELF. HE WAS A SEXUAL DEVIANT WHO GOT OFF ON DOLLS AND WHO-KNOWS-WHAT-ELSE...
HERE GOATY-GOATY...
...HE WAS PART OF A BREED WHO CANNIBALIZED THEIR DEAD...
...AND SHARED DNA WITH A CLAN THAT KILLED CHILDREN THEY DEEMED WEAK OR SICKLY. AND THOSE SPAWNS OF SHIT REJECTED HIM?!
WHY WOULDN'T HE DETEST HIS OWN EXISTENCE?
WHY WOULDN'T HE SUBCONSCIOUSLY BELIEVE HE DESERVED TO BE PUNISHED?
(HE DID.)
BUT BECAUSE HE WAS A FEEBLE-MINDED COWARD, HE COULD ONLY MUSTER THE COURAGE TO PUNISH OTHERS.

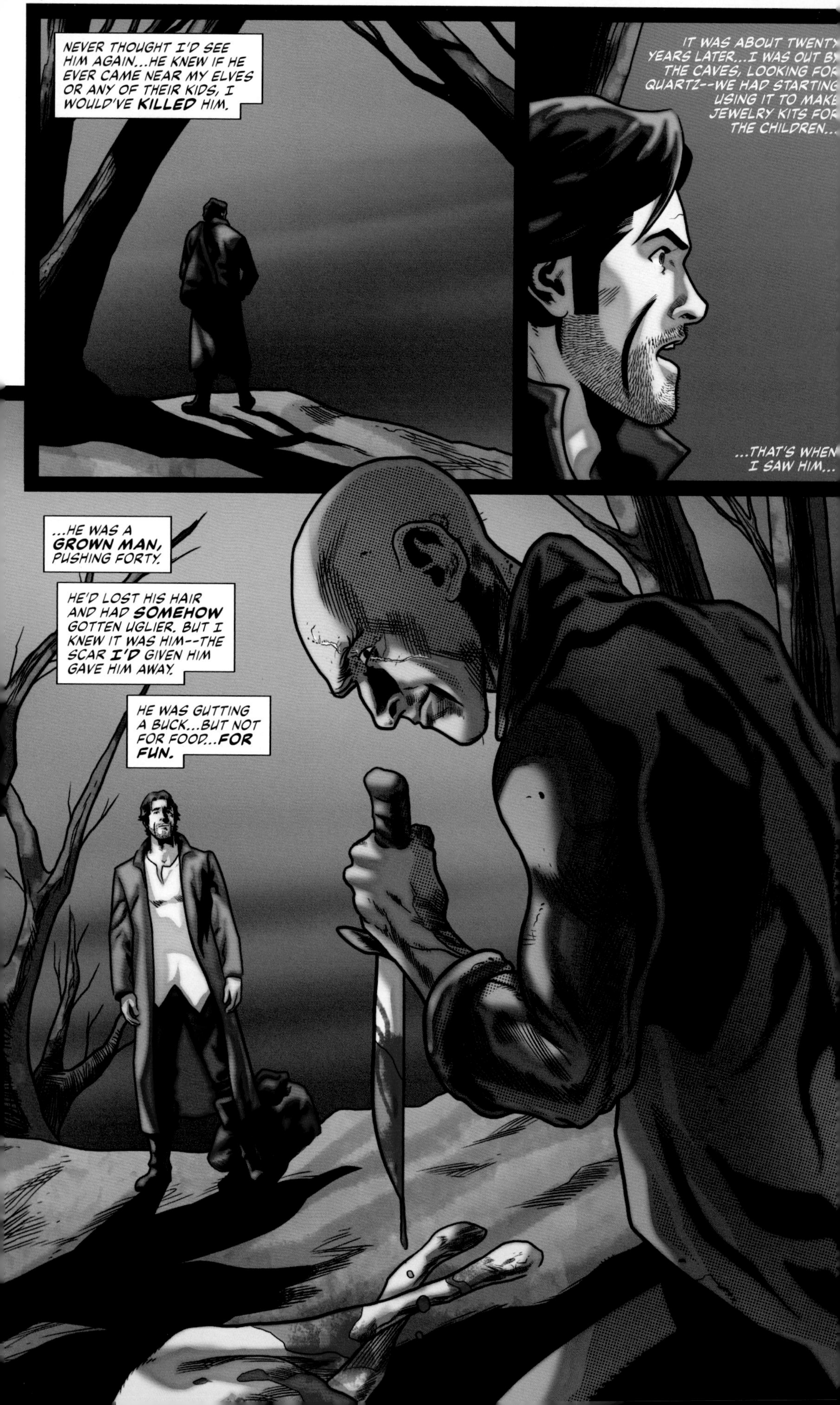
NEVER THOUGHT I'D SEE HIM AGAIN...HE KNEW IF HE EVER CAME NEAR MY ELVES OR ANY OF THEIR KIDS, I WOULD'VE **KILLED** HIM.
IT WAS ABOUT TWENTY YEARS LATER...I WAS OUT BY THE CAVES, LOOKING FOR QUARTZ--WE HAD STARTING USING IT TO MAKE JEWELRY KITS FOR THE CHILDREN...
...THAT'S WHEN I SAW HIM...
...HE WAS A **GROWN MAN,** PUSHING FORTY.
HE'D LOST HIS HAIR AND HAD **SOMEHOW** GOTTEN UGLIER. BUT I KNEW IT WAS HIM--THE SCAR **I'D** GIVEN HIM GAVE HIM AWAY.
HE WAS GUTTING A BUCK...BUT NOT FOR FOOD...**FOR FUN.**

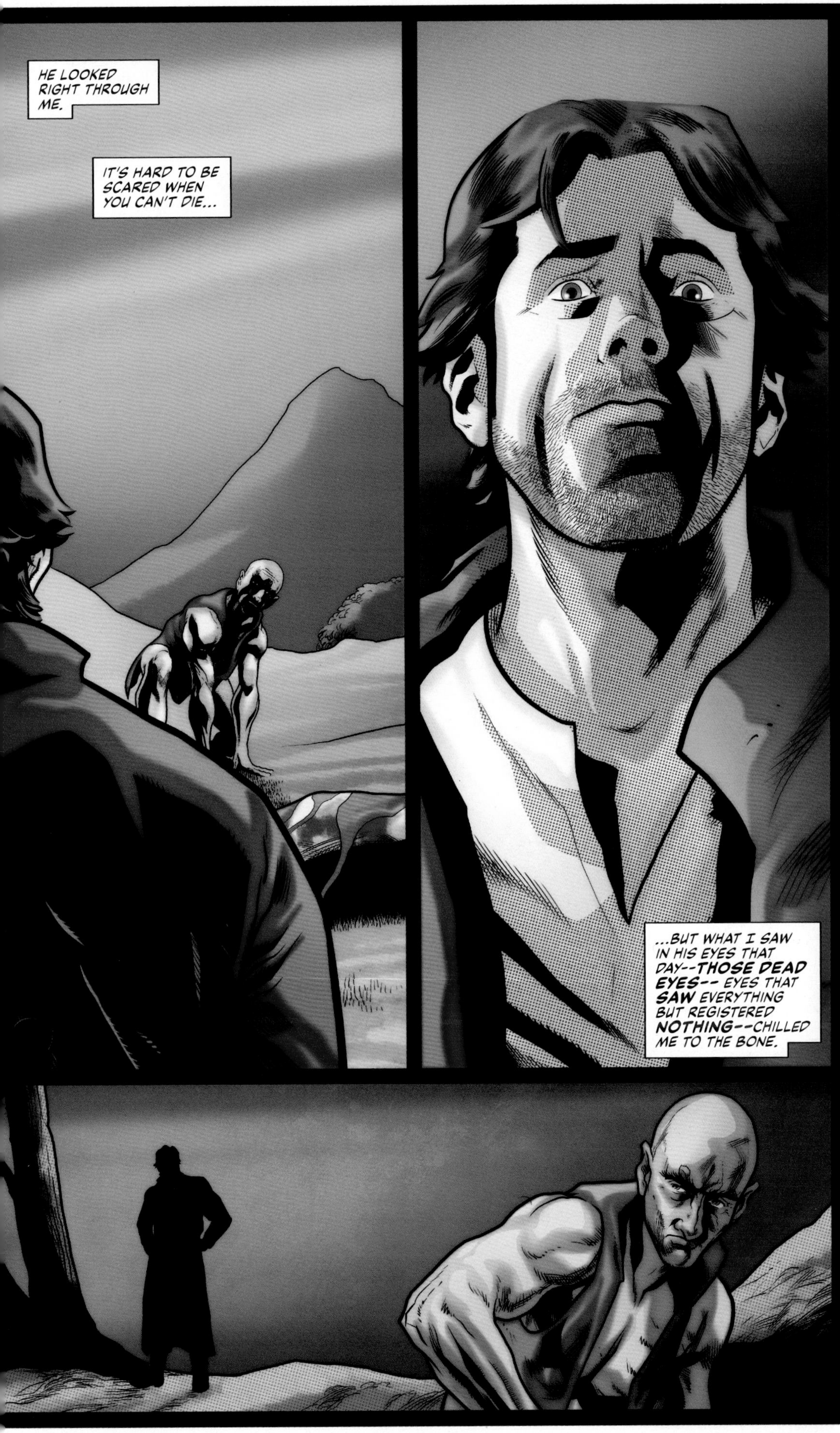
HE LOOKED RIGHT THROUGH ME.
IT'S HARD TO BE SCARED WHEN YOU CAN'T DIE...
...BUT WHAT I SAW IN HIS EYES THAT DAY--THOSE DEAD EYES-- EYES THAT SAW EVERYTHING BUT REGISTERED NOTHING--CHILLED ME TO THE BONE.

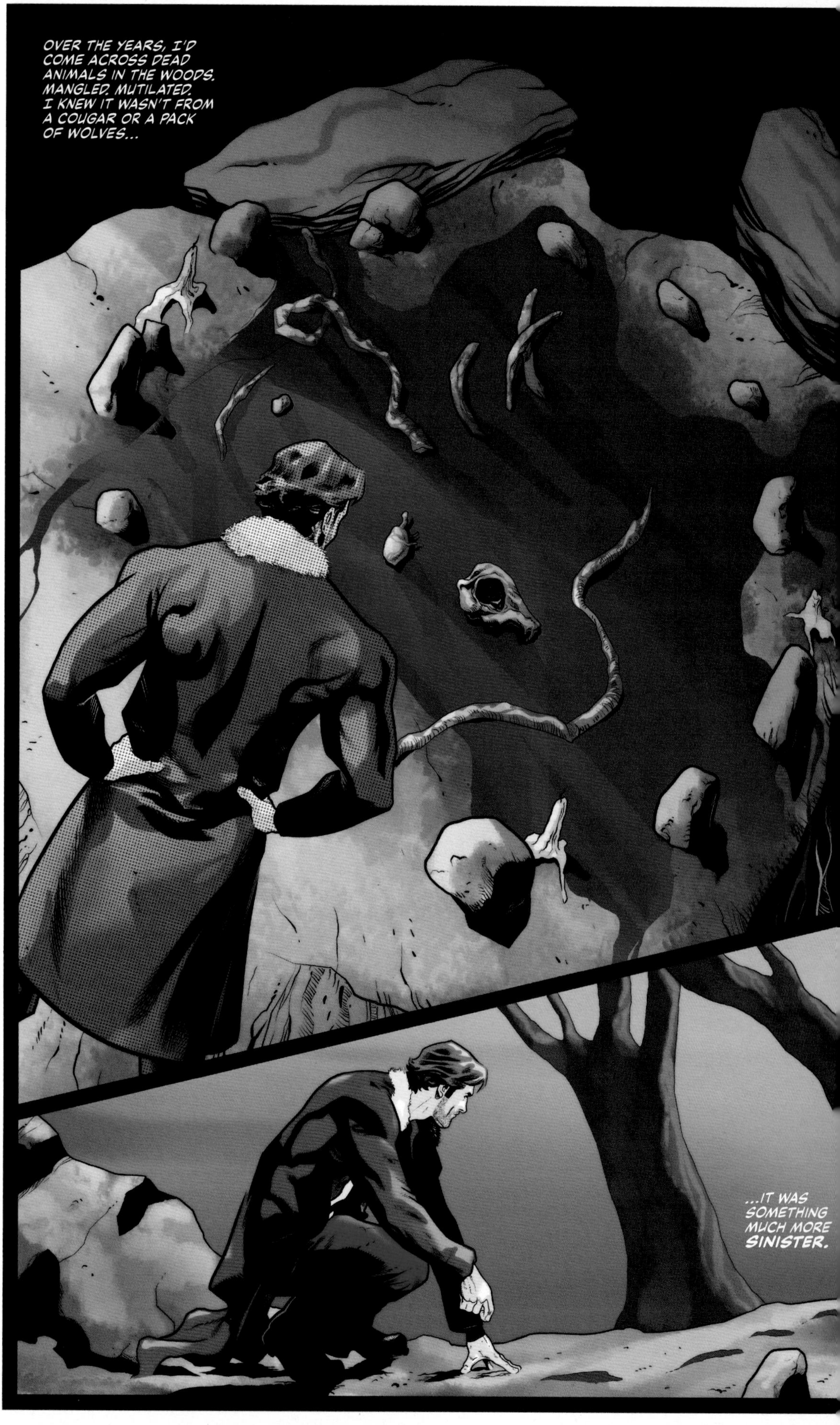
OVER THE YEARS, I'D COME ACROSS DEAD ANIMALS IN THE WOODS. MANGLED. MUTILATED. I KNEW IT WASN'T FROM A COUGAR OR A PACK OF WOLVES...
...IT WAS SOMETHING MUCH MORE SINISTER.

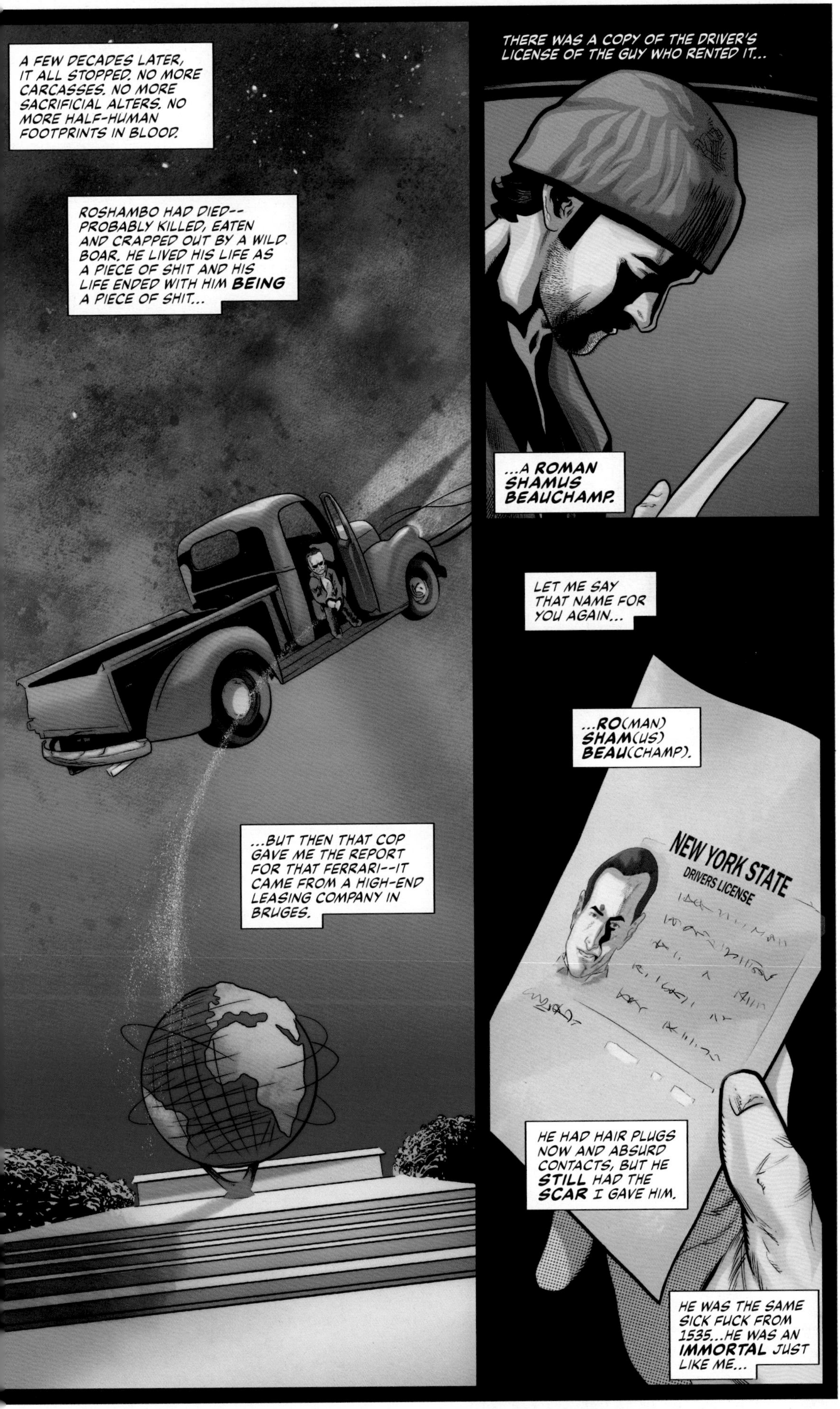

A FEW DECADES LATER, IT ALL STOPPED. NO MORE CARCASSES. NO MORE SACRIFICIAL ALTERS. NO MORE HALF-HUMAN FOOTPRINTS IN BLOOD.
ROSHAMBO HAD DIED-- PROBABLY KILLED, EATEN AND CRAPPED OUT BY A WILD BOAR. HE LIVED HIS LIFE AS A PIECE OF SHIT AND HIS LIFE ENDED WITH HIM **BEING** A PIECE OF SHIT...
...BUT THEN THAT COP GAVE ME THE REPORT FOR THAT FERRARI--IT CAME FROM A HIGH-END LEASING COMPANY IN BRUGES.
THERE WAS A COPY OF THE DRIVER'S LICENSE OF THE GUY WHO RENTED IT...
...A **ROMAN SHAMUS BEAUCHAMP.**
LET ME SAY THAT NAME FOR YOU AGAIN...
...**RO**(MAN) **SHAM**(US) **BEAU**(CHAMP).
NEW YORK STATE
DRIVERS LICENSE
HE HAD HAIR PLUGS NOW AND ABSURD CONTACTS, BUT HE **STILL** HAD THE **SCAR** I GAVE HIM.
HE WAS THE SAME SICK FUCK FROM 1535...HE WAS AN **IMMORTAL** JUST LIKE ME...

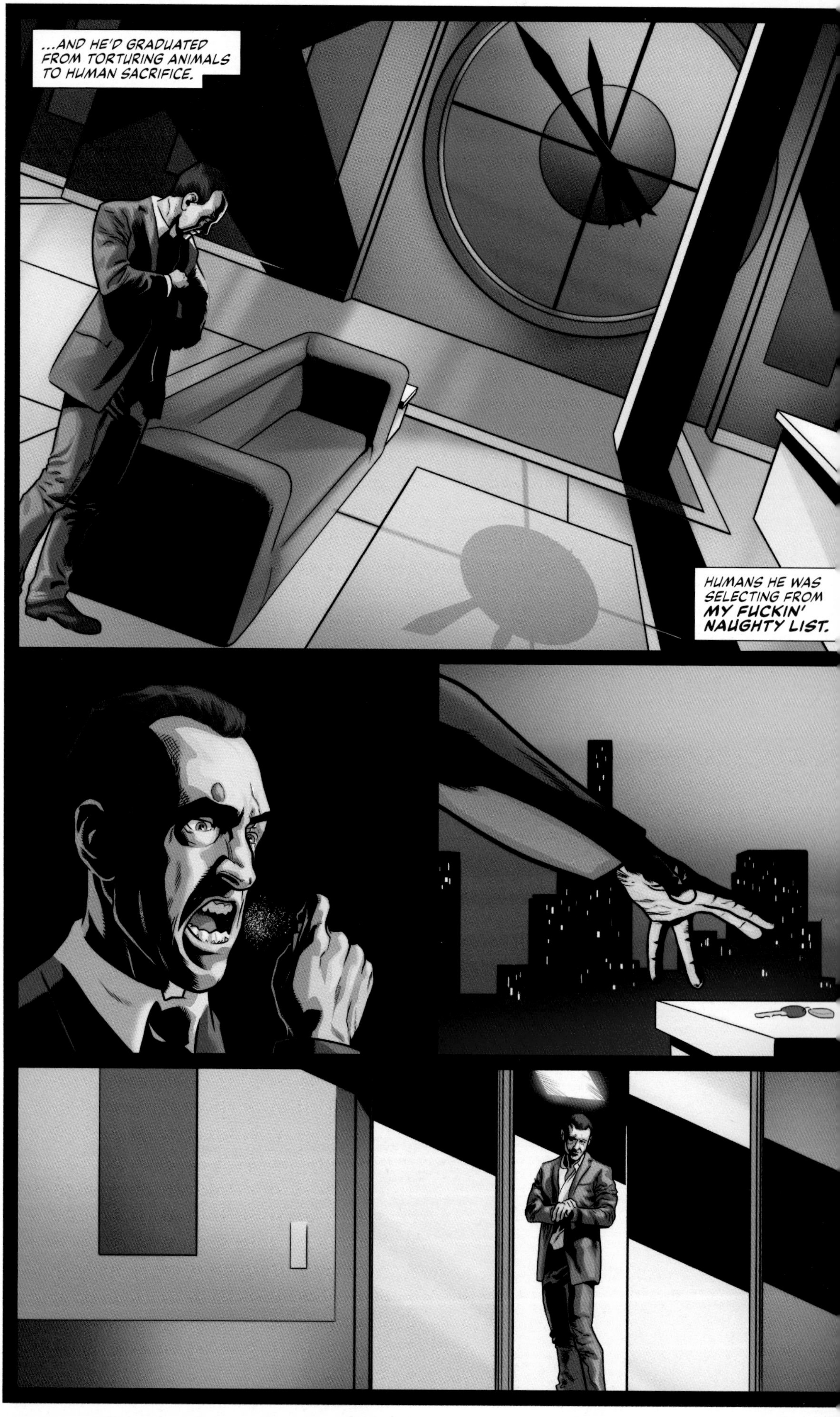
...AND HE'D GRADUATED FROM TORTURING ANIMALS TO HUMAN SACRIFICE.
HUMANS HE WAS SELECTING FROM MY FUCKIN' NAUGHTY LIST.

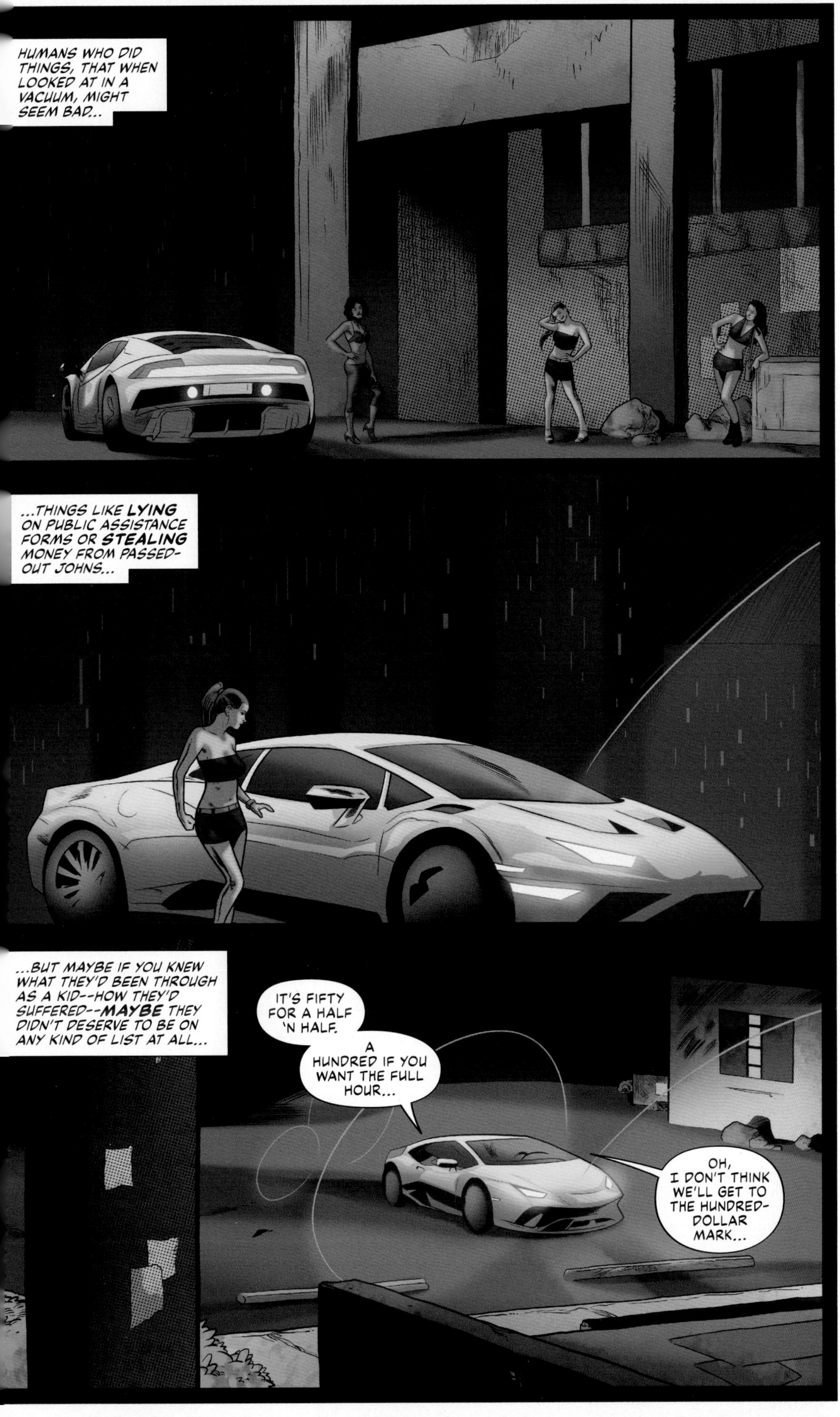
HUMANS WHO DID THINGS, THAT WHEN LOOKED AT IN A VACUUM, MIGHT SEEM BAD...
...THINGS LIKE LYING ON PUBLIC ASSISTANCE FORMS OR STEALING MONEY FROM PASSED-OUT JOHNS...
...BUT MAYBE IF YOU KNEW WHAT THEY'D BEEN THROUGH AS A KID--HOW THEY'D SUFFERED--MAYBE THEY DIDN'T DESERVE TO BE ON ANY KIND OF LIST AT ALL...
IT'S FIFTY FOR A HALF 'N HALF.
A HUNDRED IF YOU WANT THE FULL HOUR...
OH, I DON'T THINK WE'LL GET TO THE HUNDRED-DOLLAR MARK...

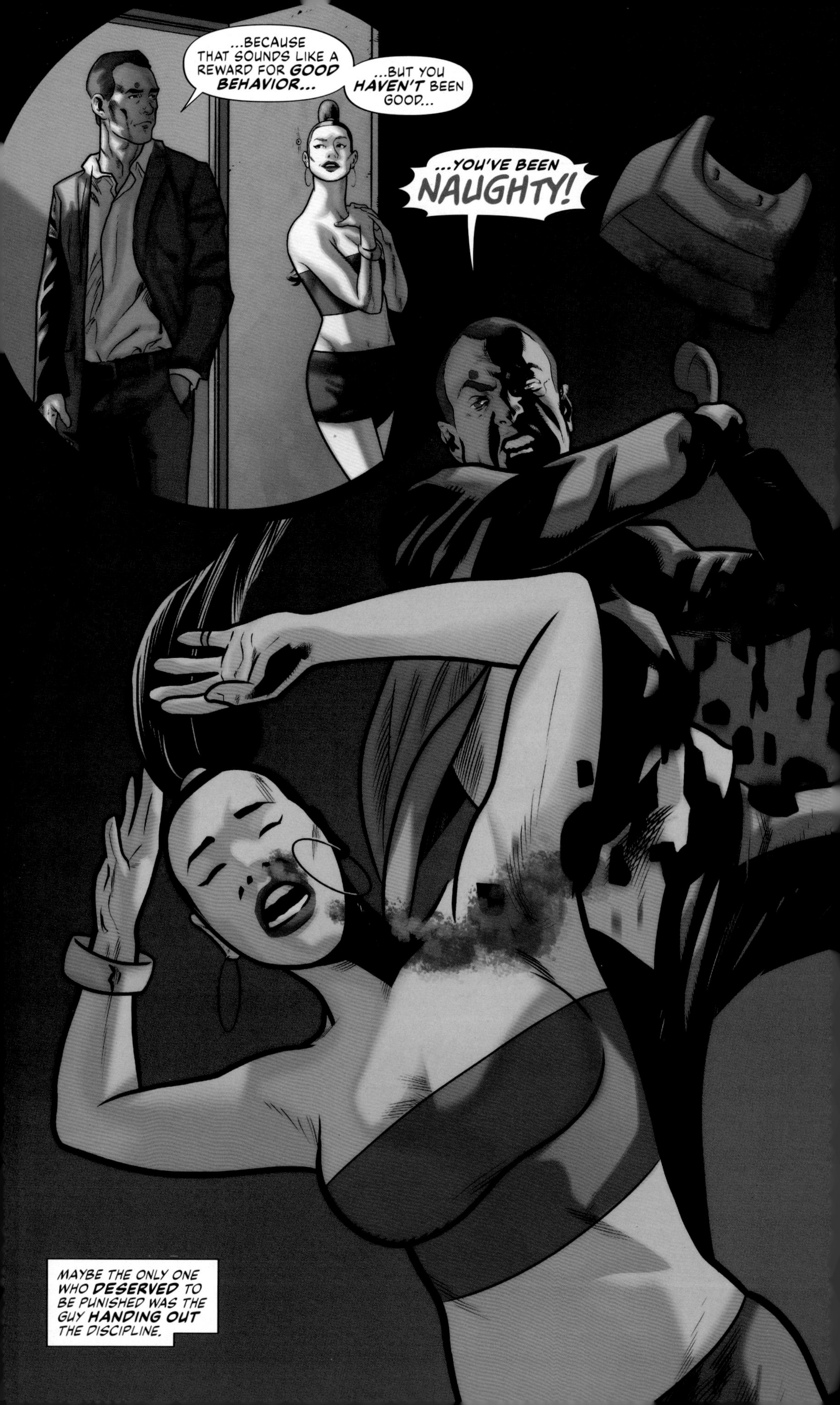
...BECAUSE THAT SOUNDS LIKE A REWARD FOR GOOD BEHAVIOR...
...BUT YOU HAVEN'T BEEN GOOD...
...YOU'VE BEEN NAUGHTY!
MAYBE THE ONLY ONE WHO DESERVED TO BE PUNISHED WAS THE GUY HANDING OUT THE DISCIPLINE.

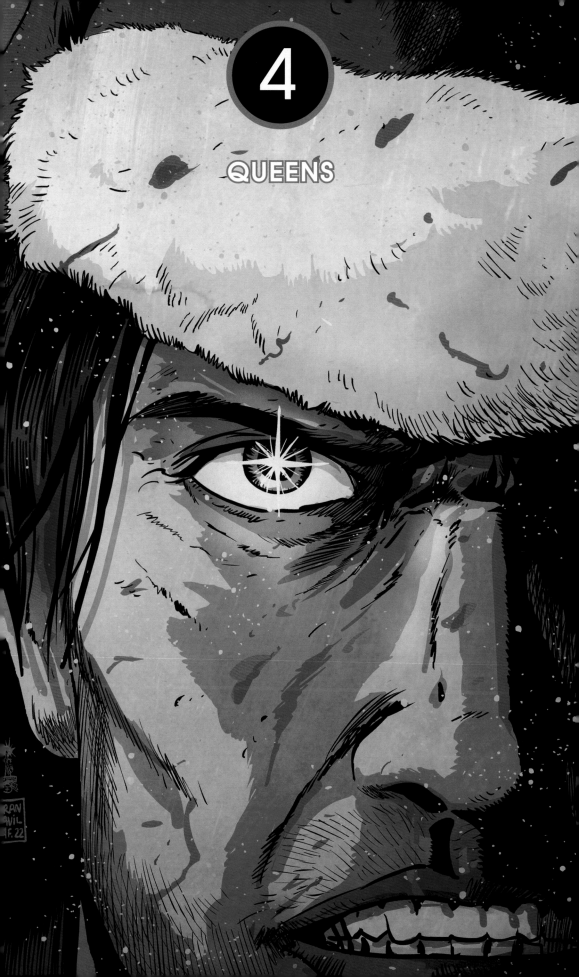

4

QUEENS

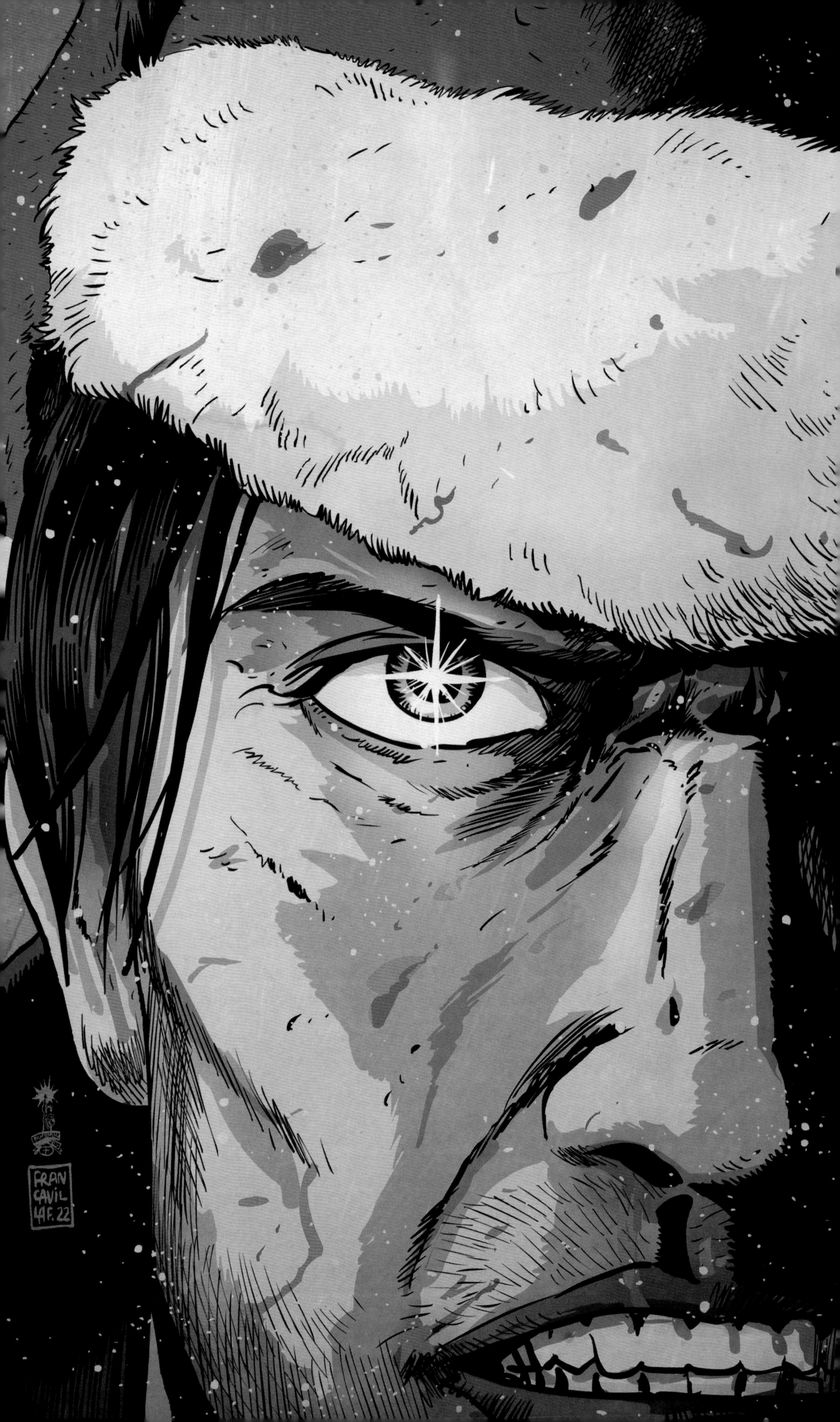
FRAN CAVIL LA F. 22

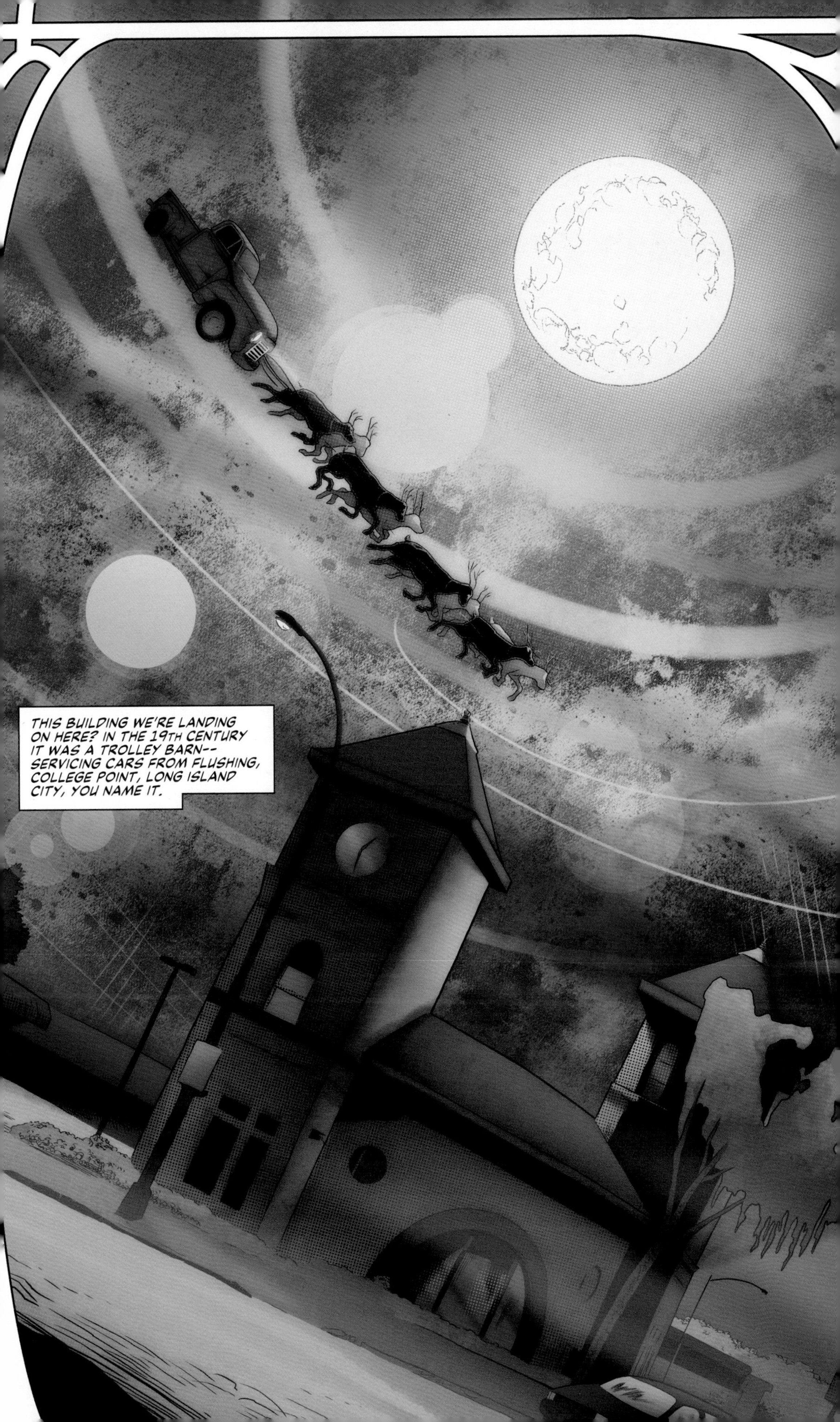
THIS BUILDING WE'RE LANDING ON HERE? IN THE 19TH CENTURY IT WAS A TROLLEY BARN--SERVICING CARS FROM FLUSHING, COLLEGE POINT, LONG ISLAND CITY, YOU NAME IT.

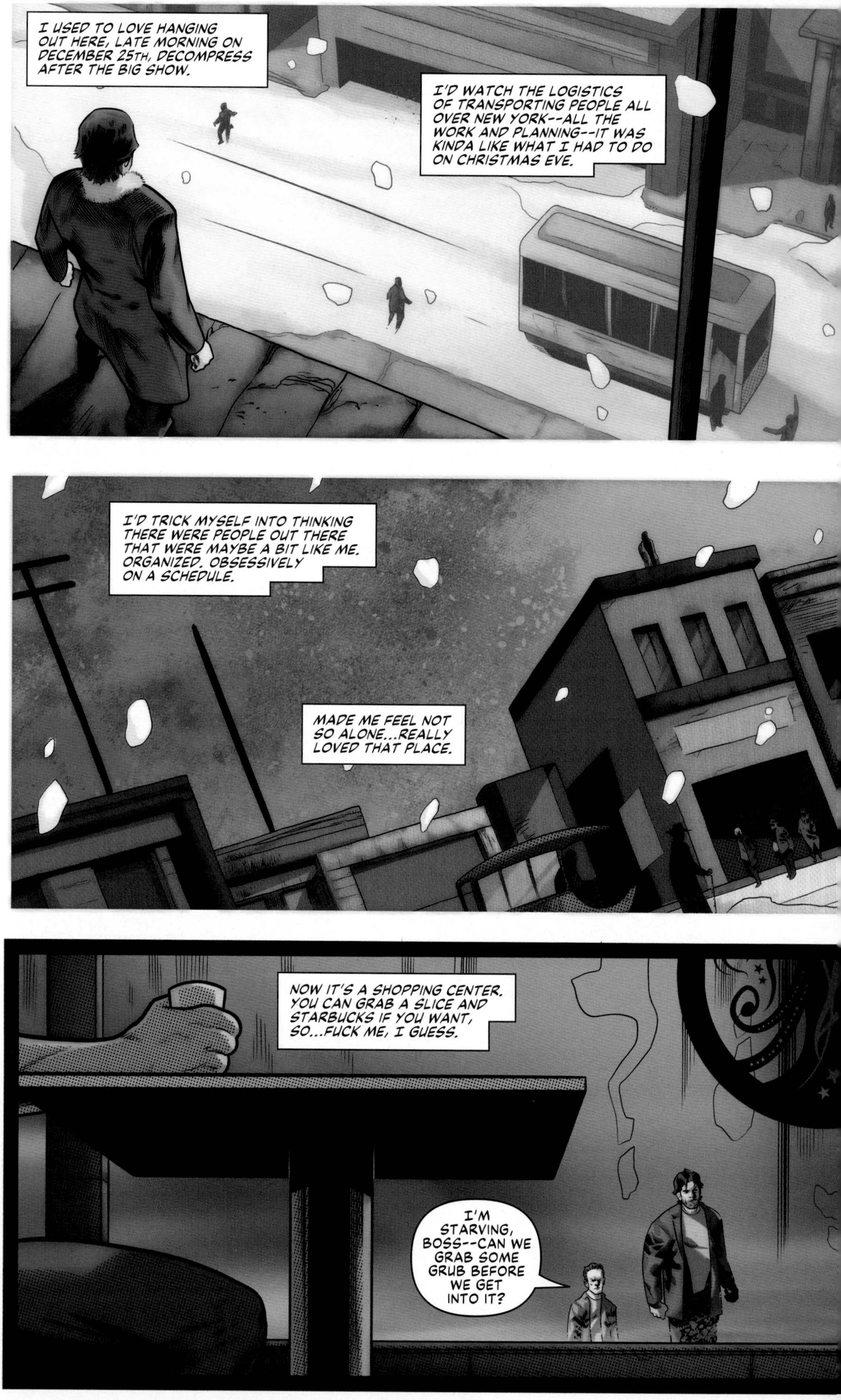
I USED TO LOVE HANGING OUT HERE, LATE MORNING ON DECEMBER 25TH, DECOMPRESS AFTER THE BIG SHOW.
I'D WATCH THE LOGISTICS OF TRANSPORTING PEOPLE ALL OVER NEW YORK--ALL THE WORK AND PLANNING--IT WAS KINDA LIKE WHAT I HAD TO DO ON CHRISTMAS EVE.
I'D TRICK MYSELF INTO THINKING THERE WERE PEOPLE OUT THERE THAT WERE MAYBE A BIT LIKE ME. ORGANIZED. OBSESSIVELY ON A SCHEDULE.
MADE ME FEEL NOT SO ALONE...REALLY LOVED THAT PLACE.
NOW IT'S A SHOPPING CENTER. YOU CAN GRAB A SLICE AND STARBUCKS IF YOU WANT, SO...FUCK ME, I GUESS.
I'M STARVING, BOSS--CAN WE GRAB SOME GRUB BEFORE WE GET INTO IT?

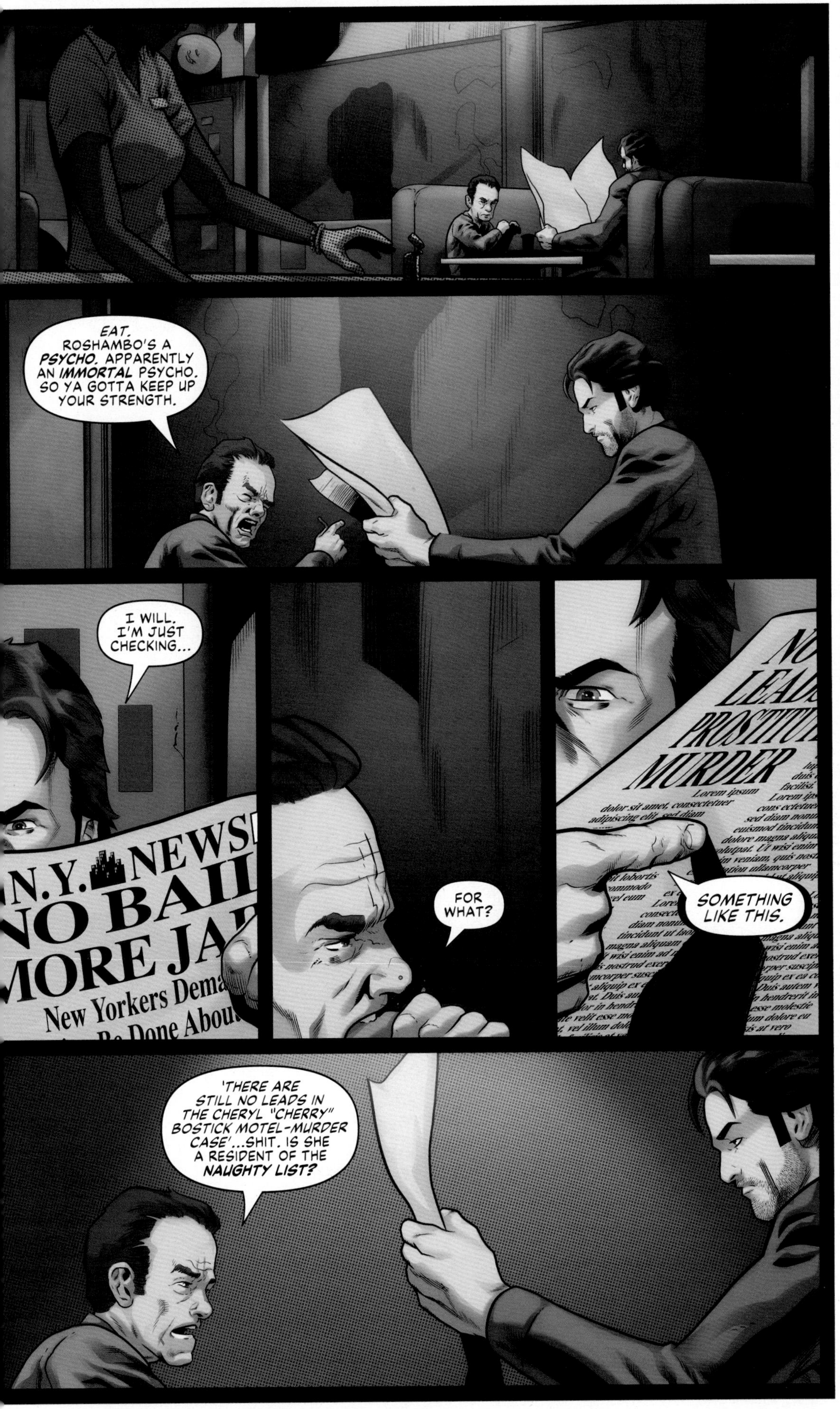
EAT. ROSHAMBO'S A *PSYCHO.* APPARENTLY AN *IMMORTAL* PSYCHO. SO YA GOTTA KEEP UP YOUR STRENGTH.
I WILL. I'M JUST CHECKING...
FOR WHAT?
SOMETHING LIKE THIS.
'THERE ARE STILL NO LEADS IN THE CHERYL "CHERRY" BOSTICK MOTEL-MURDER CASE'...SHIT. IS SHE A RESIDENT OF THE *NAUGHTY LIST?*

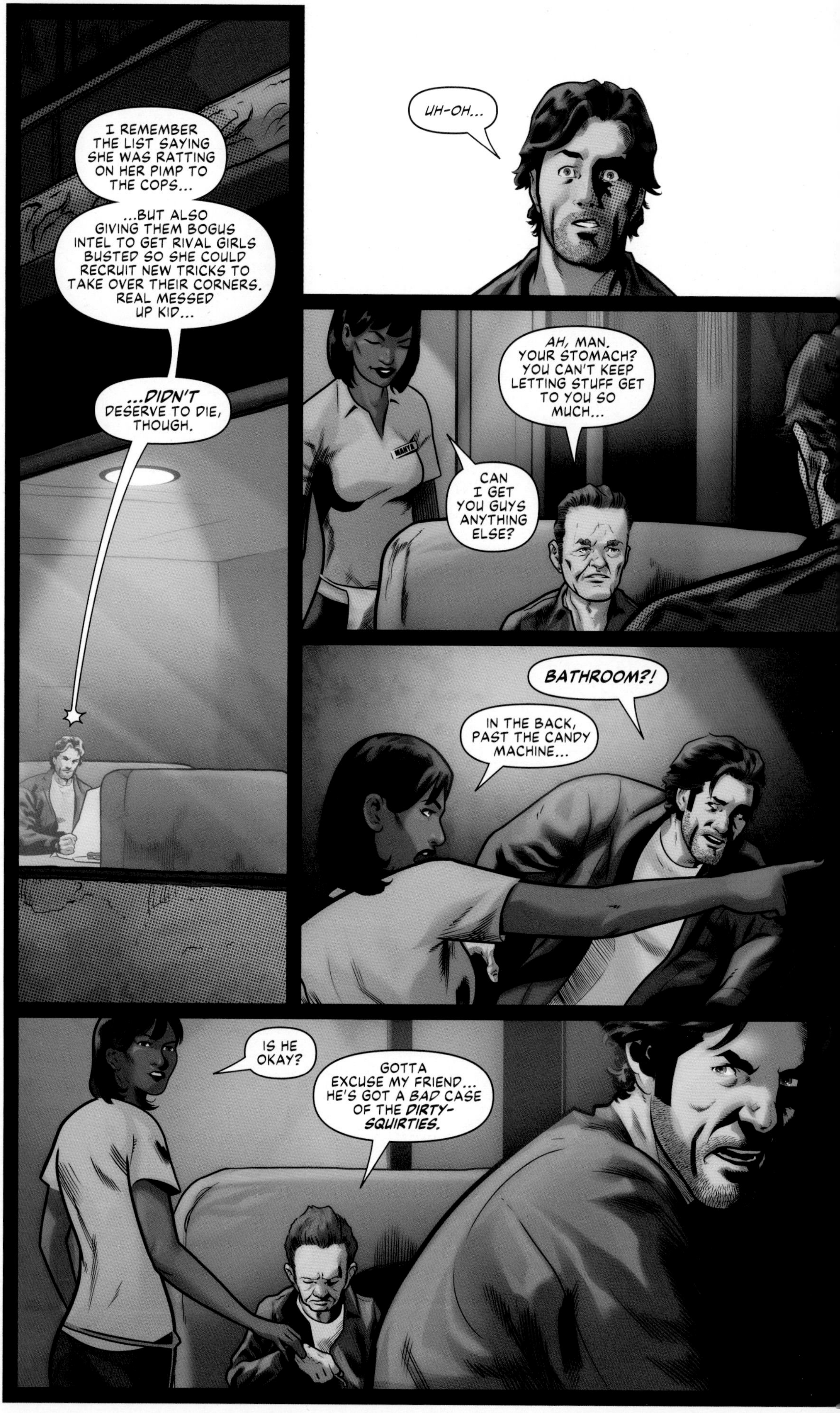
I REMEMBER THE LIST SAYING SHE WAS RATTING ON HER PIMP TO THE COPS...
...BUT ALSO GIVING THEM BOGUS INTEL TO GET RIVAL GIRLS BUSTED SO SHE COULD RECRUIT NEW TRICKS TO TAKE OVER THEIR CORNERS. REAL MESSED UP KID...
...DIDN'T DESERVE TO DIE, THOUGH.
UH-OH...
AH, MAN. YOUR STOMACH? YOU CAN'T KEEP LETTING STUFF GET TO YOU SO MUCH...
CAN I GET YOU GUYS ANYTHING ELSE?
BATHROOM?!
IN THE BACK, PAST THE CANDY MACHINE...
IS HE OKAY?
GOTTA EXCUSE MY FRIEND... HE'S GOT A BAD CASE OF THE DIRTY-SQUIRTIES.

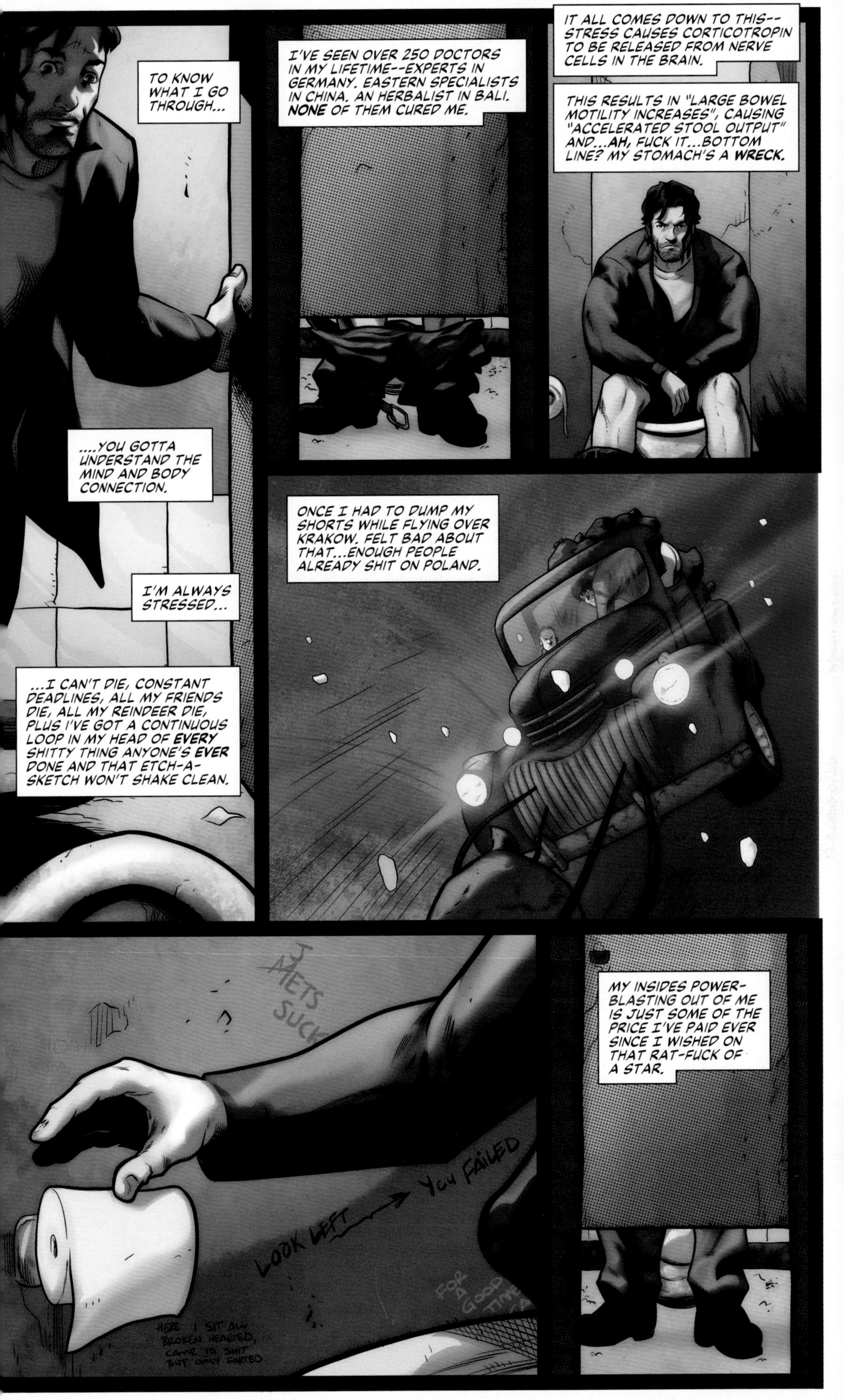
TO KNOW WHAT I GO THROUGH...
I'VE SEEN OVER 250 DOCTORS IN MY LIFETIME--EXPERTS IN GERMANY. EASTERN SPECIALISTS IN CHINA. AN HERBALIST IN BALI. **NONE** OF THEM CURED ME.
IT ALL COMES DOWN TO THIS--STRESS CAUSES CORTICOTROPIN TO BE RELEASED FROM NERVE CELLS IN THE BRAIN.
THIS RESULTS IN "LARGE BOWEL MOTILITY INCREASES", CAUSING "ACCELERATED STOOL OUTPUT" AND...**AH,** FUCK IT...BOTTOM LINE? MY STOMACH'S A **WRECK.**
....YOU GOTTA UNDERSTAND THE MIND AND BODY CONNECTION.
I'M ALWAYS STRESSED...
...I CAN'T DIE, CONSTANT DEADLINES, ALL MY FRIENDS DIE, ALL MY REINDEER DIE, PLUS I'VE GOT A CONTINUOUS LOOP IN MY HEAD OF **EVERY** SHITTY THING ANYONE'S **EVER** DONE AND THAT ETCH-A-SKETCH WON'T SHAKE CLEAN.
ONCE I HAD TO DUMP MY SHORTS WHILE FLYING OVER KRAKOW. FELT BAD ABOUT THAT...ENOUGH PEOPLE ALREADY SHIT ON POLAND.
YOU FAILED
LOOK LEFT
HERE I SIT ALL BROKEN HEARTED, CAME TO SHIT BUT ONLY FARTED
MY INSIDES POWER-BLASTING OUT OF ME IS JUST SOME OF THE PRICE I'VE PAID EVER SINCE I WISHED ON THAT RAT-FUCK OF A STAR.

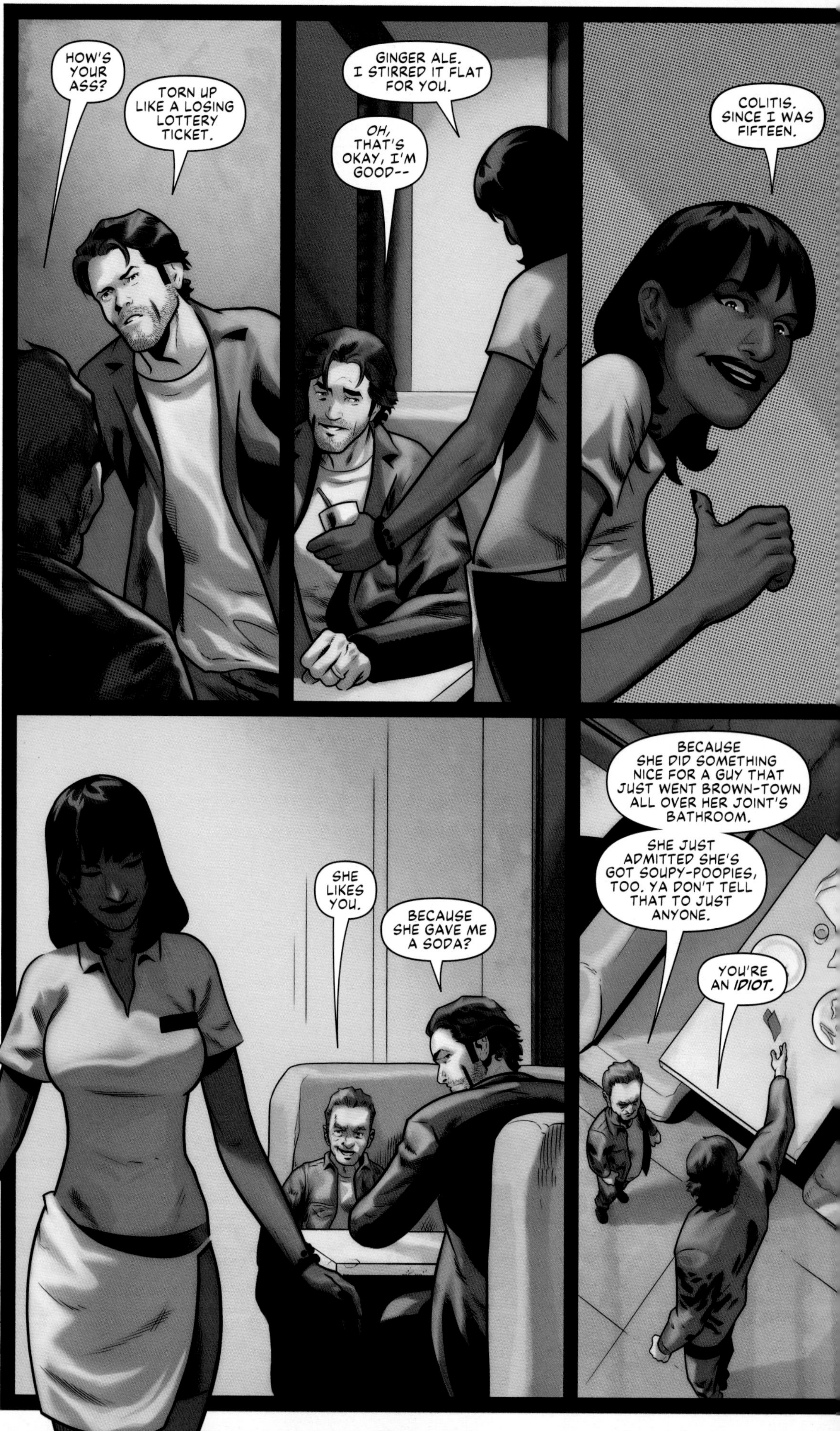
HOW'S YOUR ASS?
TORN UP LIKE A LOSING LOTTERY TICKET.
GINGER ALE. I STIRRED IT FLAT FOR YOU.
OH, THAT'S OKAY, I'M GOOD--
COLITIS. SINCE I WAS FIFTEEN.
SHE LIKES YOU.
BECAUSE SHE GAVE ME A SODA?
BECAUSE SHE DID SOMETHING NICE FOR A GUY THAT JUST WENT BROWN-TOWN ALL OVER HER JOINT'S BATHROOM.
SHE JUST ADMITTED SHE'S GOT SOUPY-POOPIES, TOO. YA DON'T TELL THAT TO JUST ANYONE.
YOU'RE AN *IDIOT.*

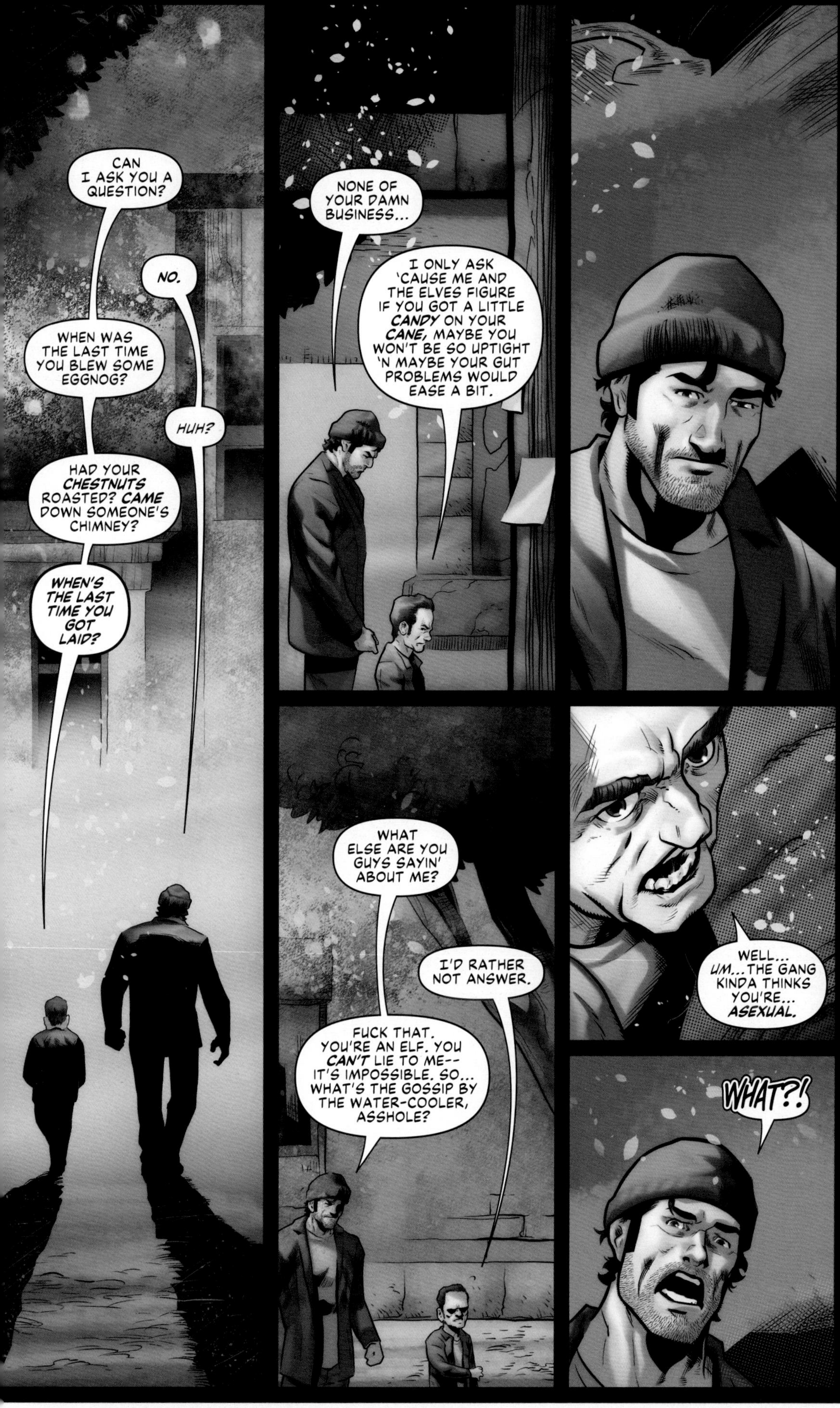
CAN I ASK YOU A QUESTION?
NO.
WHEN WAS THE LAST TIME YOU BLEW SOME EGGNOG?
HUH?
HAD YOUR CHESTNUTS ROASTED? CAME DOWN SOMEONE'S CHIMNEY?
WHEN'S THE LAST TIME YOU GOT LAID?
NONE OF YOUR DAMN BUSINESS...
I ONLY ASK 'CAUSE ME AND THE ELVES FIGURE IF YOU GOT A LITTLE CANDY ON YOUR CANE, MAYBE YOU WON'T BE SO UPTIGHT 'N MAYBE YOUR GUT PROBLEMS WOULD EASE A BIT.
WHAT ELSE ARE YOU GUYS SAYIN' ABOUT ME?
I'D RATHER NOT ANSWER.
FUCK THAT. YOU'RE AN ELF. YOU CAN'T LIE TO ME-- IT'S IMPOSSIBLE. SO... WHAT'S THE GOSSIP BY THE WATER-COOLER, ASSHOLE?
WELL... UM... THE GANG KINDA THINKS YOU'RE... ASEXUAL.
WHAT?!

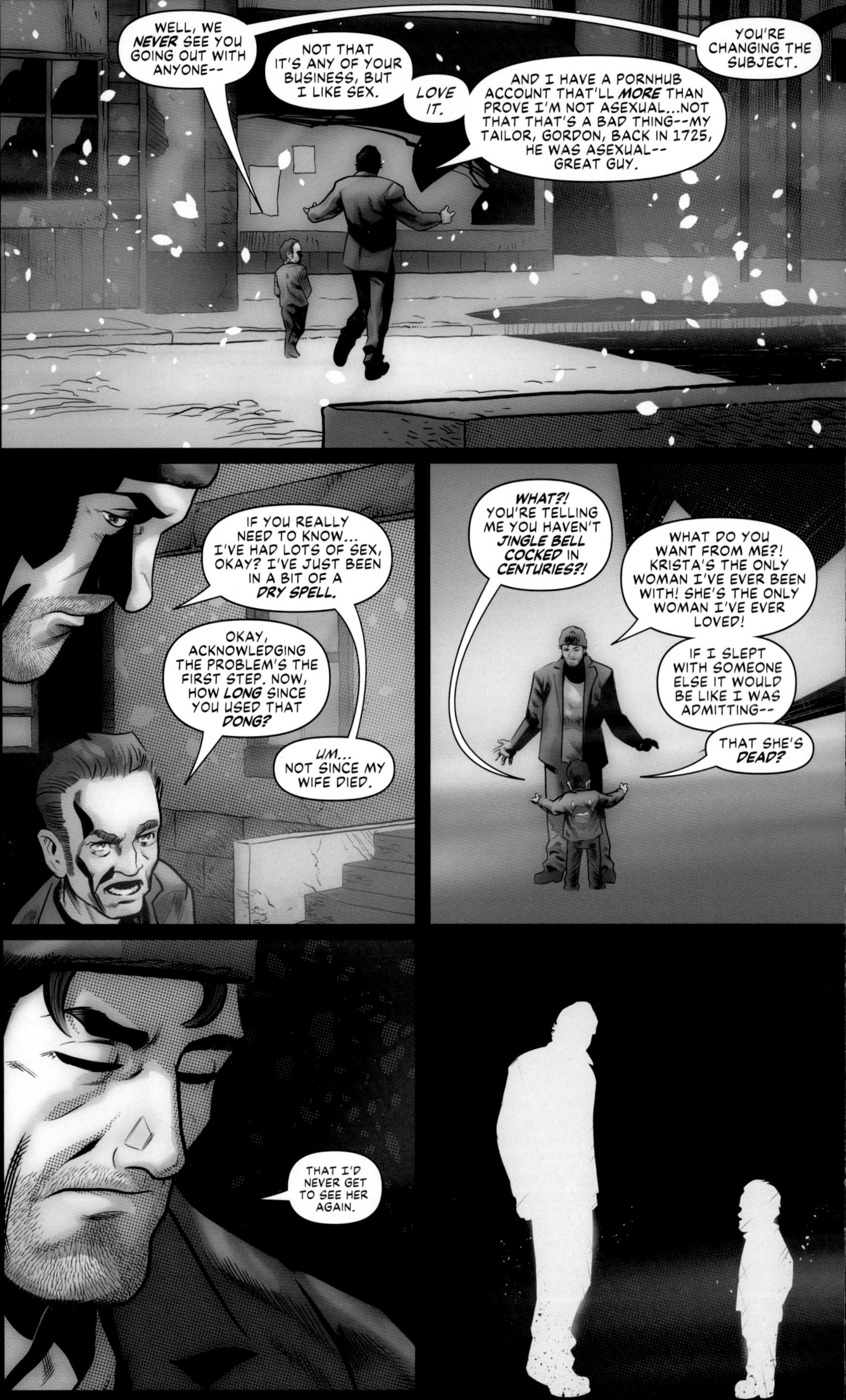
WELL, WE NEVER SEE YOU GOING OUT WITH ANYONE--
NOT THAT IT'S ANY OF YOUR BUSINESS, BUT I LIKE SEX.
LOVE IT.
AND I HAVE A PORNHUB ACCOUNT THAT'LL MORE THAN PROVE I'M NOT ASEXUAL...NOT THAT THAT'S A BAD THING--MY TAILOR, GORDON, BACK IN 1725, HE WAS ASEXUAL-- GREAT GUY.
YOU'RE CHANGING THE SUBJECT.
IF YOU REALLY NEED TO KNOW... I'VE HAD LOTS OF SEX, OKAY? I'VE JUST BEEN IN A BIT OF A DRY SPELL.
OKAY, ACKNOWLEDGING THE PROBLEM'S THE FIRST STEP. NOW, HOW LONG SINCE YOU USED THAT DONG?
UM... NOT SINCE MY WIFE DIED.
WHAT?! YOU'RE TELLING ME YOU HAVEN'T JINGLE BELL COCKED IN CENTURIES?!
WHAT DO YOU WANT FROM ME?! KRISTA'S THE ONLY WOMAN I'VE EVER BEEN WITH! SHE'S THE ONLY WOMAN I'VE EVER LOVED!
IF I SLEPT WITH SOMEONE ELSE IT WOULD BE LIKE I WAS ADMITTING--
THAT SHE'S DEAD?
THAT I'D NEVER GET TO SEE HER AGAIN.

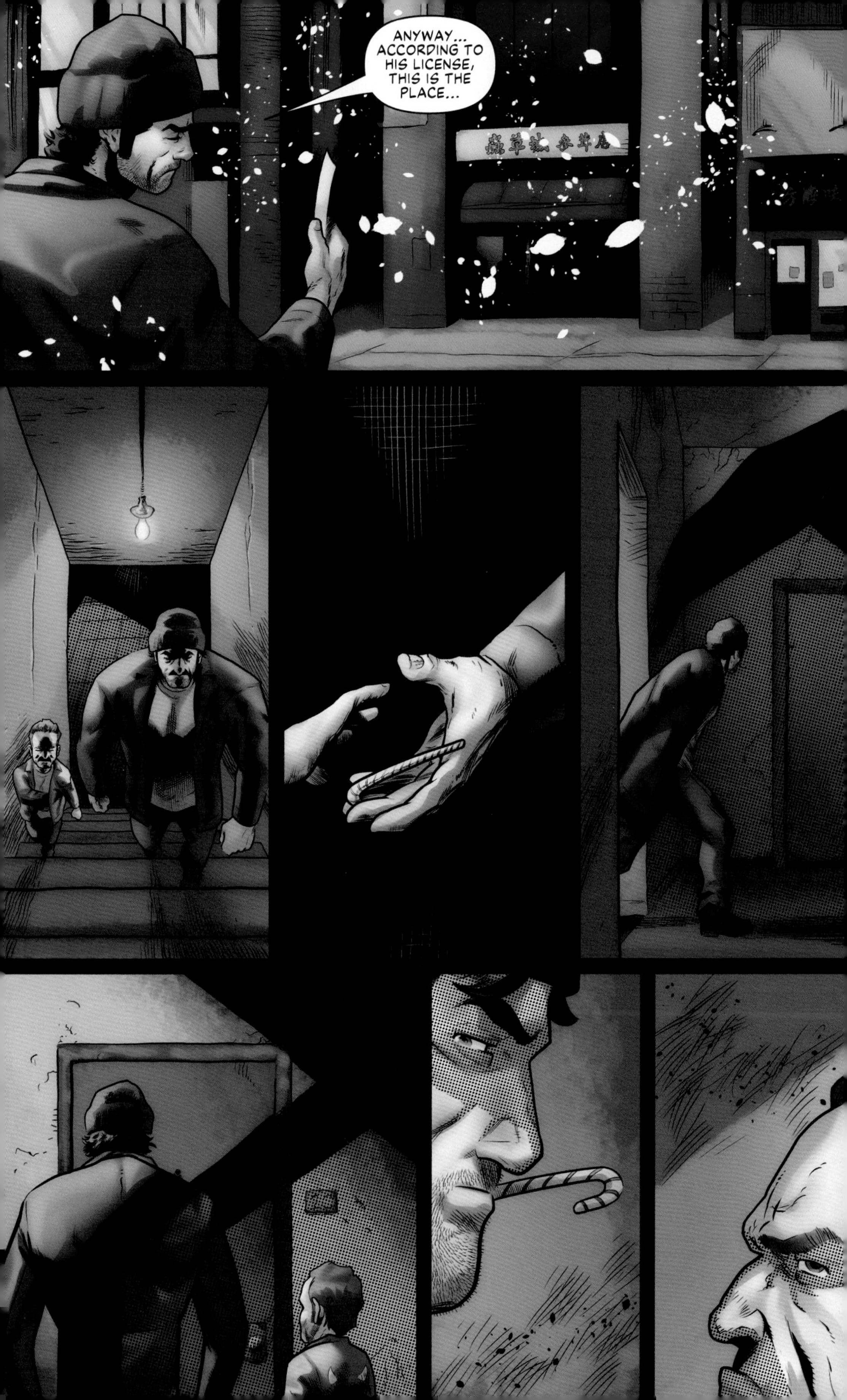
ANYWAY... ACCORDING TO HIS LICENSE, THIS IS THE PLACE...

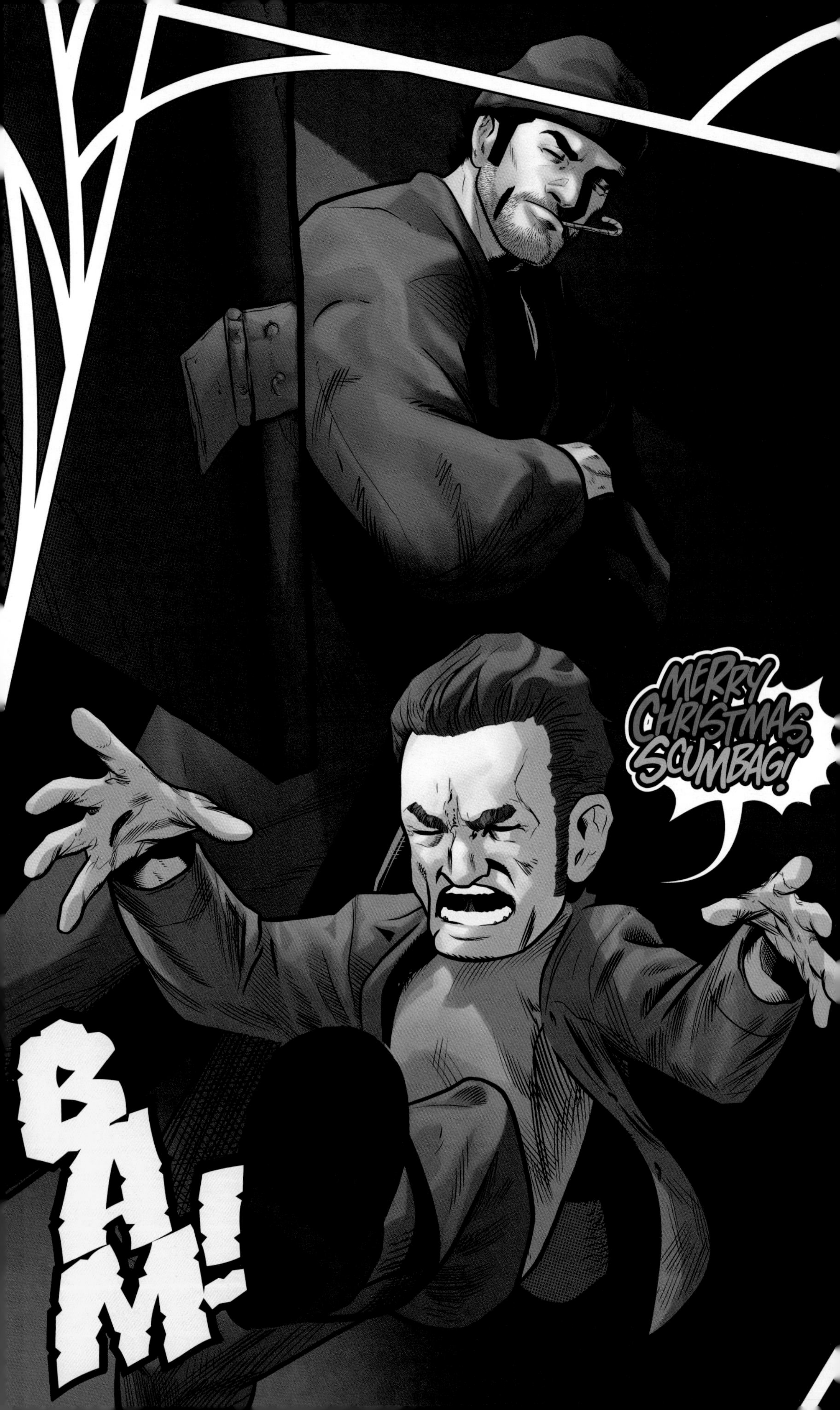
MERRY CHRISTMAS, SCUMBAG!
BAM!

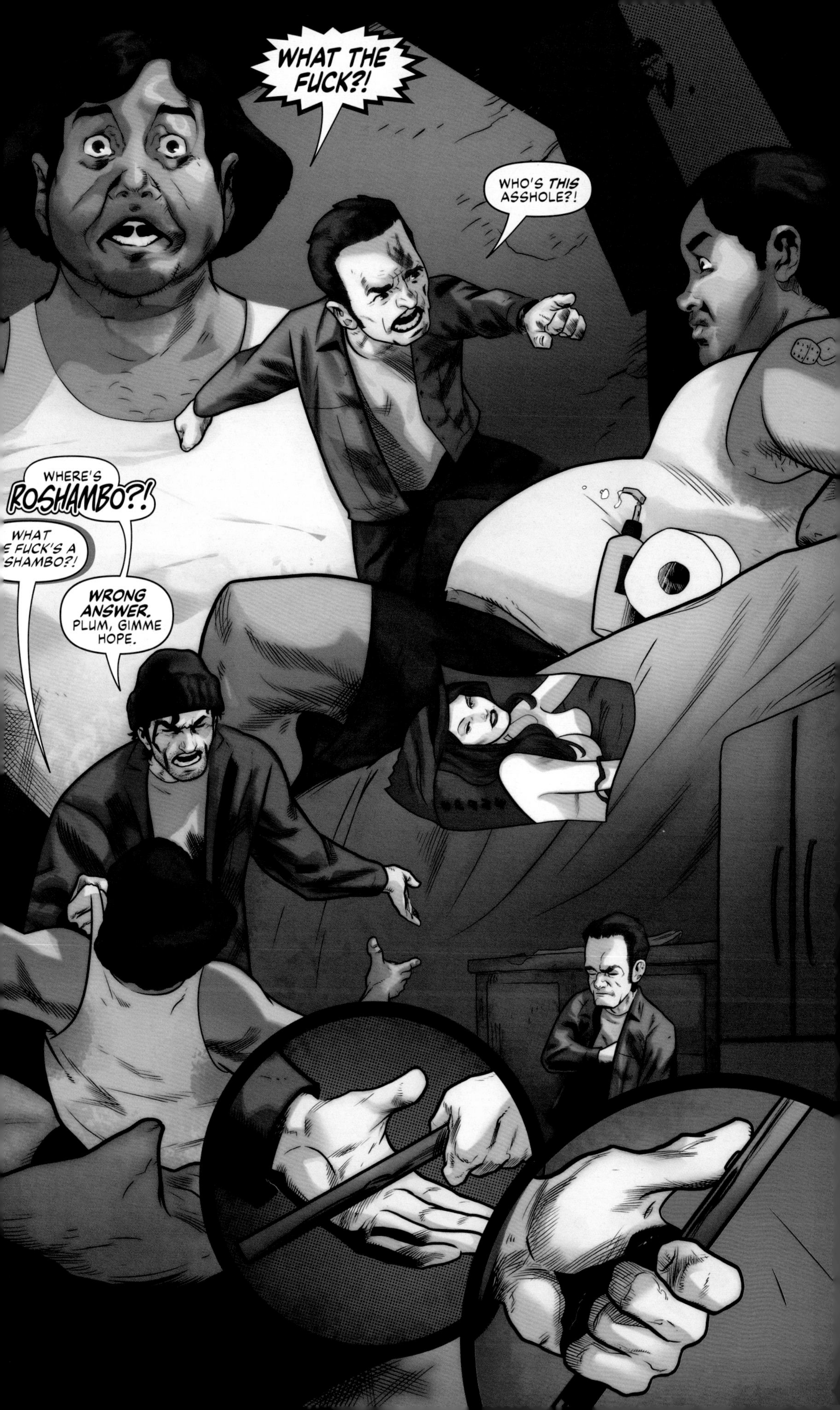
WHAT THE FUCK?!
WHO'S THIS ASSHOLE?!
WHERE'S ROSHAMBO?!
WHAT E FUCK'S A SHAMBO?!
WRONG ANSWER. PLUM, GIMME HOPE.

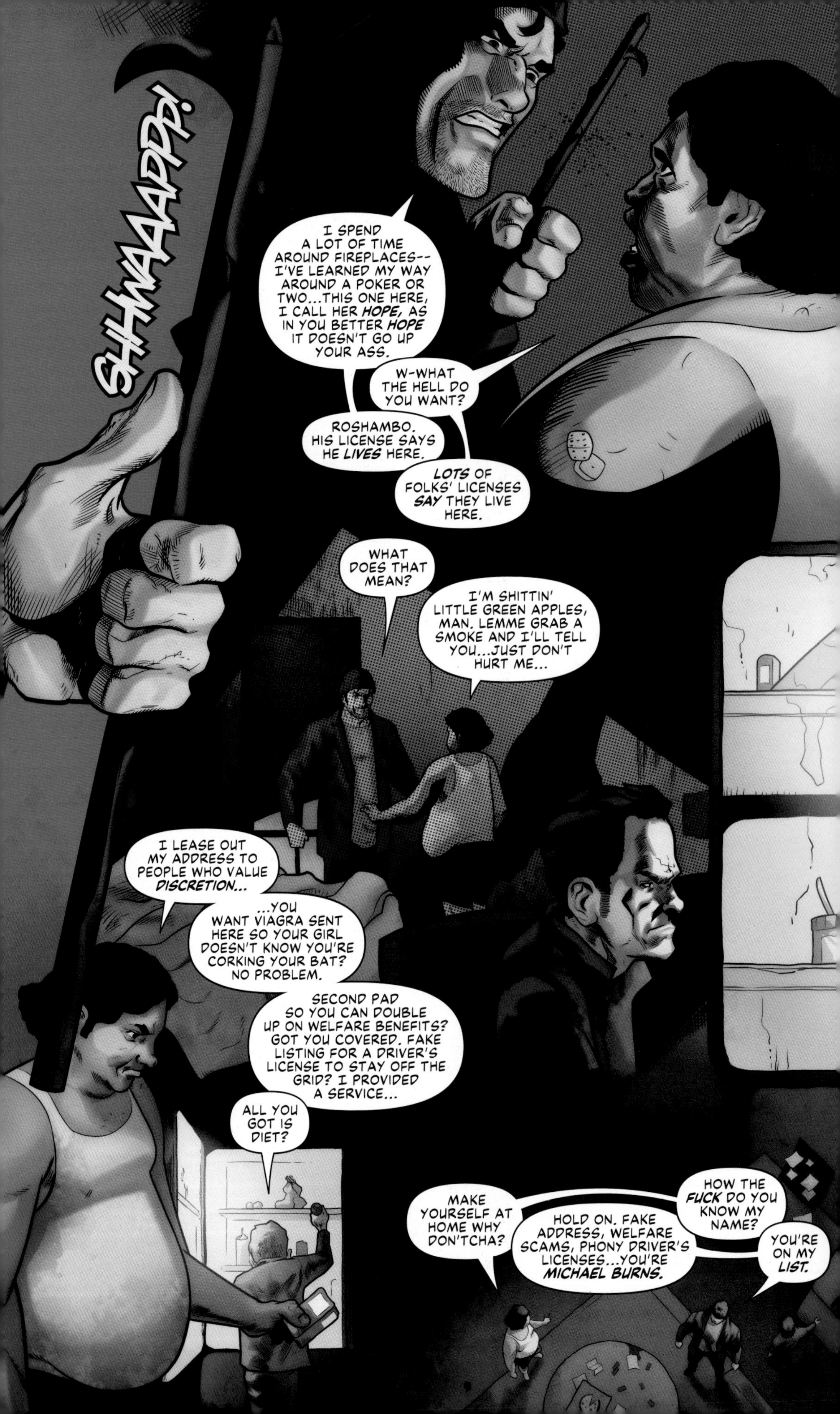
SHHWAAAAPPP!
I SPEND A LOT OF TIME AROUND FIREPLACES-- I'VE LEARNED MY WAY AROUND A POKER OR TWO...THIS ONE HERE, I CALL HER HOPE, AS IN YOU BETTER HOPE IT DOESN'T GO UP YOUR ASS.
W-WHAT THE HELL DO YOU WANT?
ROSHAMBO. HIS LICENSE SAYS HE LIVES HERE.
LOTS OF FOLKS' LICENSES SAY THEY LIVE HERE.
WHAT DOES THAT MEAN?
I'M SHITTIN' LITTLE GREEN APPLES, MAN. LEMME GRAB A SMOKE AND I'LL TELL YOU...JUST DON'T HURT ME...
I LEASE OUT MY ADDRESS TO PEOPLE WHO VALUE DISCRETION...
...YOU WANT VIAGRA SENT HERE SO YOUR GIRL DOESN'T KNOW YOU'RE CORKING YOUR BAT? NO PROBLEM.
SECOND PAD SO YOU CAN DOUBLE UP ON WELFARE BENEFITS? GOT YOU COVERED. FAKE LISTING FOR A DRIVER'S LICENSE TO STAY OFF THE GRID? I PROVIDED A SERVICE...
ALL YOU GOT IS DIET?
MAKE YOURSELF AT HOME WHY DON'TCHA?
HOLD ON. FAKE ADDRESS, WELFARE SCAMS, PHONY DRIVER'S LICENSES...YOU'RE MICHAEL BURNS.
HOW THE FUCK DO YOU KNOW MY NAME?
YOU'RE ON MY LIST.

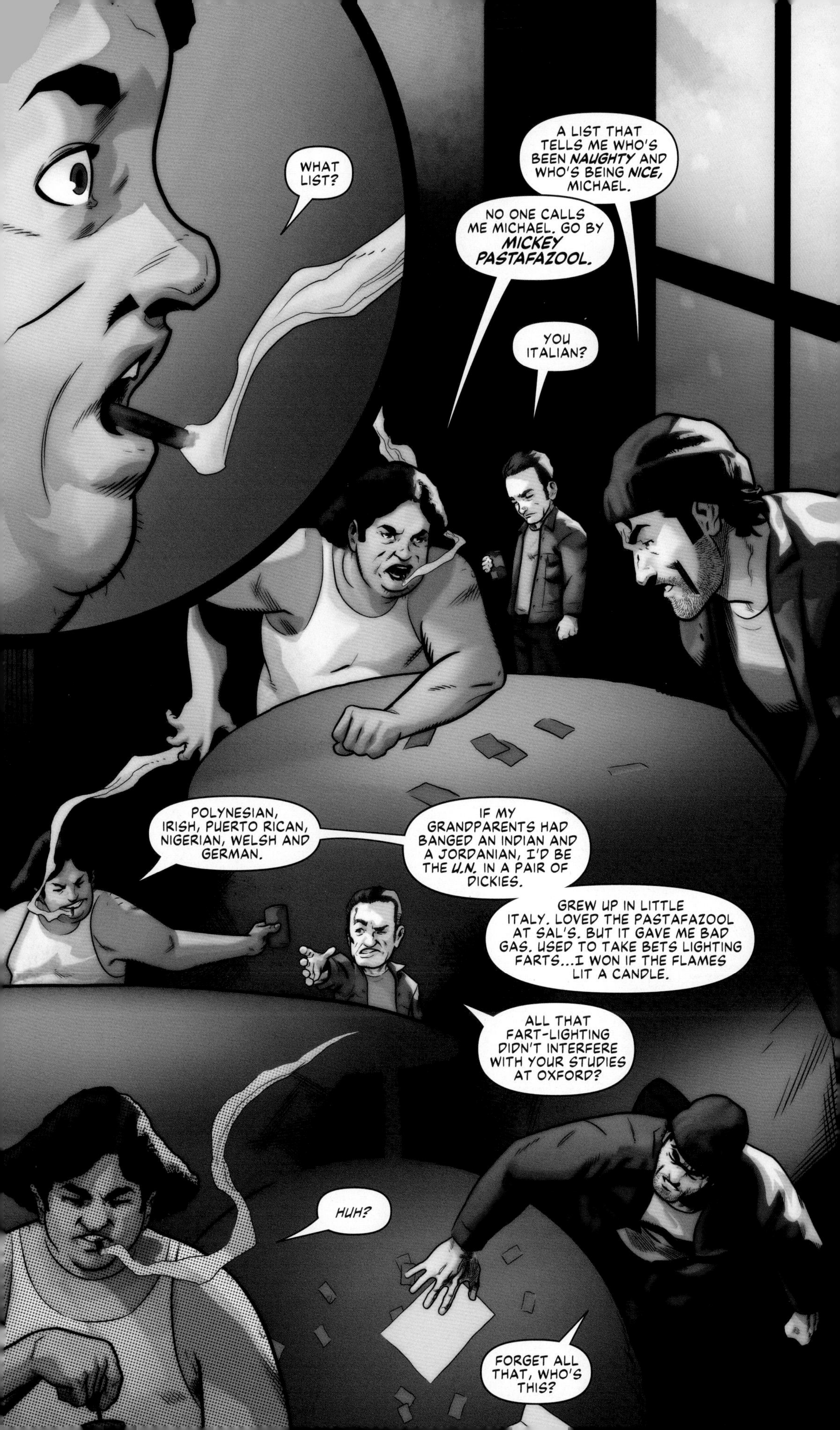
WHAT LIST?
A LIST THAT TELLS ME WHO'S BEEN NAUGHTY AND WHO'S BEING NICE, MICHAEL.
NO ONE CALLS ME MICHAEL. GO BY MICKEY PASTAFAZOOL.
YOU ITALIAN?
POLYNESIAN, IRISH, PUERTO RICAN, NIGERIAN, WELSH AND GERMAN.
IF MY GRANDPARENTS HAD BANGED AN INDIAN AND A JORDANIAN, I'D BE THE U.N. IN A PAIR OF DICKIES.
GREW UP IN LITTLE ITALY. LOVED THE PASTAFAZOOL AT SAL'S. BUT IT GAVE ME BAD GAS. USED TO TAKE BETS LIGHTING FARTS...I WON IF THE FLAMES LIT A CANDLE.
ALL THAT FART-LIGHTING DIDN'T INTERFERE WITH YOUR STUDIES AT OXFORD?
HUH?
FORGET ALL THAT, WHO'S THIS?

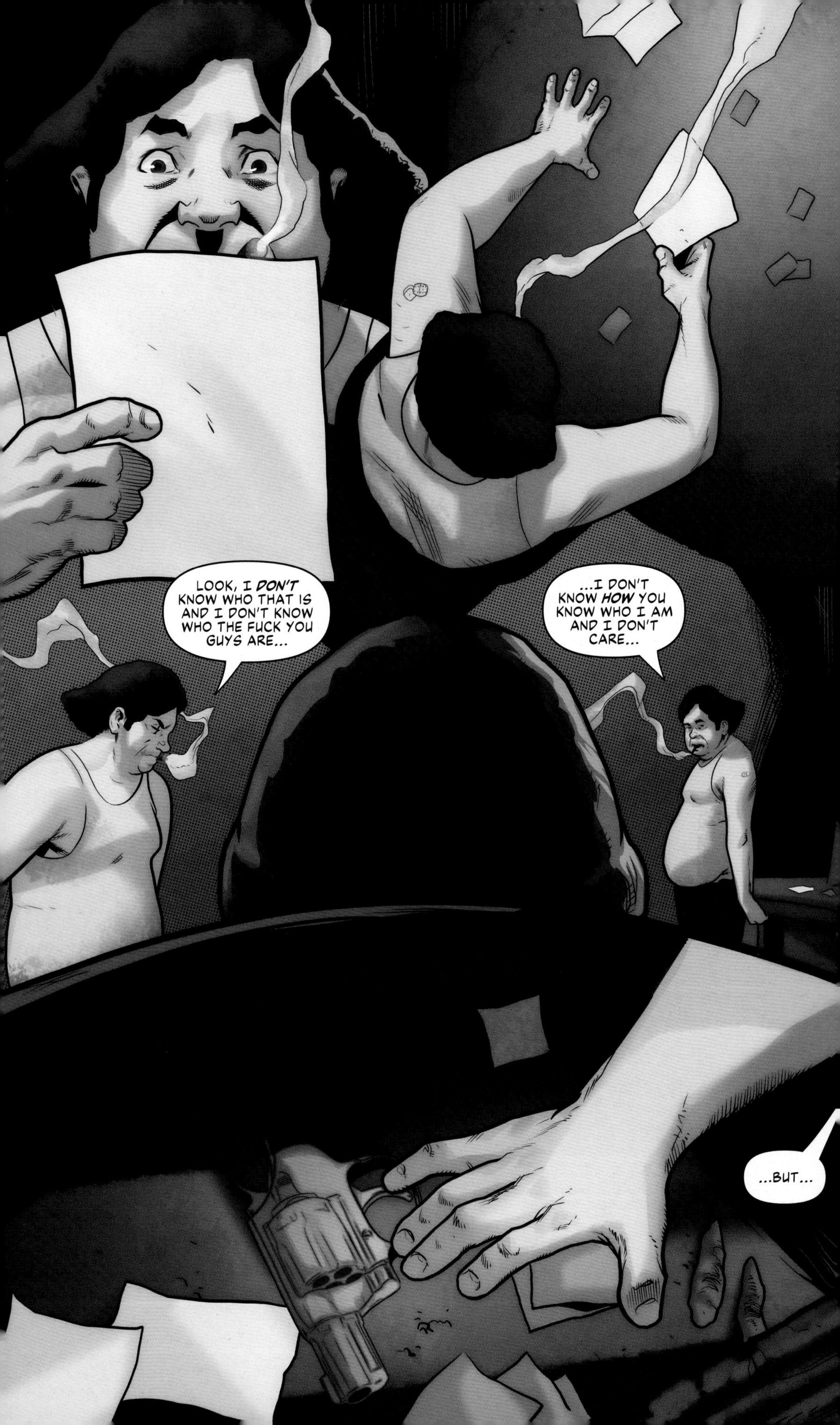
LOOK, I DON'T KNOW WHO THAT IS AND I DON'T KNOW WHO THE FUCK YOU GUYS ARE...
...I DON'T KNOW HOW YOU KNOW WHO I AM AND I DON'T CARE...
...BUT...

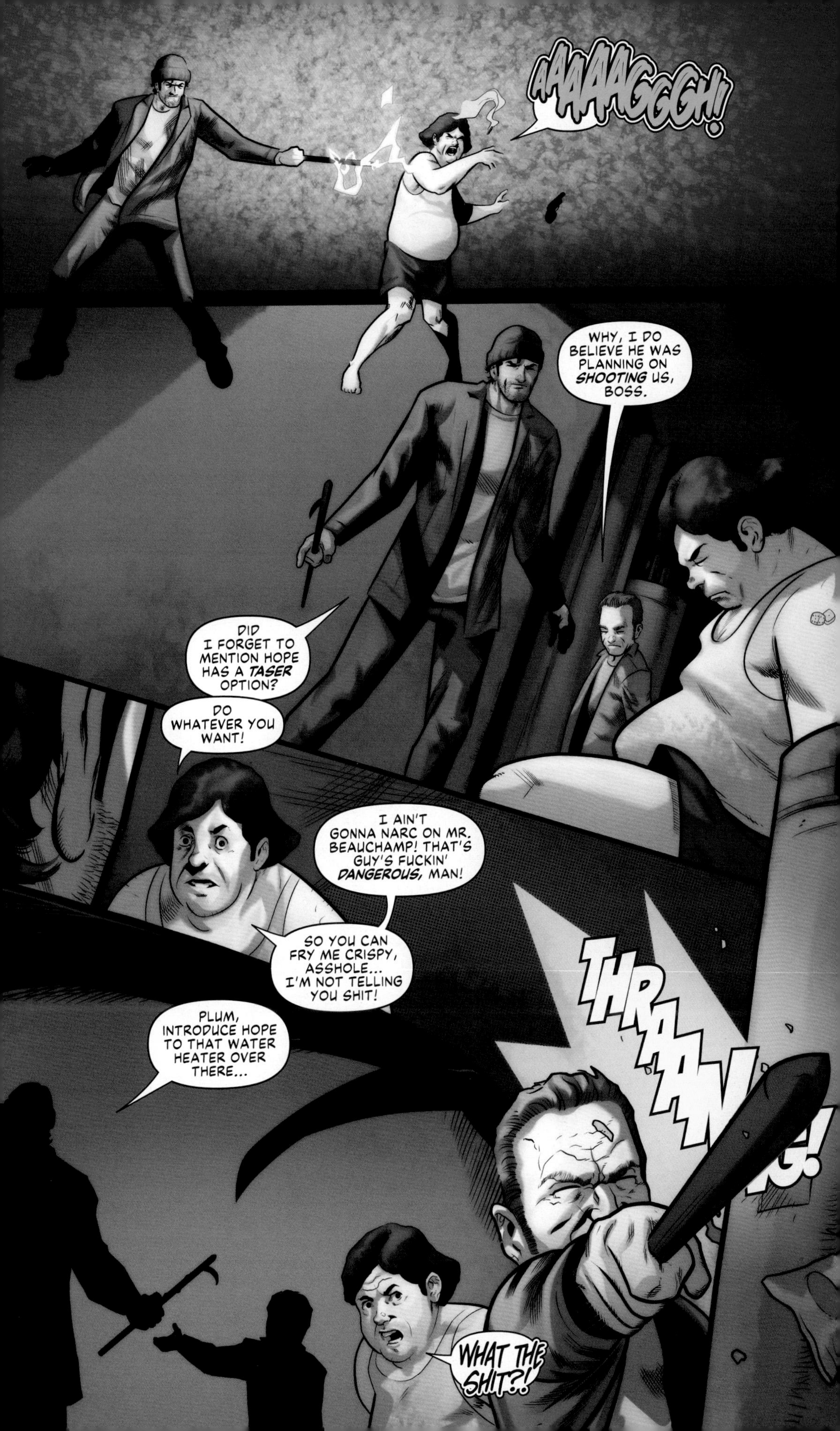
AAAAAGGGH!
WHY, I DO BELIEVE HE WAS PLANNING ON SHOOTING US, BOSS.
DID I FORGET TO MENTION HOPE HAS A TASER OPTION?
DO WHATEVER YOU WANT!
I AIN'T GONNA NARC ON MR. BEAUCHAMP! THAT'S GUY'S FUCKIN' DANGEROUS, MAN!
SO YOU CAN FRY ME CRISPY, ASSHOLE... I'M NOT TELLING YOU SHIT!
PLUM, INTRODUCE HOPE TO THAT WATER HEATER OVER THERE...
WHAT THE SHIT?!

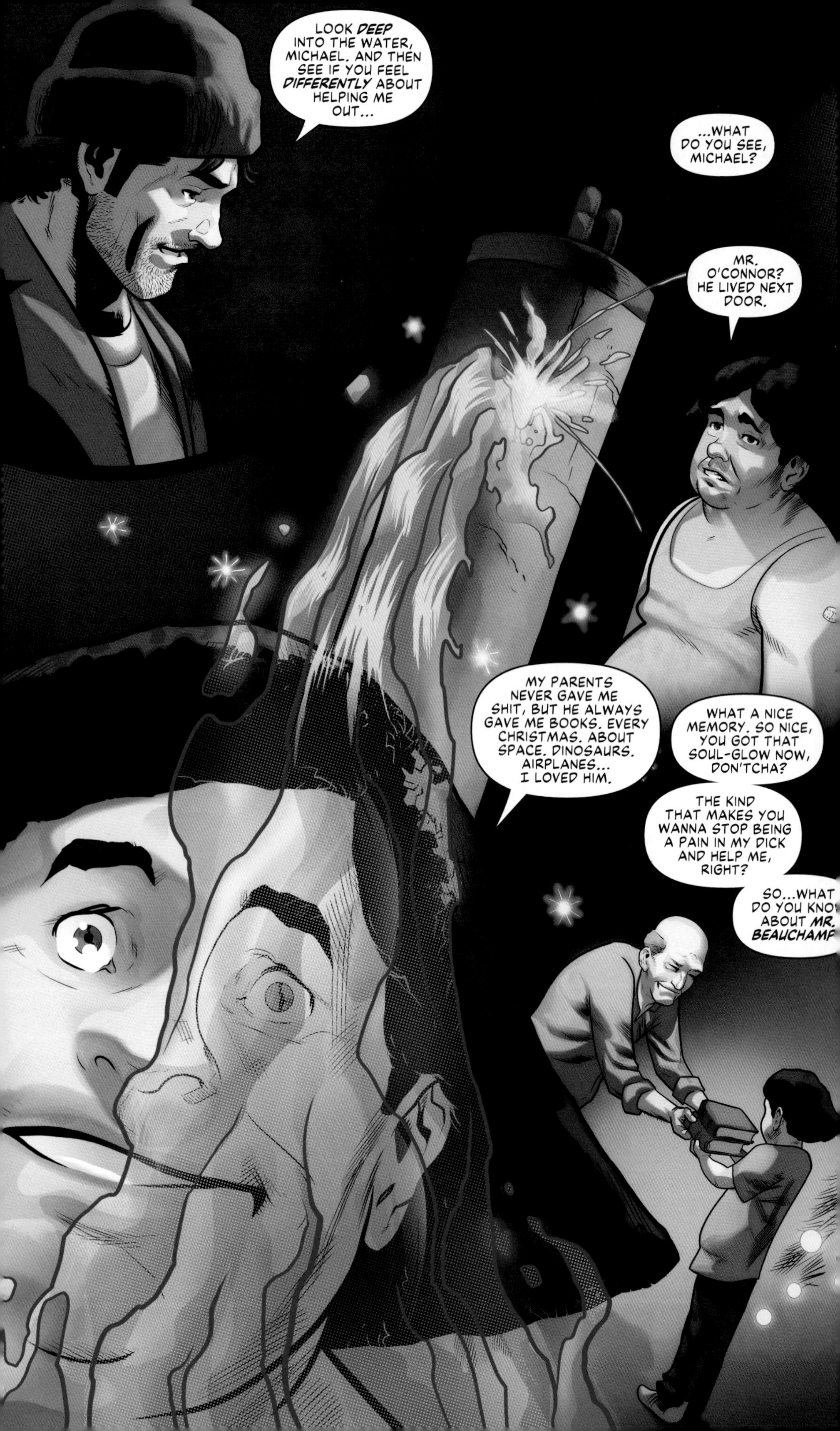
LOOK DEEP INTO THE WATER, MICHAEL. AND THEN SEE IF YOU FEEL DIFFERENTLY ABOUT HELPING ME OUT...
...WHAT DO YOU SEE, MICHAEL?
MR. O'CONNOR? HE LIVED NEXT DOOR.
MY PARENTS NEVER GAVE ME SHIT, BUT HE ALWAYS GAVE ME BOOKS. EVERY CHRISTMAS. ABOUT SPACE. DINOSAURS. AIRPLANES... I LOVED HIM.
WHAT A NICE MEMORY. SO NICE, YOU GOT THAT SOUL-GLOW NOW, DON'TCHA?
THE KIND THAT MAKES YOU WANNA STOP BEING A PAIN IN MY DICK AND HELP ME, RIGHT?
SO...WHAT DO YOU KNO ABOUT MR. BEAUCHAMP

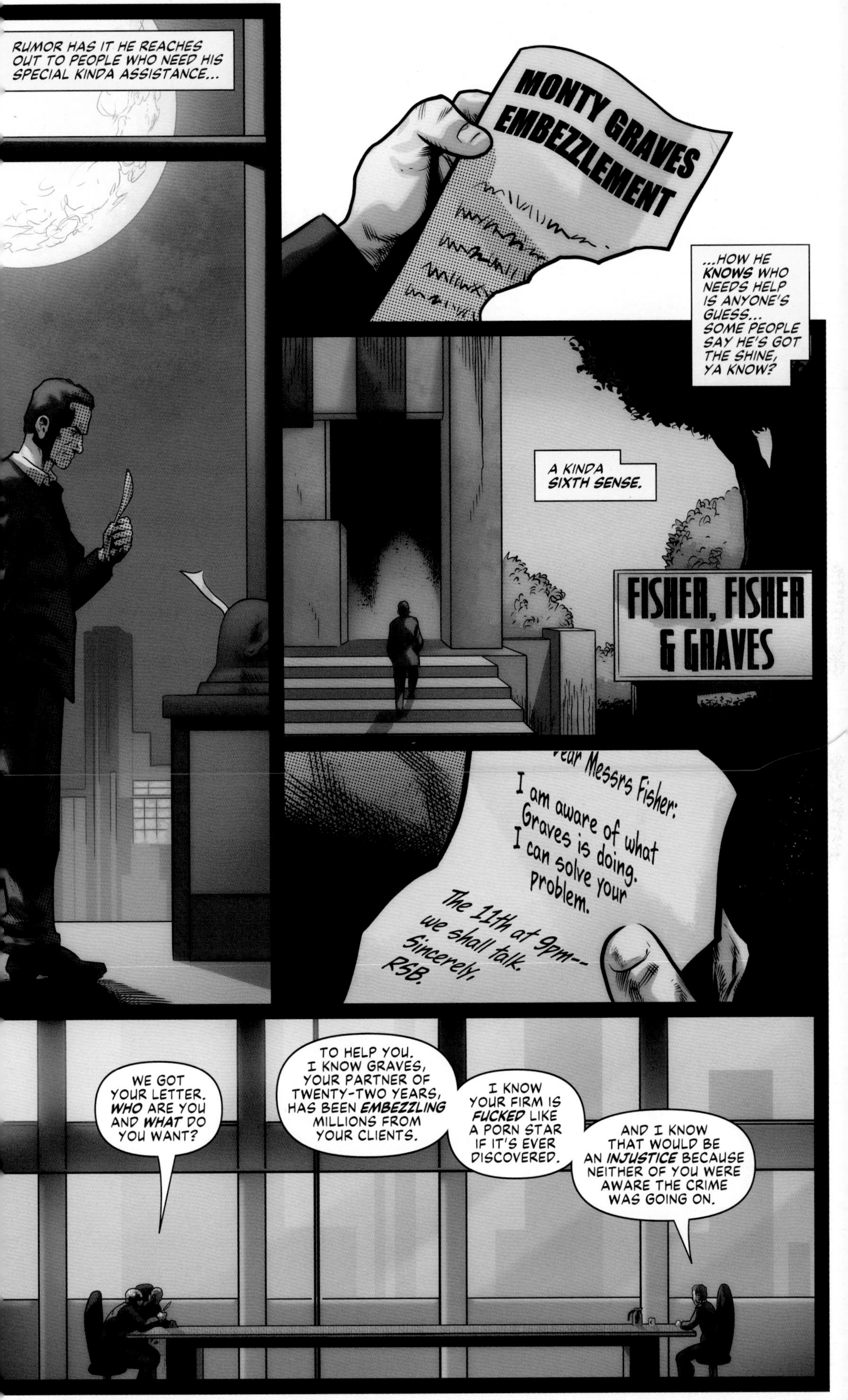
RUMOR HAS IT HE REACHES OUT TO PEOPLE WHO NEED HIS SPECIAL KINDA ASSISTANCE...
MONTY GRAVES EMBEZZLEMENT
...HOW HE KNOWS WHO NEEDS HELP IS ANYONE'S GUESS... SOME PEOPLE SAY HE'S GOT THE SHINE, YA KNOW?
A KINDA SIXTH SENSE.
FISHER, FISHER & GRAVES
Dear Messrs Fisher:
I am aware of what Graves is doing. I can solve your problem.
The 11th at 9pm-- we shall talk. Sincerely, RSB.
WE GOT YOUR LETTER. WHO ARE YOU AND WHAT DO YOU WANT?
TO HELP YOU. I KNOW GRAVES, YOUR PARTNER OF TWENTY-TWO YEARS, HAS BEEN EMBEZZLING MILLIONS FROM YOUR CLIENTS.
I KNOW YOUR FIRM IS FUCKED LIKE A PORN STAR IF IT'S EVER DISCOVERED.
AND I KNOW THAT WOULD BE AN INJUSTICE BECAUSE NEITHER OF YOU WERE AWARE THE CRIME WAS GOING ON.

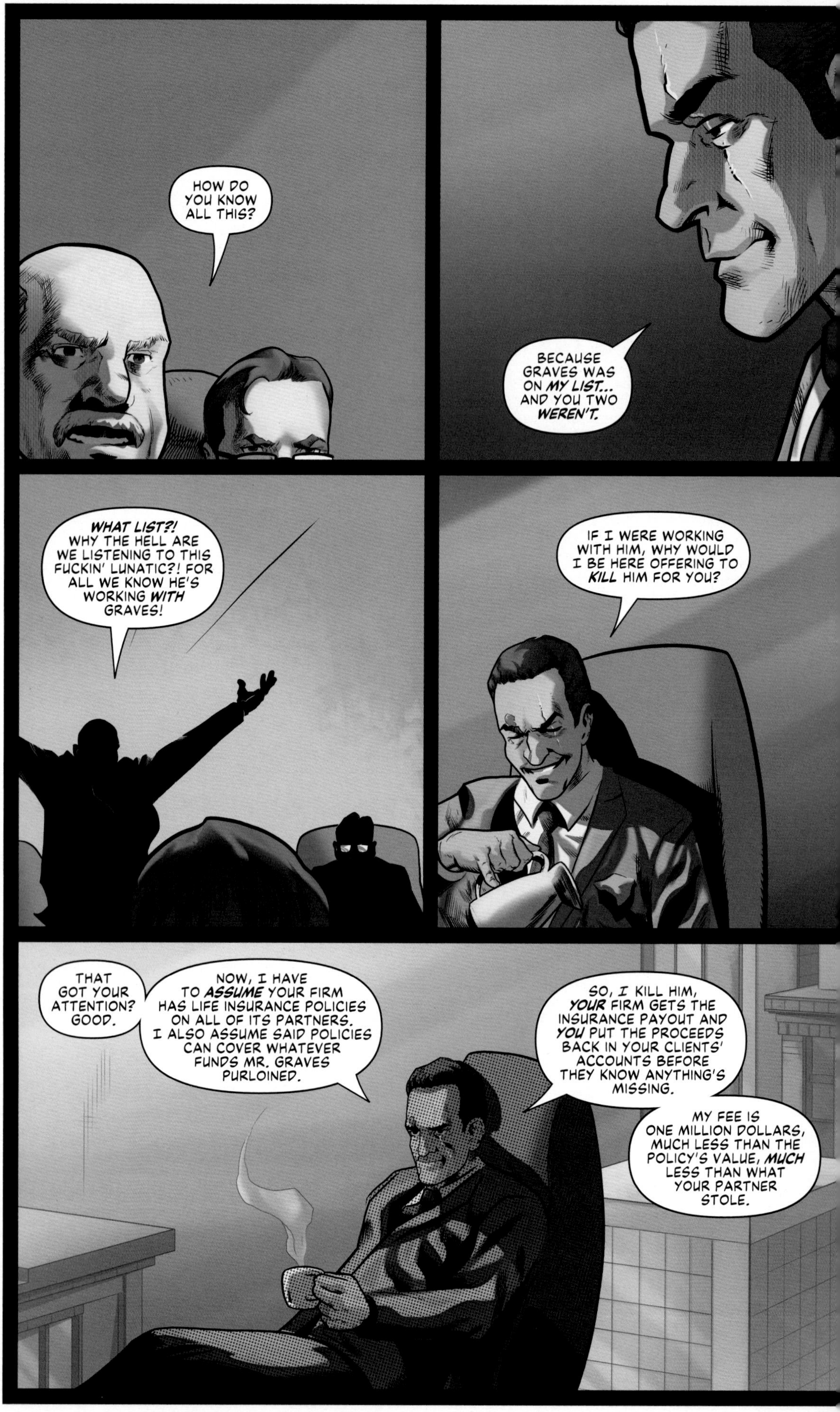
HOW DO YOU KNOW ALL THIS?
BECAUSE GRAVES WAS ON MY LIST... AND YOU TWO WEREN'T.
WHAT LIST?! WHY THE HELL ARE WE LISTENING TO THIS FUCKIN' LUNATIC?! FOR ALL WE KNOW HE'S WORKING WITH GRAVES!
IF I WERE WORKING WITH HIM, WHY WOULD I BE HERE OFFERING TO KILL HIM FOR YOU?
THAT GOT YOUR ATTENTION? GOOD.
NOW, I HAVE TO ASSUME YOUR FIRM HAS LIFE INSURANCE POLICIES ON ALL OF ITS PARTNERS. I ALSO ASSUME SAID POLICIES CAN COVER WHATEVER FUNDS MR. GRAVES PURLOINED.
SO, I KILL HIM, YOUR FIRM GETS THE INSURANCE PAYOUT AND YOU PUT THE PROCEEDS BACK IN YOUR CLIENTS' ACCOUNTS BEFORE THEY KNOW ANYTHING'S MISSING.
MY FEE IS ONE MILLION DOLLARS, MUCH LESS THAN THE POLICY'S VALUE, MUCH LESS THAN WHAT YOUR PARTNER STOLE.

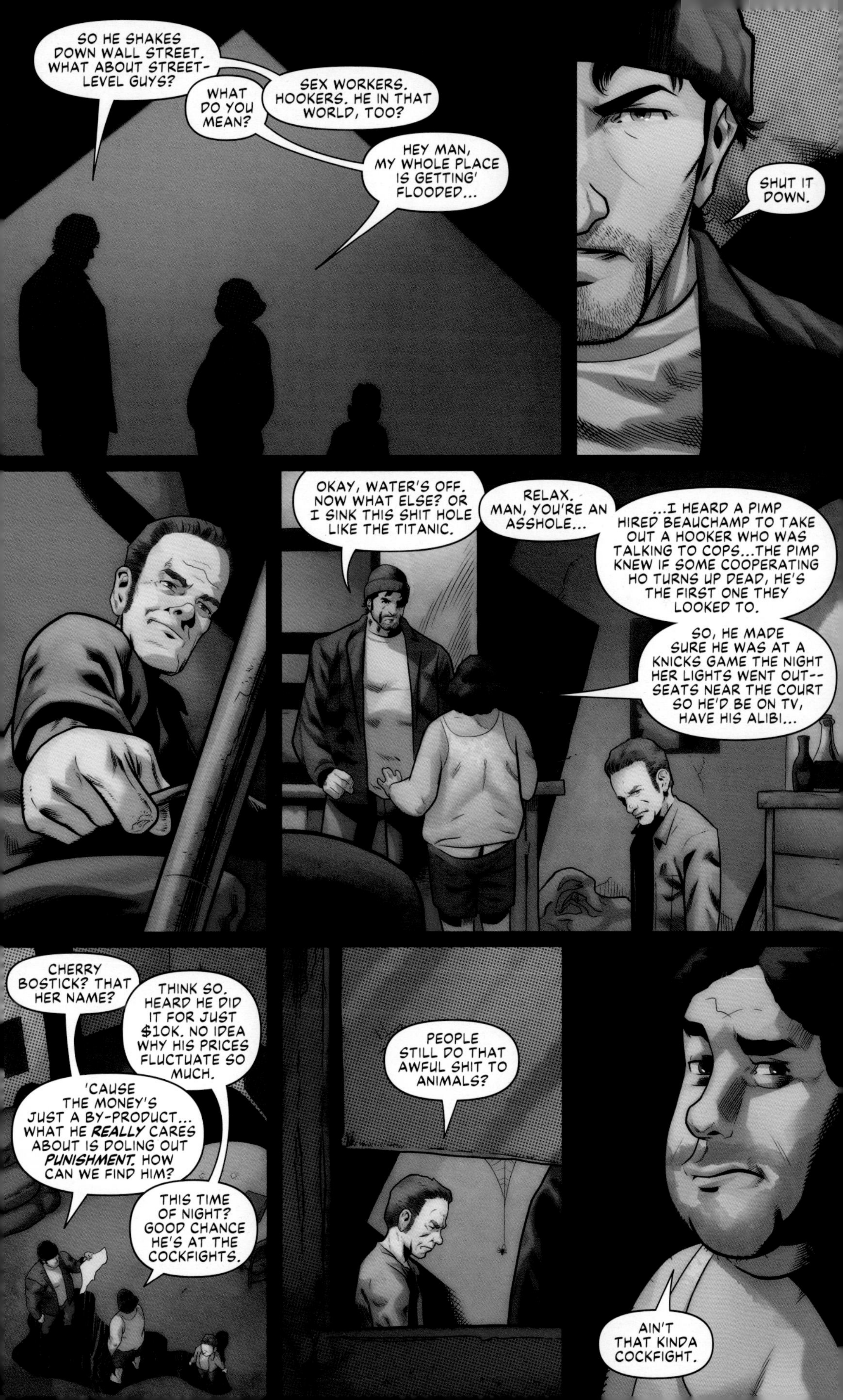
SO HE SHAKES DOWN WALL STREET. WHAT ABOUT STREET-LEVEL GUYS?
WHAT DO YOU MEAN?
SEX WORKERS. HOOKERS. HE IN THAT WORLD, TOO?
HEY MAN, MY WHOLE PLACE IS GETTING' FLOODED...
SHUT IT DOWN.
OKAY, WATER'S OFF. NOW WHAT ELSE? OR I SINK THIS SHIT HOLE LIKE THE TITANIC.
RELAX. MAN, YOU'RE AN ASSHOLE...
...I HEARD A PIMP HIRED BEAUCHAMP TO TAKE OUT A HOOKER WHO WAS TALKING TO COPS...THE PIMP KNEW IF SOME COOPERATING HO TURNS UP DEAD, HE'S THE FIRST ONE THEY LOOKED TO.
SO, HE MADE SURE HE WAS AT A KNICKS GAME THE NIGHT HER LIGHTS WENT OUT--SEATS NEAR THE COURT SO HE'D BE ON TV, HAVE HIS ALIBI...
CHERRY BOSTICK? THAT HER NAME?
THINK SO. HEARD HE DID IT FOR JUST $10K. NO IDEA WHY HIS PRICES FLUCTUATE SO MUCH.
'CAUSE THE MONEY'S JUST A BY-PRODUCT... WHAT HE *REALLY* CARES ABOUT IS DOLING OUT ***PUNISHMENT.*** HOW CAN WE FIND HIM?
THIS TIME OF NIGHT? GOOD CHANCE HE'S AT THE COCKFIGHTS.
PEOPLE STILL DO THAT AWFUL SHIT TO ANIMALS?
AIN'T THAT KINDA COCKFIGHT.

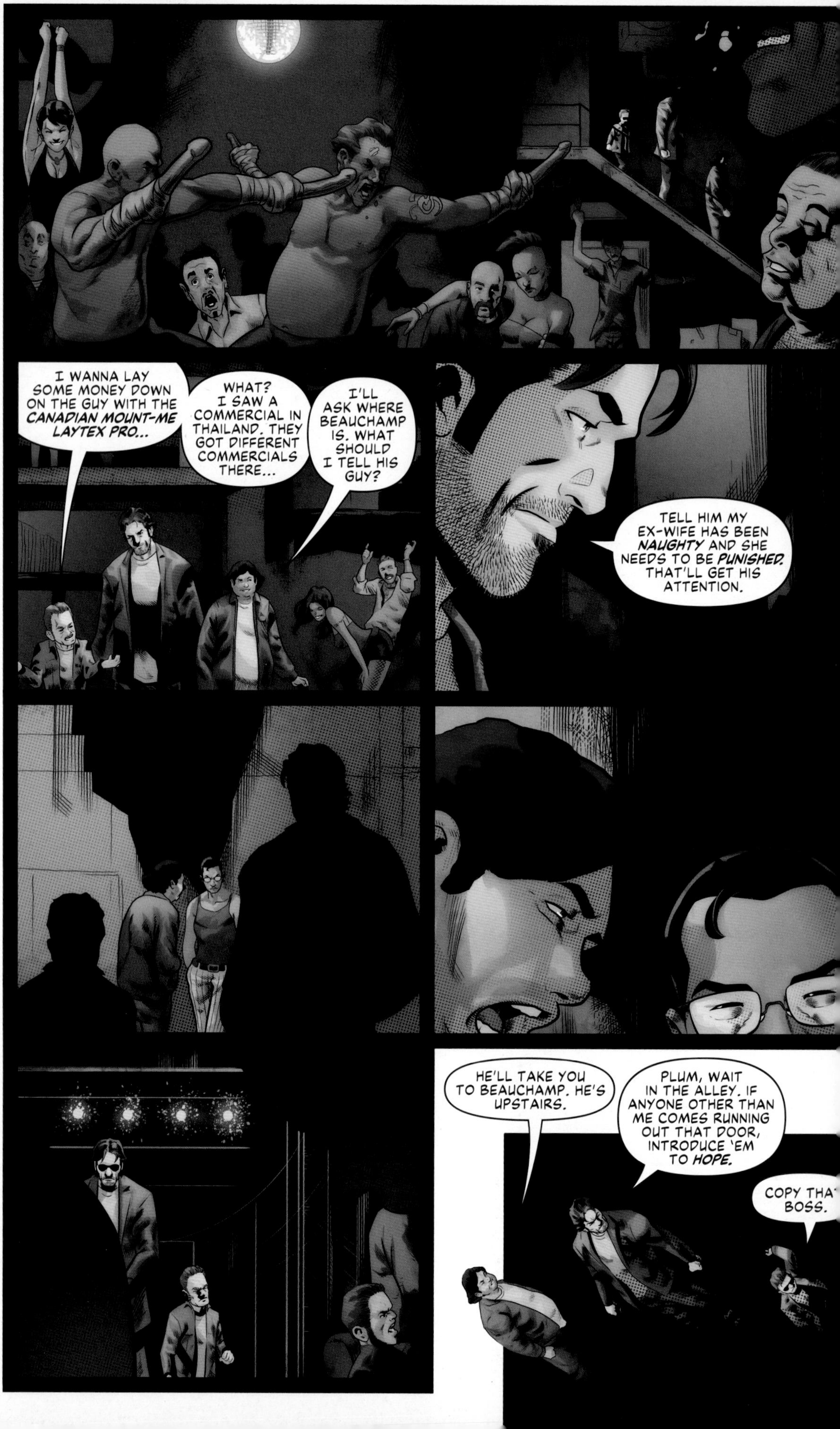
I WANNA LAY SOME MONEY DOWN ON THE GUY WITH THE *CANADIAN MOUNT-ME LAYTEX PRO...*
WHAT? I SAW A COMMERCIAL IN THAILAND. THEY GOT DIFFERENT COMMERCIALS THERE...
I'LL ASK WHERE BEAUCHAMP IS. WHAT SHOULD I TELL HIS GUY?
TELL HIM MY EX-WIFE HAS BEEN *NAUGHTY* AND SHE NEEDS TO BE *PUNISHED.* THAT'LL GET HIS ATTENTION.
HE'LL TAKE YOU TO BEAUCHAMP. HE'S UPSTAIRS.
PLUM, WAIT IN THE ALLEY. IF ANYONE OTHER THAN ME COMES RUNNING OUT THAT DOOR, INTRODUCE 'EM TO *HOPE.*
COPY THA BOSS.

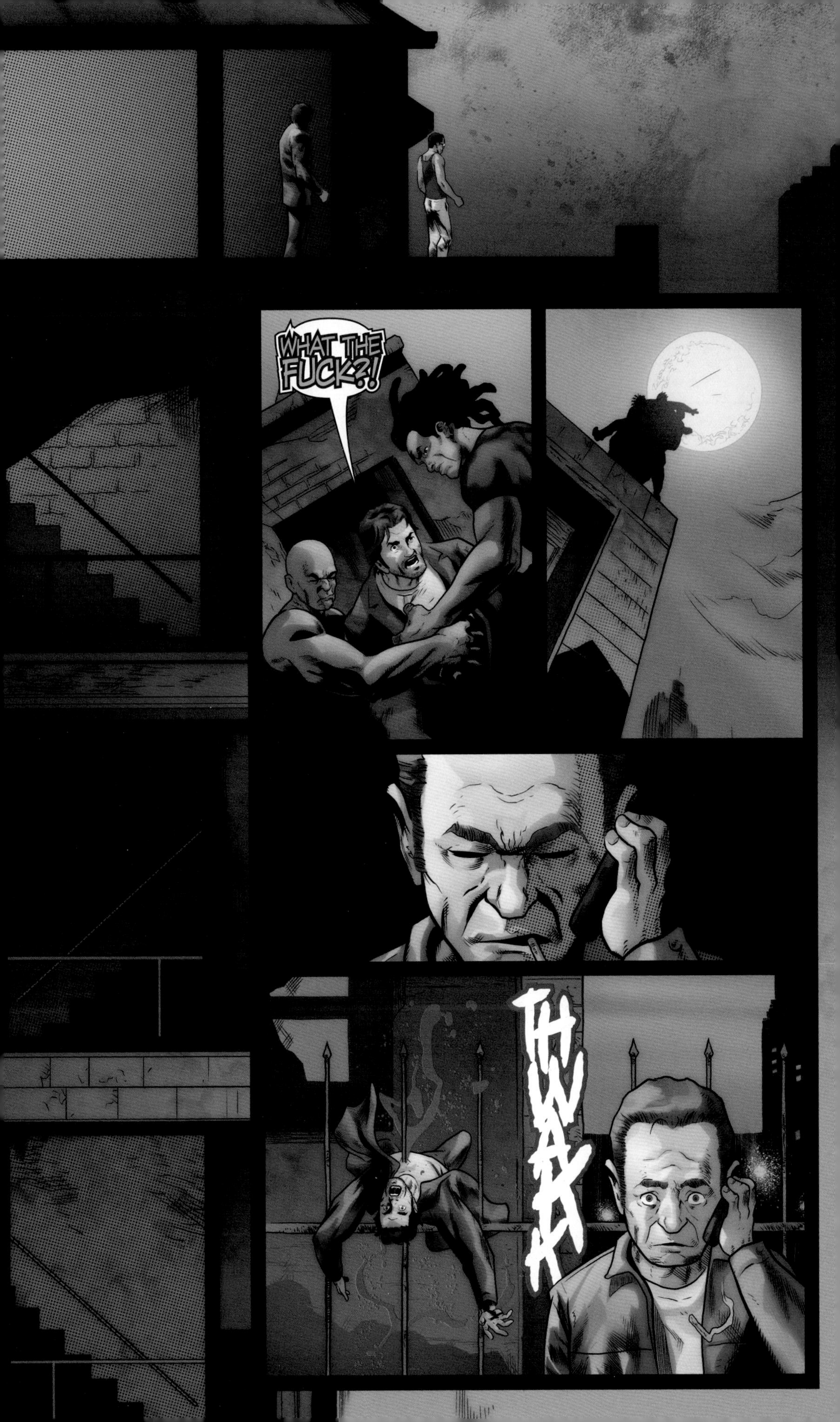
WHAT THE FUCK?!
THWAK

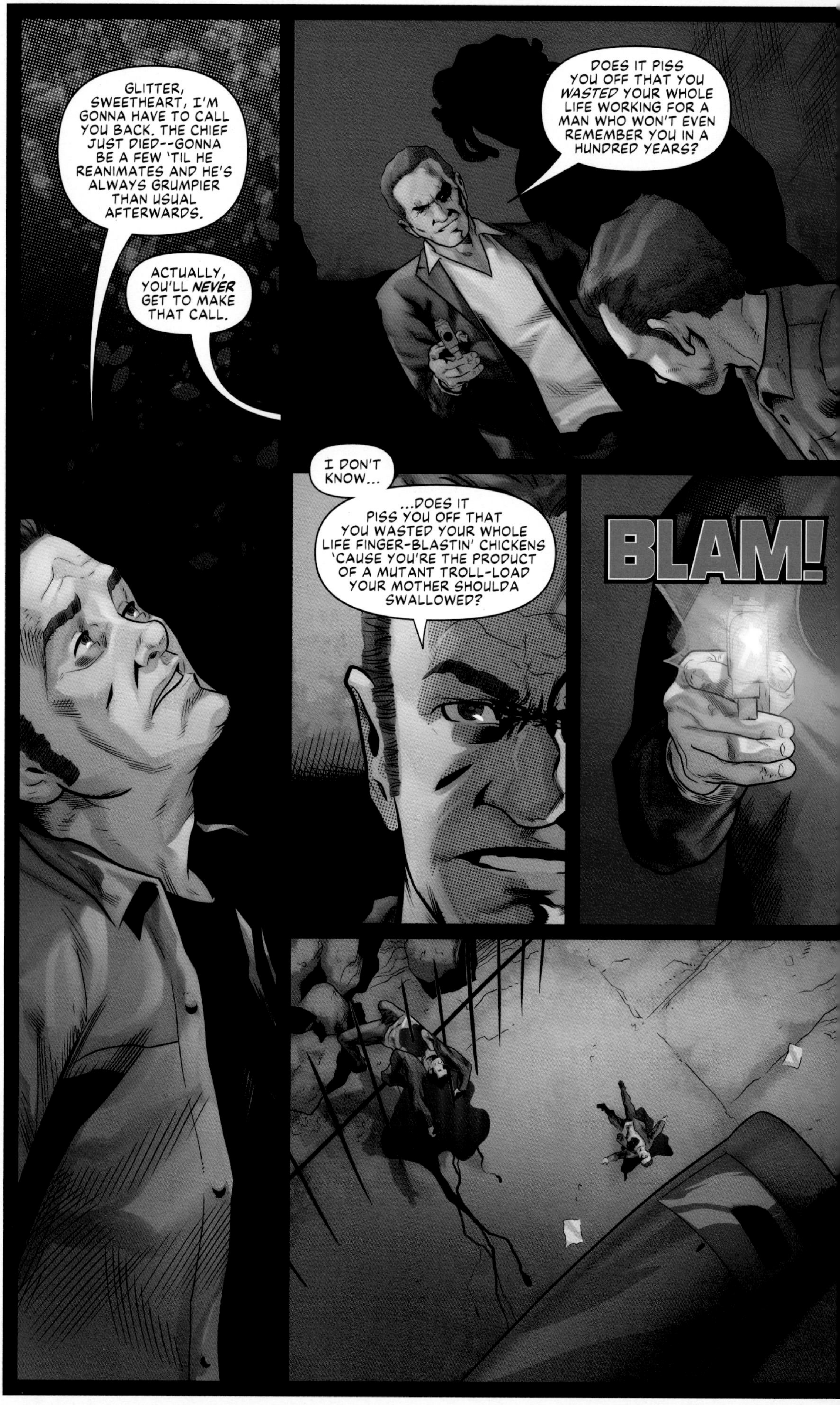
GLITTER, SWEETHEART, I'M GONNA HAVE TO CALL YOU BACK. THE CHIEF JUST DIED--GONNA BE A FEW 'TIL HE REANIMATES AND HE'S ALWAYS GRUMPIER THAN USUAL AFTERWARDS.
ACTUALLY, YOU'LL *NEVER* GET TO MAKE THAT CALL.
DOES IT PISS YOU OFF THAT YOU *WASTED* YOUR WHOLE LIFE WORKING FOR A MAN WHO WON'T EVEN REMEMBER YOU IN A HUNDRED YEARS?
I DON'T KNOW...
...DOES IT PISS YOU OFF THAT YOU WASTED YOUR WHOLE LIFE FINGER-BLASTIN' CHICKENS 'CAUSE YOU'RE THE PRODUCT OF A MUTANT TROLL-LOAD YOUR MOTHER SHOULDA SWALLOWED?
BLAM!

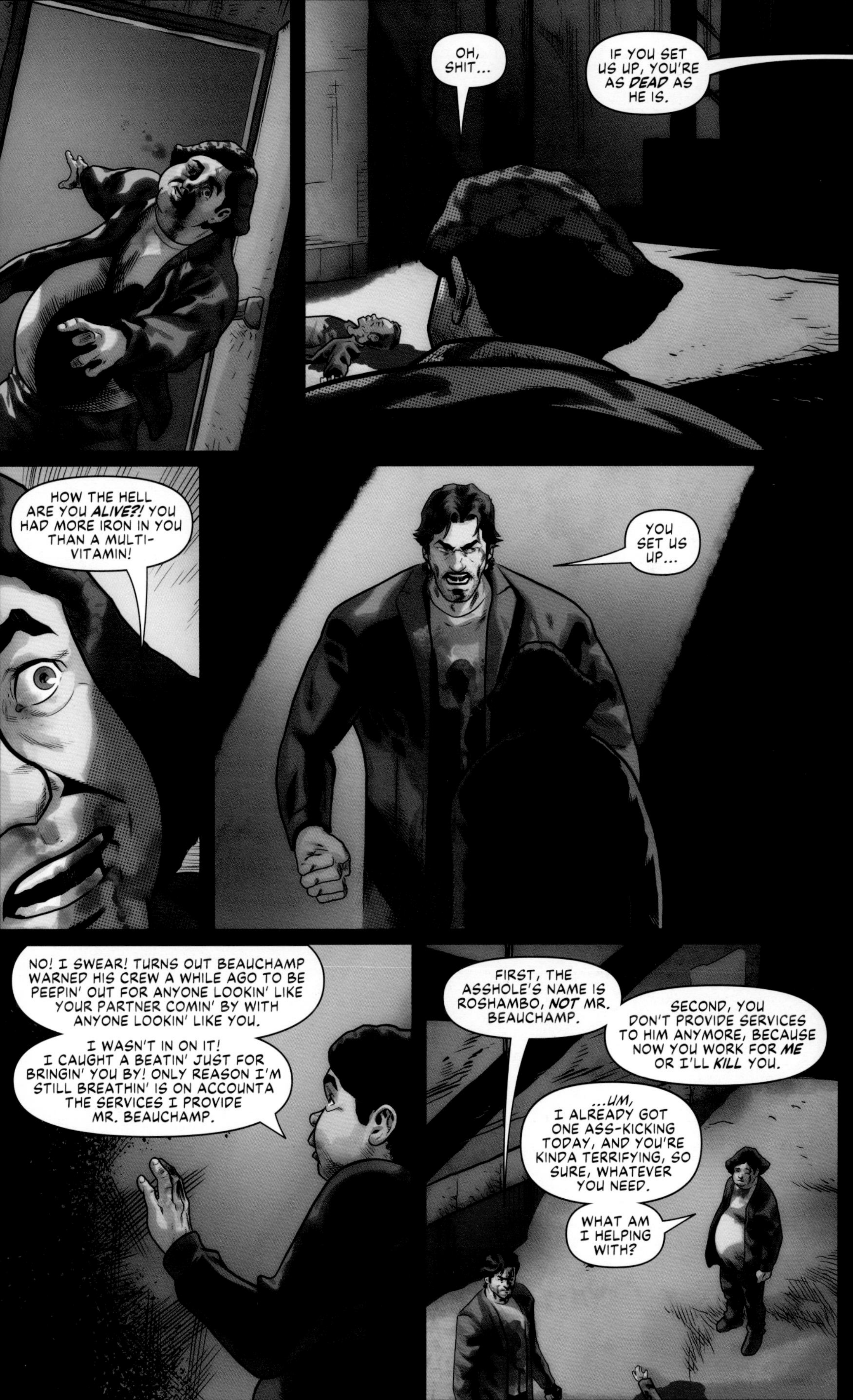
OH, SHIT...
IF YOU SET US UP, YOU'RE AS *DEAD* AS HE IS.
HOW THE HELL ARE YOU *ALIVE?!* YOU HAD MORE IRON IN YOU THAN A MULTI-VITAMIN!
YOU SET US UP...
NO! I SWEAR! TURNS OUT BEAUCHAMP WARNED HIS CREW A WHILE AGO TO BE PEEPIN' OUT FOR ANYONE LOOKIN' LIKE YOUR PARTNER COMIN' BY WITH ANYONE LOOKIN' LIKE YOU.
I WASN'T IN ON IT! I CAUGHT A BEATIN' JUST FOR BRINGIN' YOU BY! ONLY REASON I'M STILL BREATHIN' IS ON ACCOUNTA THE SERVICES I PROVIDE MR. BEAUCHAMP.
FIRST, THE ASSHOLE'S NAME IS ROSHAMBO, *NOT* MR. BEAUCHAMP.
SECOND, YOU DON'T PROVIDE SERVICES TO HIM ANYMORE, BECAUSE NOW YOU WORK FOR *ME* OR I'LL *KILL* YOU.
...*UM,* I ALREADY GOT ONE ASS-KICKING TODAY, AND YOU'RE KINDA TERRIFYING, SO SURE, WHATEVER YOU NEED.
WHAT AM I HELPING WITH?

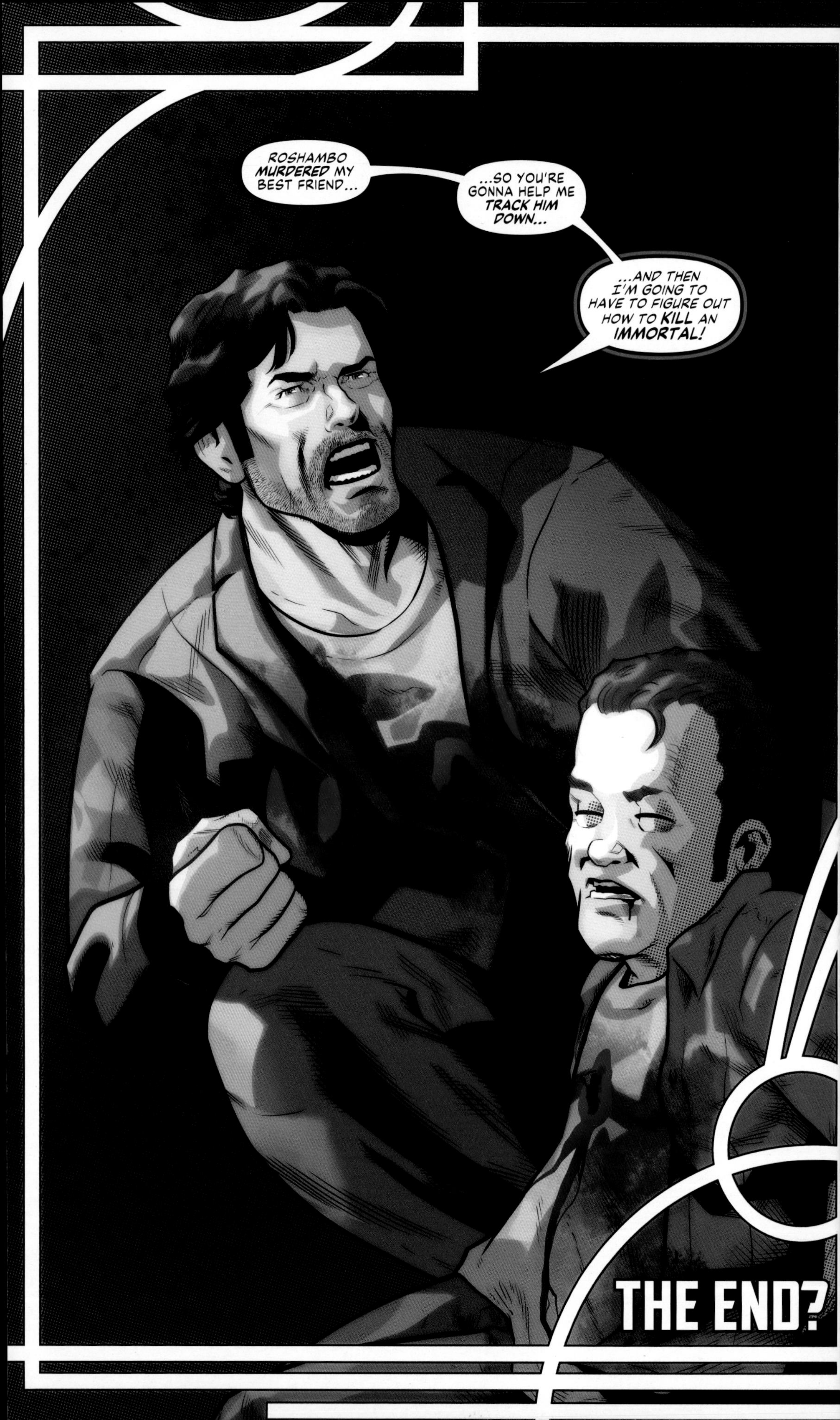
ROSHAMBO MURDERED MY BEST FRIEND...
...SO YOU'RE GONNA HELP ME TRACK HIM DOWN...
...AND THEN I'M GOING TO HAVE TO FIGURE OUT HOW TO KILL AN IMMORTAL!
THE END?

NAUGHTY LIST™

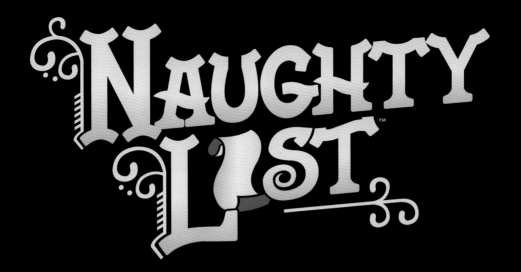

EXTRAS

9 RULES FOR WORKPLACE SAFETY

1. No eggnog on the job.

2. Do not eat candy canes near open machinery.

3. Remove all bells from clothing and shoes before entering workshop floor.

4. Mistletoe is for decoration only – harassment of any kind will not be tolerated.

5. Clean reindeer dung from boots before exiting locker room.

6. *Do They Know It's Christmas* is not a Christmas song! If you play it, you're fired.

7. Secret Santa is not fun or permitted. If you suggest it, you're fired.

8. The Christmas Tree must be watered every day. Dry trees = fires.

9. Use a ladder to place the star. Elf-stacking is strictly prohibited.

TAKE CARE!

Employee of the Month

TRACK DOWN TD & TRY TO CONVINCE HIM TO LET US TAKE HIS PHOTO

NS

Paste ee Photo ere

Presented to:

Turtle Dove
aka TD

Division: Wind-Ups

Years Employed: 12

Reason Selected: TD only missed two days of work after a brutal elk attack outside The Blinking Lights Tavern. He suffered two broken ribs and required facial stitches, but still met his quota for both Tops and Race Cars.

Santa Says: "TD knew it was our busy season, so he sucked it up and got the job done. He's a good shit."

Employee Says: "If I find out who left the Elk gate open again, I'm shoving a box of ornament hooks straight up their ass!"

THIS WEEKEND!

ANTLER DOWNS

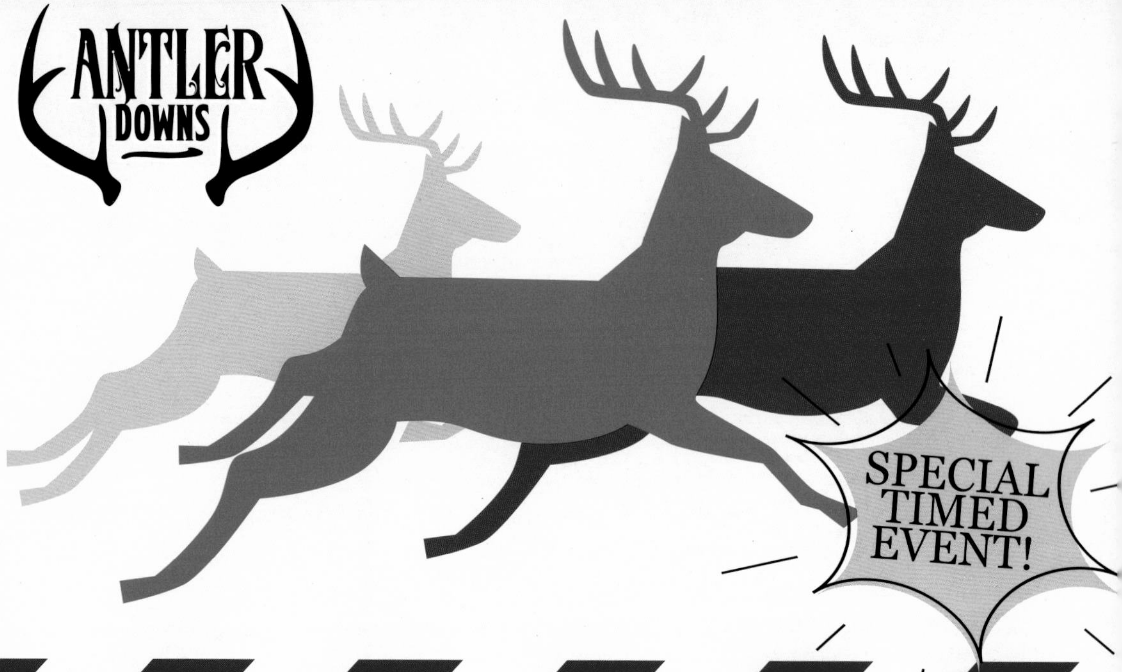
SPECIAL
TIMED
EVENT!

FEATURING COMET 18!

Admission

Adults: $12.00
Kids Under 10: Free

Senior Citizen & Veteran Discounts Honored

AFTER THE RACES, MAKE SURE TO VISIT THE BIG BUCKS LOUNGE

Dance to the sounds of
NIRVANNA ROCK WITH YOU
the Northland's best and only
Kurt Cobain/Michael Jackson tribute band!

Ladies drink half-off 'til midnight.
Losing Tickets of $100 or more gets you a
FREE PITCHER!

1 MILE

	WIN	PLACE	SHOW

MAKE SELECTION BY NUMBER

1 YULE LOGARITHM

09Mar	7SA	ft	6f ^{85}	:21^{72}	:44^{23}	01:08^{22}	F	**105**	3	3
02Nov	6SA	ft	7f ^{76}	:22^{19}	:44^{19}	01:20^{75}	F	**114**	9	9
22Oct	6Kee	ft	6f ^{34}	:22^{67}	:45^{59}	01:09^{08}	F	**114**	1	4

2 SLEIGH IT AIN'T SO

09Mar	8SA	ft	7f ^{63}	:21^{60}	:43^{13}	01:08^{22}	F	**108**	6	3
02Nov	6SA	ft	8f ^{22}	:23^{18}	:43^{29}	01:20^{75}	F	**123**	4	9
22Oct	6Kee	ft	7f ^{44}	:21^{67}	:44^{23}	01:09^{08}	F	**123**	4	4

3 REBEL WITHOUT A CLAUS

09Mar	7SA	ft	7f ^{63}	:21^{45}	:45^{23}	01:02^{11}	F	**111**	6	3
02Nov	6Kee	ft	6f ^{11}	:21^{23}	:45^{12}	01:02^{12}	F	**111**	4	8
22Oct	6Kee	ft	6f ^{23}	:21^{49}	:46^{72}	01:04^{89}	F	**114**	7	5

4 CHIMNEY CRICKET

02Nov	6SA	ft	8f ^{22}	:32^{18}	:43^{29}	01:20^{75}	F	**123**	4	9
22Oct	6Kee	ft	8f ^{44}	:32^{67}	:44^{23}	01:09^{08}	F	**123**	4	4
12Sep	9SA	ft	8f ^{61}	:32^{60}	:43^{13}	01:08^{22}	F	**108**	6	3

5 RESTING GRINCH FACE

02Nov	5SA	ft	9f ^{12}	:22^{39}	:43^{73}	01:08^{29}	F	**138**	4	10
22Oct	6SA	ft	8f ^{44}	:22^{38}	:43^{29}	01:08^{17}	F	**138**	3	3
12Sep	8SA	ft	8f ^{45}	:22^{18}	:43^{10}	01:08^{23}	F	**138**	3	3

6 RUDOLPH LUNDGREN

02Nov	8SA	ft	9f ^{23}	:21^{98}	:48^{35}	01:32^{17}	F	**198**	2	2
22Oct	6Kee	ft	9f ^{63}	:21^{43}	:48^{87}	01:36^{27}	F	**223**	4	2
03Jul	7MD	ft	9f ^{34}	:21^{32}	:47^{18}	01:34^{29}	F	**190**	8	3

7 GREG

02Nov	6Kee	ft	8f ^{13}	:31^{45}	:42^{25}	01:10^{75}	F	**123**	4	9
22Oct	6Kee	ft	8f ^{18}	:32^{24}	:42^{23}	01:11^{08}	F	**123**	4	4
12Sep	9SA	ft	8f ^{23}	:32^{89}	:43^{25}	01:11^{24}	F	**108**	6	3

Issue 1
LEE FERGUSON & JOSE VILLARRUBIA
Incentive Cover

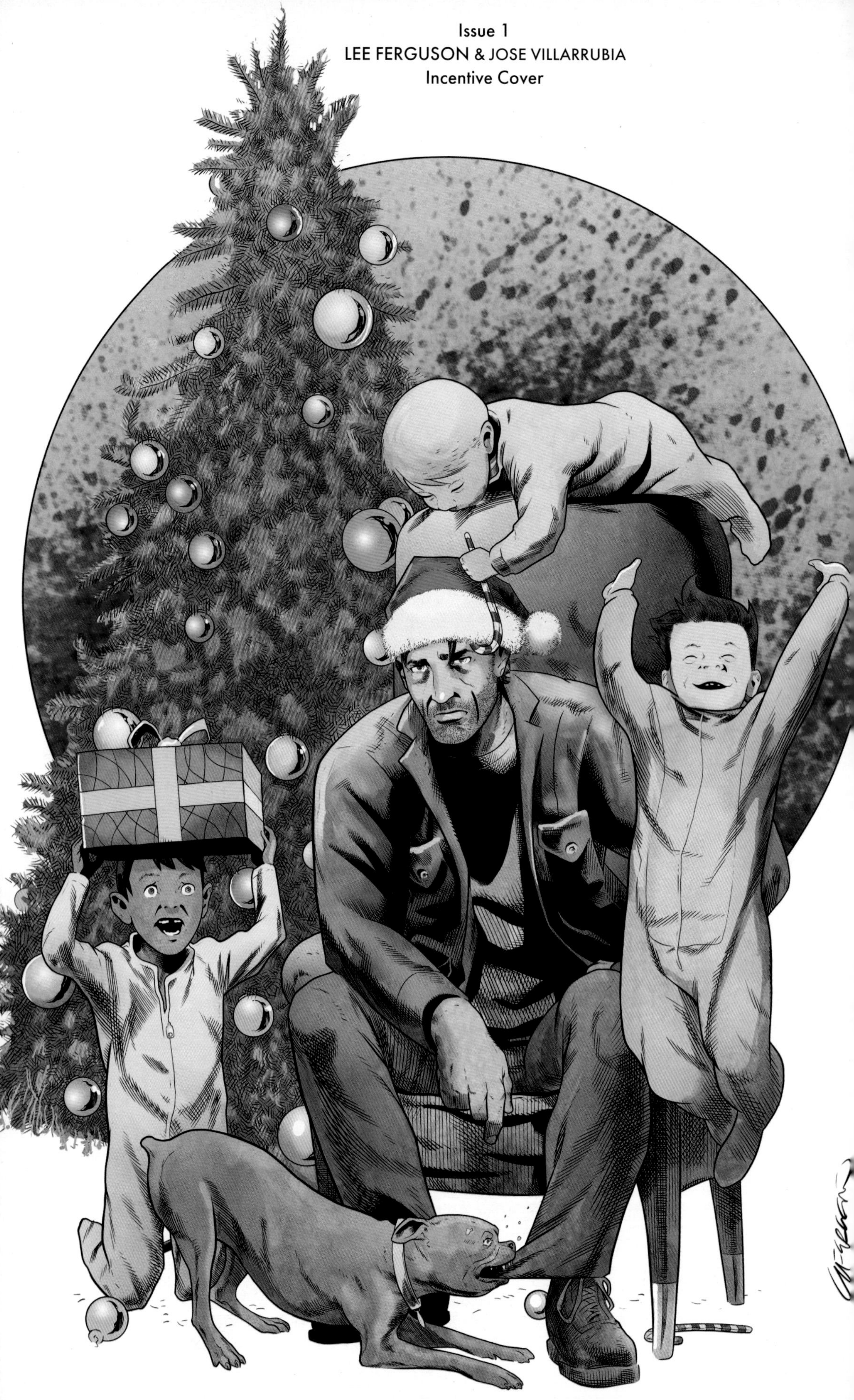

SKETCHBOOK
LEE FERGUSON

AFTERSHOCK COMICS: What were your influences behind the overall look of NAUGHTY LIST?

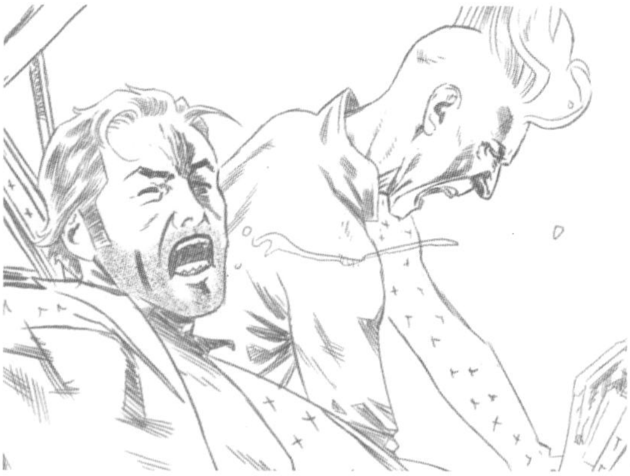

LEE FERGUSON: You know, I'm always reading, watching and looking at things, and I think new bits are always adding themselves to my list of influences whether I'm aware at the time or not... but the big "new" influence I *tried* to get into this was Norman Rockwell. I really wanted things like that variant cover, or the shot with Nick and the kids and all the faces around the frame to have that Rockwell holiday feel. I wanted each of them to feel like something you'd see on a holiday card and know you had just caught a moment in time, and there was a tale to be told there.

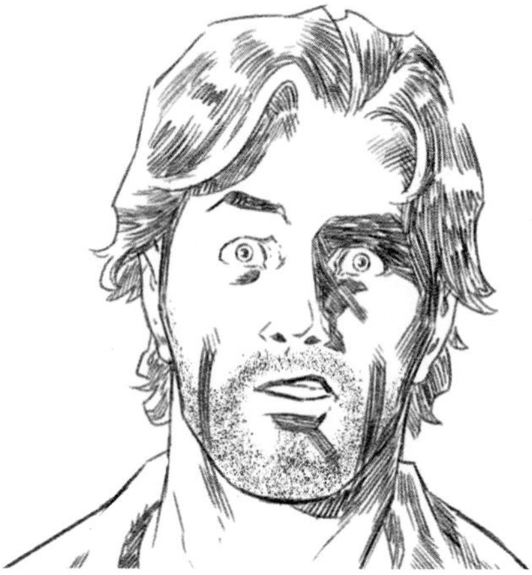

ASC: What was your favorite scene to illustrate?

LF: This is gonna sound weird, but probably the first twelve pages of the first issue, actually. I really liked the way we got to speed through Nick's whole sad history. It was kind of brutal and awesome to see what he'd been through. And I really enjoyed working out that clock page.

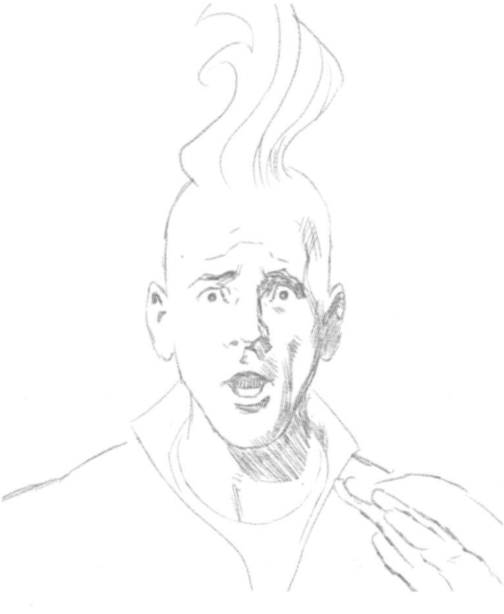

ASC: If you had a pet reindeer, what would you name them?

LF: You know, you gotta meet the reindeer, get to know them...*THEN* come up with a fitting name, right?

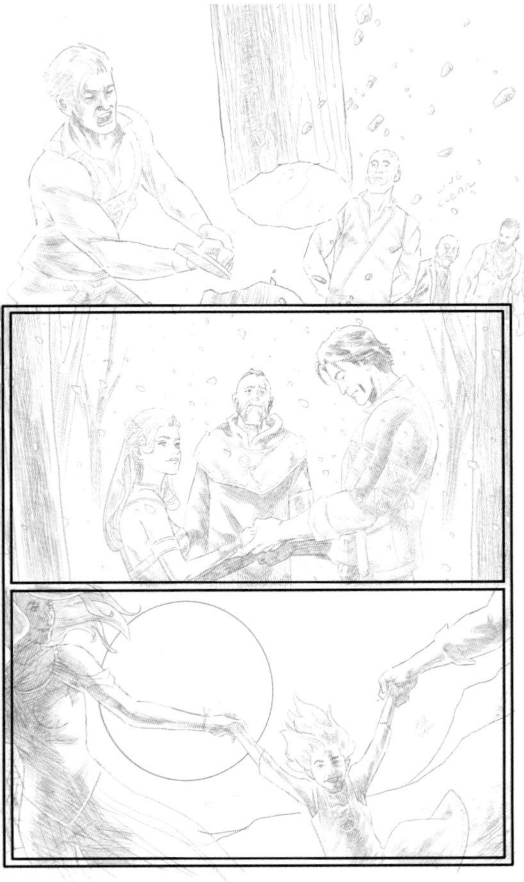

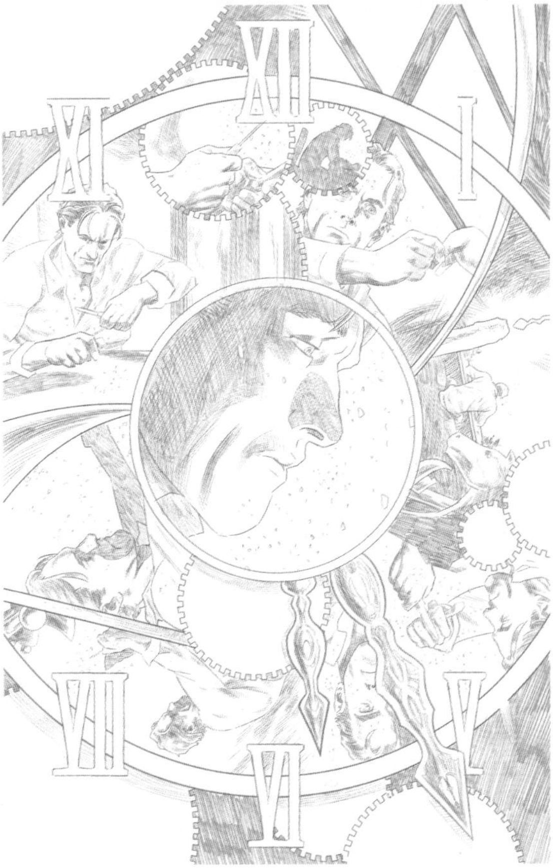
XII
I
XI
VII
VI
V

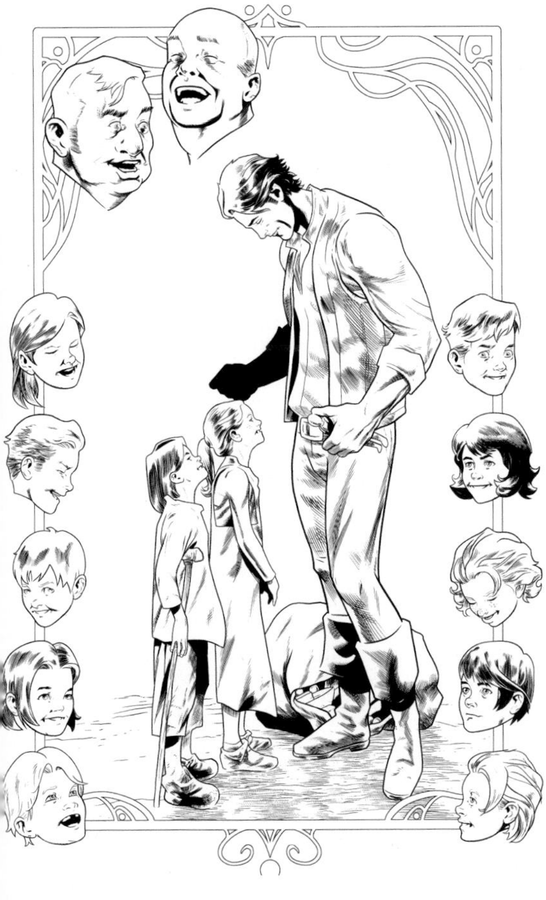

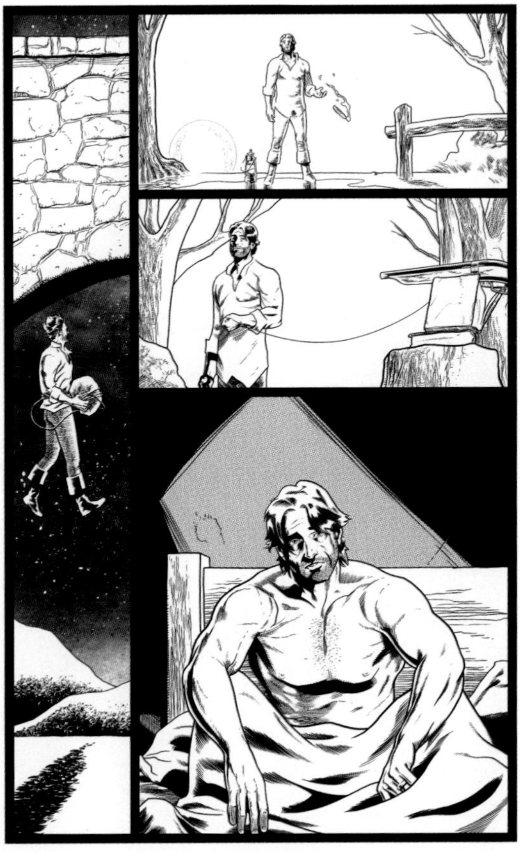

ASC: What was your favorite Plum moment to illustrate?

LF: Definitely the scene where the guy at the racetrack blows Plum some crap, and Plum proceeds to annihilate the guy and then trash talks him for good measure. That was perfect. I'm also really partial to the page in issue four where he's on the phone, looking down, then we snap zoom out on his eyes widening as Nick lands behind him. I imagine Plum had a lot of those moments in his life.

ASC: What was the most challenging aspect for you when illustrating NAUGHTY LIST?

LF: Well, I haven't drawn a lot of reindeer in my life, so those were probably the major drawing challenge. That said, for me, the most challenging part of any book is breaking down the script into an actual comic. But it's also my favorite part by far.

ASC: If you could pick any vehicle to act as your sleigh, what would you choose?

LF: I would probably just stick with a sleigh. I'm a pretty traditional guy!

ASC: Was there any moment when illustrating the scripts you laughed out loud?

LF: Well, I enjoyed a lot of the banter between Nick and Plum throughout, but the fight club at the end of issue four definitely got a chuckle out of me... ;)

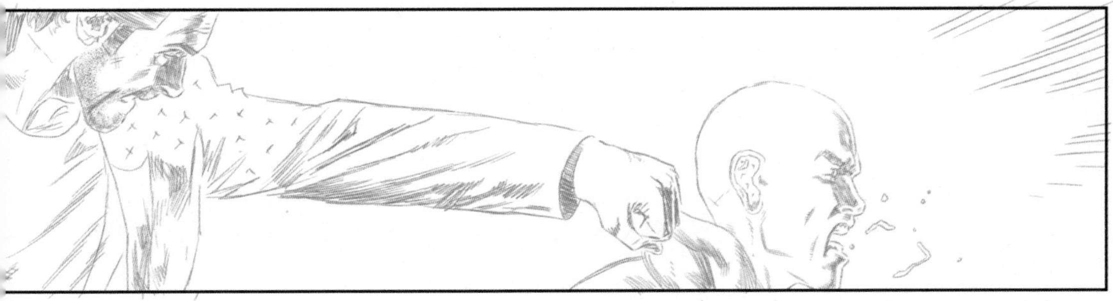

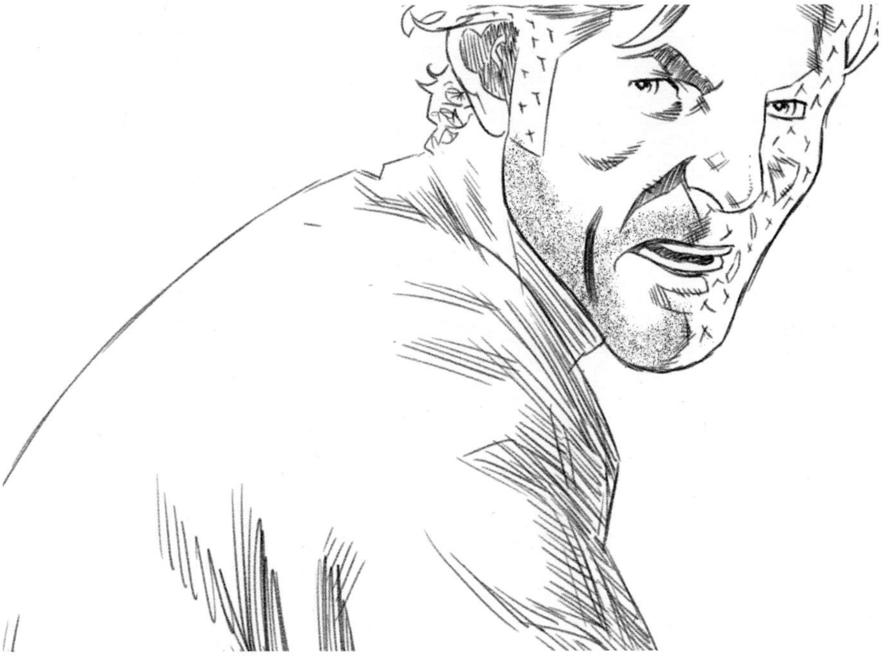

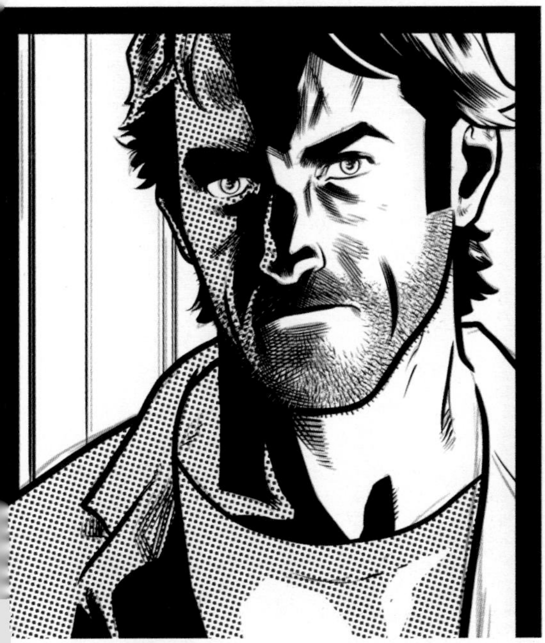

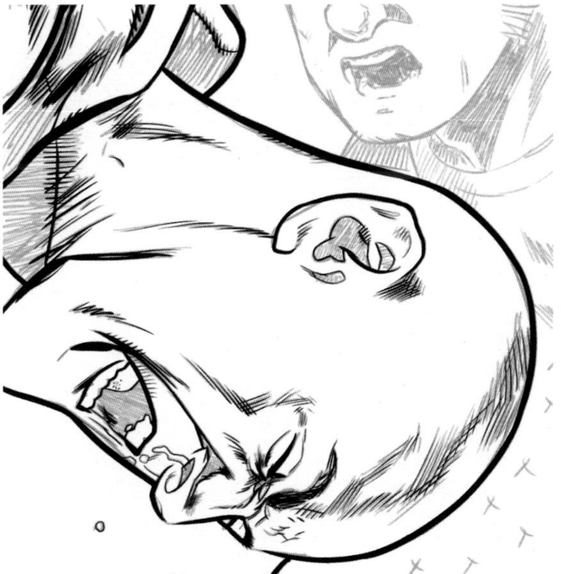

NICK SANTORA writer

Nick Santora is an Emmy-nominated writer and producer who has worked with talented teams on shows such as *The Sopranos*, *Law & Order*, *Prison Break*, *Breakout Kings*, *Most Dangerous Game* and *Reacher*. Nick has also succeeded in unscripted television and feature films, having created and executive produced the hit reality show, *Beauty & the Geek* and the films *The Punisher: War Zone*, *The Longshots*, *Dog Gone* and *Safety*. Besides his film and tv credits, Nick is a best-selling novelist with his novels *Slip & Fall*, *Fifteen Digits* and his children's book *I Want An Alien For Christmas*.

LEE FERGUSON artist

🐦 @LeeMFerguson

Artist Lee Ferguson lives in Florida, and has drawn books for Marvel, DC, IDW, and Dynamite, working on characters like Wolverine, the Joker, Nick Fury, Black Canary, Snake Eyes and Flash Gordon. He has also worked on a line of children's books for DC featuring Wonder Woman, Superman, the Flash and more. Along the way, Lee has made the time to put out a few creator-owned projects in his career, including *The Many Adventures of Miranda Mercury* (with co-creator and writer Brandon Thomas) at Archaia, *Sam and His Talking Gun* (with his son Drew) at Scout Comics, and his own book, *Freak*, at Image Comics, with more to come...

JUANCHO! colorist

📷 juancho.velez25

JUANCHO! is a burger and cereal lover, who also happens to color and draw comics! You can find him in Bogotá, Colombia doing his freelance duties, but you never know where he might travel next to taste new burgers. Online, he's at juancho25.artstation.com.

PIPPA BOWLAND colorist

🐦 @PippaBowland

Pippa Bowland has been coloring comics for about two years. During this time, she has worked with 2000AD, as well as Ahoy, Dynamite and other publishers. Now, she is thrilled to be a part of the AfterShock family. Pippa lives in North West England and works alongside husband, and letterer, Simon Bowland, and their tabby cat, Jess.

SIMON BOWLAND letterer

🐦 @SimonBowland

Simon has been lettering comics for over a decade and is currently working for DC, Image, Valiant, Dark Horse, Dynamite, 2000AD and IDW, amongst others. His debut AfterShock project was UNHOLY GRAIL. Born and bred in England, Simon still lives there today alongside his wife and their tabby cat.

DAVE SHARPE letterer

🐦 @DaveLSharpe

Upon graduating from the Joe Kubert School in 1990, he went on to work at Marvel Comics as an in-house letterer, eventually running their lettering department in the late 90s and early 00s. Over the years, Dave has lettered hundreds of comics, such as *Spider-Girl*, *She-Hulk* and *The Defenders* for Marvel, and *Green Lantern*, *Harley Quinn*, and *Batgirl* for DC Comics. Dave now works on both *X-O Manowar* and *Faith* for Valiant Comics in addition to his lettering duties on several AfterShock titles.